New World
Parrots in Crisis

Solutions from Conservation Biology

Edited by Steven R. Beissinger and Noel F. R. Snyder

Foreword by Joseph M. Forshaw

with Abstracts in Spanish

Smithsonian Institution Press   **Washington and London**

Library of Congress Cataloging-in-Publication Data

New World parrots in crisis : solutions from conservation biology /
    editors, Steven R. Beissinger and Noel F. R. Snyder.
        p.   cm.
    Includes bibliographical references and index.
    ISBN 1-56098-110-5   ISBN 1-56098-136-9 (pbk.)
    1. Parrots—Latin America—Congresses. 2. Birds, Protection of—Latin
America—Congresses. 3. Rare birds—Latin America—Congresses. 4. Parrot
industry—Congresses. I. Beissinger, Steven R. II. Snyder, Noel F. R.
QL696.P7N49   1991
333.95'8—dc20   91-52867
                                                                                    CIP

British Library Cataloguing-in-Publication is available.

The paper used in this publication meets the minimum requirements of the
American National Standard for Permanence of Paper for Printed Library
Materials Z39.48-1984.

Printed in the United States of America.
97 96 95 94 93 92   5 4 3 2 1

For permission to reproduce individual illustrations appearing in the book, please
correspond directly with the owner of the image as listed in the caption or the
contributor of the individual chapter.

Cover: Red-and-Green Macaws (*Ara chloroptera*) on a clay lick on the middle Manu
River, Peru. (Photograph by Eduardo Nycander and Charles Munn)

Contents

Foreword

The second meeting of the Parrot Working Group of the International Council for Bird Preservation (ICBP) was held on the Caribbean island of St. Lucia in April 1980 and focused attention on the plight of Neotropical parrots. Prior to that meeting, there were growing concerns for the conservation of these birds, especially for the spectacular *Amazona* species of the Lesser Antilles, and this was the reason for holding the meeting on St. Lucia. However, I doubt that at the time there was full appreciation of the seriousness of the situation, and certainly there was no adequate forewarning of the critical problems that we would be addressing a decade later.

At the St. Lucia meeting, I pointed out that parrots are particularly disadvantaged in that not only must they contend with the pressures that confront most wildlife, notably habitat destruction and the indiscriminate use of pesticides, but they also face additional threats, such as those posed by the rapacious live bird trade. This multiplicity of pressures makes conservation of these birds especially difficult.

The same theme was taken up by Christoph Imboden, the director of ICBP, in his preface to the proceedings of the meeting. He warned that trade in parrots had reached such alarming proportions that, coupled with loss of habitat, it was pushing many species to the verge of extinction. I suggest that this assessment was no exaggeration. We have now witnessed the almost certain extinction of Spix's Macaw (*Cyanopsitta spixii*) in the wild, and the dramatic declines in many other parrot populations continue unabated. If we do not act with the urgency demanded by this rapidly deteriorating situation, I have little doubt that by the end of this century, other species will have joined Spix's Macaw.

What has taken place since the St. Lucia meeting, and are we now better positioned to come up with an effective conservation strategy for Neotropical parrots? In their introduction to this book, Steve Beissinger and Noel Snyder emphasize that there have been few detailed studies of parrots in the wild and that overall biological knowledge of these birds is still quite limited. While this is true, I am encouraged that in very recent years there has been a marked improvement in our knowledge of parrots, and researchers now are giving increasing attention to the group. In the early 1970s, when the first edition of my *Parrots of the World* was published, the lack of recorded information on the family was appalling. The dearth of knowledge was especially acute in the Neotropics. In contrast, in his foreword to the third edition of my book, published in 1989, Dean Amadon commented on advances made in recent years and pointed out that exciting findings are coming from field studies being undertaken on parrots in a number of regions.

Significant advances have been made in my own country, where biologists in the Division of Wildlife and Ecology of the Commonwealth Scientific and Industrial Research Organisation (CSIRO) have carried out major studies on species of economic importance usually associated with their impacts on agriculture. I suggest that the findings from these projects could be applied in many instances to the management of parrot populations in the New World.

In their contribution "Toward a Conservation Strategy for Neotropical Psittacines," Noel Snyder, Frances James, and Steve Beissinger briefly review the state of implementation of recommendations from the St. Lucia meeting, especially relating to habitat preservation and trade. Although it is true that some action has been taken on many of these recommendations, I remain most disappointed at the levels of implementation. Habitat loss continues at a frightening pace, and the gains made through the establishment of reserves need to be consolidated by effective management of all natural areas, whether in reserves or not. However, it is in combating the effects of trade, a matter largely the prerogative of authorities in consumer nations, that implementation has been singularly ineffective.

Whenever mention is made of trade in wildlife, attention turns to the Convention on International Trade in Endangered Species of Wild Fauna and Flora (CITES), which is the international regime set up to control such trade. In the past, I have been strongly critical of the effectiveness of CITES in combating the ever-expanding trade in wild birds, and I shall maintain that criticism until a fundamental change is made by CITES in its approach to the problem. Since CITES came into force, the live-bird trade has increased enormously, with parrots being most affected, and it continues to expand despite the still meager knowledge of the status and ecology of most species.

Some parrot species presumably can withstand trade, especially if their wild populations are managed comprehensively. However, it must be acknowledged that trade in parrots or other live birds is utilization of wildlife and, as such, must be based on sound principles of sustained yield harvesting. Before trade in any species can be undertaken, it is necessary to ascertain whether the wild populations of that species can sustain trade and, if so, at what level. When those data are at hand, regulated trade could be permitted, with periodic checks put in place to monitor the effects of trade. Such monitoring procedures should incorporate assessments of recruitment rates to ensure that harvesting is directed at appropriate age cohorts of the population, usually the younger, non-breeding birds. Wasteful and inhumane methods of capture, such as felling nest trees in the hope of securing chicks, or shooting adults in the hope that one or two will recover from injuries, must be eliminated. Harvesting programs need to be sufficiently flexible to enable action to be taken promptly to restrict trade, or even halt it altogether, if monitoring studies detect declines in the population. Present methods, as effected through CITES, adopt a totally inappropriate approach in that evidence of scarcity becomes a prerequisite for the imposition of trade controls. Surely, the capability of wild populations to withstand harvesting must be established before trade is permitted.

On a number of occasions, I have stressed that when birds are transferred from one locality to another there is potential for significant biological consequences at the place of origin and the place of destination. It is obvious that taking large numbers of birds for the live-bird trade can be a drain on wild populations. But not so obvious are the threats at places of destination where endemic populations can be stressed by competition from feral populations of exotic species, and where feral populations can have substantial impacts on agriculture.

A report carried in the *Los Angeles Times* of March 11, 1991, stated that there may be as many as a thousand feral parrots in southern California. This report seems to have aroused few concerns, other than from a pet store owner in Van Nuys who complained that people would not buy birds from him if they could see them in their backyards! I have spent time watching feral *Amazona* parrots in and around Los Angeles, where for many years the birds were considered a novelty and little attention was paid them. However, numbers are building up significantly, breeding is well established, and authorities already are faced with nuisance problems in residential districts. Whether severe long-term biological and economic problems may result from continued increases in these feral populations is still unknown, but certainly there are substantial potential hazards.

Against this background, a concerted campaign has been mounted to relax the prohibition on exports of native birds from Australia so that species known to cause damage to crops can be exported. I am amazed that any credence at all could be given to such a campaign. Exports of so-called "pest species" from Australia, South America, or elsewhere certainly will not alleviate conflicts with agriculture in the exporting countries, but could pose real problems for agri-cultural interests in importing countries. To further highlight the lack of sound biological input to policy-making, I point to the absurdity of having on one hand a campaign to export from Australia so-called "pest species," while at the same time moves are being made to allow imports into Australia of species with pest potential. Australia has the world's most significant parrot fauna, so importation of foreign parrots has a much greater potential for adverse impacts there than in countries without native parrots.

If trade is to continue, then the issues that I have raised should be addressed, and an administering regime must be set up to ensure that protection of wild populations is the paramount consideration. It has been pointed out correctly that the majority of exporting countries are developing nations without the resources required for monitoring studies of their parrot populations. For a possible solution to this difficulty we need to look at hunting, which is utilization of wildlife on a grand scale, and the controls put in place to safeguard game species. Here we find strong reliance on the "user pays" principle, and I suggest that the same principle should apply to the live-bird trade. If a country in South America wishes to export an apparently common and widespread species, there should arise immediately a requirement for studies of that species in the wild to determine whether the population can withstand harvesting and, if so, at what levels and with what age groups. Also, there must be comprehensive surveys to identify areas in which harvesting could take place and other areas, such as favored nesting places, where the species could be fully protected. A developing nation in South America could not be expected to allocate the resources necessary for these studies without assistance, and that assistance should come from trade interests. Funding for fieldwork undertaken by resident ccologists or to meet the costs of bringing in the required expertise could be provided by license fees paid by those engaged in trade, just as hunting licenses provide funding for monitoring of game populations.

I recognize that establishment of an administering framework for such a regime will be difficult, but it can be done. The first step would be to look at appropriateness of an existing international body to oversee the operations worldwide, and, of course, CITES stands out as the most likely candidate. Already, the CITES Secretariat is administering quotas in wildlife trade, so it could set up a unit to oversee a sustained yield harvesting regime for the international live-bird trade.

A not-unexpected response from conservation bodies in developed nations has been a call to ban importation of all exotic birds, and that was the resolution submitted to the American Ornithologists' Union in 1989. Not surprisingly, that resolution generated lively debate and a decision was not reached, but it seems to me that good arguments can be brought forward to support imposition of a moratorium on trade until an effective administering regime is in place.

When such bans are under discussion, I am often asked about experiences in Australia, where a prohibition on trade in live birds, other than the export of non-native species, has been in force for more than thirty years. I would not presume to suggest that what is good for Australia would necessarily be good for all countries. The Australian ban has to be appraised within the overall context of our national wildlife management practices. Nevertheless, it cannot be denied that parrot populations are far healthier in Australia than in neighboring countries where trade is permitted. It is true that prohibition generates illicit trafficking, but this is primarily an enforcement problem. There is some smuggling of Australian parrots, but this is being counteracted fairly successfully by increased surveillance and imprisonment penalties for convicted offenders. The positive result is that resources can be directed to conservation and management programs, especially habitat protection or rehabilitation and minimizing competition for nest sites from introduced species.

One of my primary concerns is that unless populations in Neotropical countries are afforded a respite while we set up an effective regime for administering trade, they could decline to such low numbers that any capacity to make shifts in habitat preferences will be lost. In many parts of their worldwide range, parrots are adopting to secondary growth, plantations, and even urban gardens, but I fear their ability to do this will be undermined by large-scale trapping to satisfy the international market. I suspect that time has already run out for some parrot species, and we cannot allow continuation of trade motivated primarily by profit potential, with scant regard for the conservation of wild populations, and with inherent high levels of mortality.

Above all, there must be a decision on whether there is to be any trade at all. If trade is to continue, then we must ensure that it does not threaten wild populations. I hope the information presented and opinions expressed in the pages of this book will assist in the critical decision-making that cannot be postponed any longer.

Joseph M. Forshaw

Introduction

Steven R. Beissinger and Noel F. R. Snyder

School of Forestry & Environmental Studies, Yale University, New Haven,
Connecticut 06511; and Wildlife Preservation Trust International, P.O. Box 426,
Portal, Arizona 85632

New World parrots are being imported from less developed countries to developed countries in astounding quantities, primarily to supply a demand for aviculture and the pet trade. More than 1.8 million parrots legally entered the international trade during a recent 5-year period. In addition to pressures from commerce, these birds are also threatened from widespread habitat destruction and shooting for food or to protect crops. At least 30% of the 140 parrot species found in the Western Hemisphere are now threatened with extinction. Yet, Neotropical psittacines remain among the least known of birds in the world.

Biological knowledge of parrots is poor in part because most species are difficult to catch and band, have large home ranges, are tropical forest dwellers, and nest in elevated tree cavities that are difficult to observe or reach. Also, most ornithologists live in countries lacking native parrots. Although parrots are commonly kept in captivity, this has served more to stigmatize these birds than to encourage their study. Most ornithologists and ecologists today are nearly completely ignorant of the biology of these birds and the extent of their conservation problems. There have been so few detailed studies of psittacines in the wild that parrot biology could be considered one of the present "frontiers" of ornithology.

Many of the basic questions to be answered about parrot behavior and ecology have a fundamental bearing on ecological theory as well as conservation. For example, why do the few parrot societies that have been studied in detail appear to have such a large proportion of nonbreeding adults (over 50%), many occurring as mated pairs defending territories? Yet, helping behavior rarely occurs in this group. Furthermore, why do parrots exhibit some of the most striking hatching asynchronies known in birds? A resolution of questions such as these can be expected to have far-reaching implications not only for advancing our understanding of population regulation mechanisms, but also for effective management of wild populations to promote their survival.

This book is about contemporary problems in conservation science. The various chapters cover topics ranging from the "straight and narrow road" of rigorous biology to the difficult and tortuous arena of social science, where black-and-white answers can quickly become gray. While biologists are often called upon to find proximate solutions to conservation problems, the ultimate causes of many of these problems often originate in the behavior of people or human institutions. Long-term solutions lie as much in good politics as in good biology. The need for sound biological understanding is inescapable, but such understanding is not sufficient to ensure successful conservation in most cases.

The presentations in this book are derived primarily from a symposium entitled "The Conservation Crisis of New World Parrots" that was held at the American Ornithologists' Union (AOU) annual meetings in Los Angeles in June 1990. The stimulus for the symposium was a resolution submitted to the AOU in 1989 to ban all importation of exotic birds (mainly parrots) into the United States. When this proposal resulted in lively but indecisive controversy at the annual meetings held in Pittsburgh, we decided to organize a comprehensive forum that would serve to educate scientists, policymakers, and the general public not only about the trade issue but also about other important issues in parrot conservation.

As the title of this book suggests, the main theme of the symposium was the conservation problems facing New World parrots, although many comparisons with conservation problems of other wildlife species were also presented. Neotropical parrots certainly have some unique characteristics, but this book should

APPROACHES TO PARROT CONSERVATION

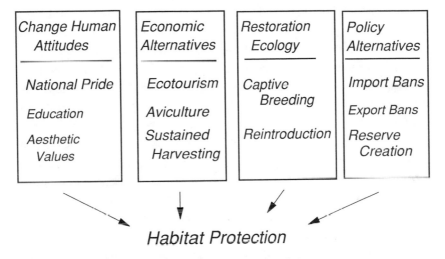

Fig. 1. A general schema of approaches to conserving Neotropical parrots.

not be viewed strictly as a taxonomically or regionally based book. The conservation problems or forces that threaten parrots include the main elements in the set of factors that threaten most biological diversity. Likewise, many of the approaches to conservation that are featured in this book are representative of the strategies being developed throughout the field of conservation biology. In general, New World parrots serve only as a case study of the principles and solutions that have application to many other species.

Contributions to this book were selected to represent a wide range of parrot species as well as approaches to conservation. In addition to reviewing their fields of expertise, authors were invited to analyze carefully the benefits and limitations of the particular approach to conservation that they represented. Several of the approaches are so new that it is too early to assess their full potentials. Others have now established sufficient records of accomplishment that their full potentials are more certain.

The book begins with an overview of the distribution and diversity of threatened New World parrots and the causes of their decline. Then a variety of approaches to the problems of parrot conservation are presented (Fig. 1).

These approaches can be classified as those that act primarily to change human attitudes, that promote economic alternatives which are part of the "use it or lose it" approach to conservation also known as sustainable development, that function as salvage operations to restore critically endangered forms to the wild, or that act through legal mechanisms to restrict harmful practices. Each of these approaches results, either directly or indirectly, in habitat protection. The approaches considered certainly do not qualify as all inclusive, but represent certain dominant directions in a continuum of options for dealing with these problems.

The importance of education and local participation in conservation is demonstrated with great clarity by an innovative campaign to conserve the large amazon parrots of the Lesser Antilles. Two primarily economic approaches to sustainable development using parrots are discussed: ecotourism projects in Peru that generate funds by luring tourists to the rainforest to see free-ranging macaws, and projects in Venezuela and Argentina to determine the feasibility of harvesting certain parrots in a manner that sustains populations. The relevance of the pest status of certain parrot species to conservation is explored in some depth. Salvage operations for critically endangered species are discussed in chapters on captive breeding and reintroduction, two techniques that are frequently used and abused by conservation biologists. Finally, legal remedies are discussed primarily in the context of regulation of the international trade in parrots.

Can commercial aviculture, a major cause of the decline of parrots, be changed to benefit the conservation of psittacines? What are the limitations and potentials of captive breeding to conserve these species? To what extent can parrots be conserved through sustained harvest schemes or ecotourism? To what extent should the current trade in parrots be curtailed? These are but a few of the central topics of debate in parrot conservation today, and a sampling of the topics given thoughtful discussion in this volume. Finally, in accord with the special emphasis on trade issues, which currently are being debated at national and international levels, the book includes a round-table discussion from the AOU symposium focused on this subject.

This book has developed principally as a result of the labors of each contributor. Each author deserves special credit for summarizing his or her special field of expertise in a timely fashion so that hard-won insights can be rapidly disseminated for the benefit of practical conservation efforts. We thank the AOU for providing a forum to bring attention to the crisis facing New World parrots. We also acknowledge the financial support of Warren King, the U.S. Fish and Wildlife Service Office of International Affairs, and the International Council for Bird Preservation-U.S. Section for help with publication costs of this book. The Yale University School of Forestry and Environmental Studies provided important financial support toward the logistics of coordinating this effort. Carlos Guindon translated the abstracts into Spanish. James Gibbs, Carlos Guindon, Kathy Sestrich, and Nellie Tsipoura helped with production.

1. Dimensions and Causes of the Parrot Conservation Crisis

N. J. Collar and A. T. Juniper

International Council for Bird Preservation,
32 Cambridge Road, Girton, Cambridge CB3 0PJ, United Kingdom

Abstract.—The New World harbors around 140 species of parrots, of which no fewer than 42 (30%) may be considered at some risk of extinction. This very high proportion has mainly resulted from a combination of habitat destruction and exploitation for the pet trade. Central America (including Mexico) holds 4 threatened parrots; the Caribbean 7; northern South America 4; the Andes of northwestern South America 11; the central savannas (chiefly Brazil and Bolivia) 6 (all macaws); and the Atlantic Forest region of Brazil and Argentina 9 (these numbers are subject to constant revision). Of these 42 species, 17 are at risk from habitat loss only, 7 from trade, 15 from a mixture of the two, and 3 from other factors. Of the 98 non-threatened parrot species, almost all are declining and many require conservation measures to offset the current impacts of habitat conversion and trade.

PARROTS IN PERSPECTIVE

As reviewed by Homberger (1985) and Forshaw (1989), the majority of the world's 330-odd parrot species are found in tropical regions. Most are forest dwellers, the lowlands being especially rich in species. However, some species penetrate temperate latitudes (e.g., *Psittacula derbiana, Enycognathus lepto-rhynchus*), while others (e.g., *Bolborhynchus orbygnesius, Neopsittacus pulli-cauda*) are associated with temperate vegetation at high altitude within the tropics. A few species are shoreline specialists, and three are exclusively ter-restrial and nocturnal.

Most parrots are sedentary, although they may make substantial local move-ments between roosting and feeding areas. Seasonal migrations are very un-usual, but arid-land species, notably in Australia, are commonly nomadic. With only one exception, all species eat seeds or nuts, always husked before swallowing, but the diet extends to fruit, pollen, nectar, roots, and lichens, and sometimes also insects. Most species are gregarious and forage in flocks.

Pairs can mate for life but a few species change partners annually (Forshaw 1989, Waltman and Beissinger unpubl. MS). Many parrots live in pairs throughout the year. Nests are usually in hollow trees (the presence or preser-vation of dead trees or limbs can be a critical factor in conservation), although some species breed in cliffs or termite mounds. Some parrots are colonial, most notably the Monk Parakeet (*Myiopsitta monachus*), which constructs enormous stick nests in the tops of trees and is a serious crop pest in its native southern South America. Usually females lay two to five eggs but sometimes clutches reach 10 eggs (Forshaw 1989, Beissinger and Waltman 1991). Eggs hatch after 14 to 32 days of incubation. Parental care is shared, and the young may remain with their parents until the next breeding season.

Although dispersed widely through the Pacific Ocean and Old World in general, parrots reach their maximum diversity in South America, southeast Asia, and Australia (Forshaw 1989). Stattersfield (1988) lists 12 species known to have become extinct since 1600 and there is evidence for the former existence of others, mostly in the accounts of early explorers (e.g., see Snyder et al. 1987, and Butler 1991). The majority of parrots, and indeed all extinct birds, in Stattersfield's list were confined to islands (10 species). The cause of their loss was usually uncertain but presumably involved habitat loss within restricted ranges, direct human persecution, and competition and predation from introduced species. Natural causes probably compounded these factors. Stattersfield's two continental forms, both lost during the twentieth century, were the Carolina Parakeet (*Conuropsis carolinensis*) of the United States, which was once the most northerly occurring parrot in the world, and the Glaucous Macaw (*Anodorhynchus glaucus*), which used to be found in southern Brazil, northern Argentina, Uruguay, and Paraguay. However, this form, like the Paradise Parrot (*Psephotus pulcherrimus*) of Australia, is regarded in the analyses below as still just possibly extant.

DIMENSIONS OF THE CRISIS

Numbers At Risk

Despite the extinctions suffered by the Psittacidae in recent centuries, past trends do not prepare us for the dimensions of the current conservation crisis facing the family. Collar and Andrew (1988) suggested that 71 parrot species (21.5% of the Psittacidae) were at risk of extinction, and listed 29 more species as near-threatened. Birds in this second category were either genuine borderline cases, or species considered most vulnerable to decline in the future. Hence no fewer than 100, or 30% of the Psittacidae's 330 species, were identified as giving cause for concern or worse.

Of these 100 species, 52 (38 threatened and 14 near-threatened) are Neotropical (out of a total of some 140 species in the region). (For the purposes of this paper, the "Neotropics" is used as a synonym for the New World, and hence includes species in Mexico that occur north of the strict biogeographical boundary of the Neotropical region). Forty of these species are found primarily on the continent (31 threatened and 9 near-threatened), while 12 are island species (7 threatened and 5 near-threatened). The proportion of continental to island forms that are endangered in the Neotropics (3.3:1) is reversed compared to the locations of threatened parrot species in the rest of the world (1:3.8), where island forms are typically at risk.

Threatened species lists are always subject to change, and that in Collar and Andrew (1988) was in any case preliminary. Subsequent information has led to some adjustments to the figures above, involving the deletion of *Pyrrhura hypoxantha* (an invalid species), the relegation of *Amazona xanthops* to near-threatened status, and the promotion to threatened status of *Amazona leucocephala*,

Pyrrhura orcesi, Hapalopsittaca fuertesi, H. pyrrhops, Amazona dufresniana, and *A. tucumana.* Currently, therefore, the International Council for Bird Preservation (ICBP) considers 42 Neotropical parrot species at risk of extinction, and these are detailed in the Appendix. This list is thus more extensive than that of Silva (1989), who based his criteria on the listing of forms in CITES (Convention on International Trade in Endangered Species) Appendix I or the listing of "endangered" forms (although this term was misunderstood) in the previous single-volume Red Data Book (King 1977–1979).

All but one of the threatened Neotropical species are distributed within six general areas (Fig. 1). Central America (including Mexico) holds four species (*Rhynchopsitta pachyrhyncha, R. terrisi, Amazona viridigenalis,* and the island form *Aratinga brevipes*). Seven species inhabit Caribbean islands (*Aratinga euops, Amazona leucocephala, A. vittata, A. versicolor, A. arausiaca, A. guildingii, A. imperialis*). The lowland forests of northern South America support four species (*Guaruba guarouba, Pyrrhura perlata, Amazona dufresniana, A. barbadensis*). The Andes of northwestern South America hold 11 species (*Leptosittaca branickii, Ognorhynchus icterotis, Pyrrhura orcesi, P. albipectus, P. calliptera, Bolborhynchus ferrugineifrons, Brotogeris pyrrhopterus, Touit stictoptera, Hapalopsittaca amazonina, H. fuertesi, H. pyrrhops*). On its own in the Andean foothills of Argentina is *Amazona tucumana.* The interior savanna lowlands of South America hold six species (*Anodorhynchus hyacinthinus, A. glaucus, A. leari, Cyanopsitta spixii, Ara glaucogularis, A. rubrogenys*). Finally, the Atlantic Forest region of Brazil, together with adjacent areas of Paraguay and Argentina, holds nine threatened parrots (*Aratinga auricapilla, Pyrrhura cruentata, Touit melanonota, T. surda, Amazona pretrei, A. brasiliensis, A. rhodocorytha, A. vinacea, Triclaria malachitacea*).

The areas in question are extensive (Fig. 1) and many of the threatened species do not occur sympatrically. Nevertheless, it is obviously important to look for areas of overlap between threatened species to identify especially important areas for the establishment of reserves. Many of the species do occur in existing protected areas. But for most species it is not known if these reserves are large enough to hold viable populations (Soulé 1987) or can meet the species' requirements throughout their life cycles. Indeed, detailed information on the distribution and natural history of most species is very limited and

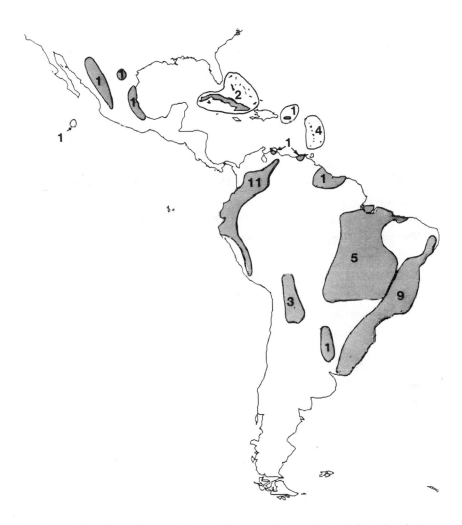

Fig. 1. Ranges of Neotropical psittacines at risk of extinction (See Appendix for explanation). The number of species occupying a range is given. Note that the regions with the most threatened species are the Caribbean Islands (7 species), the Andes of northwestern South America (11 species), and the Atlantic Forest of Brazil (9 species).

in some cases almost completely lacking. This renders the task of determining conservation priorities for particular areas very problematic. Although essential, such priorities should always be framed so as to reflect their provisional nature.

Mexico

The two species of *Rhynchopsitta*, both threatened, inhabit coniferous forests in the Sierra Madre Occidental (*pachyrhyncha*) and Oriental (*terrisi*). *Amazona viridigenalis* is confined to lowland gallery forest and dry open pine-oak ridges extending up the Sierra Madre Oriental. All three species require effective key site conservation for their long-term survival, although at present it is not clear which are the most important areas to protect. Meanwhile, the prospects for these birds could be enhanced through the development of forestry practices that take better account of their feeding and nesting requirements (although *R. terrisi* nests in cliffs).

Aratinga brevipes, confined to Socorro, clearly stands to benefit from current interest in a comprehensive recovery program for the Revillagigedos Islands.

Caribbean

The rainforest on the northern slope of Morne Diablotin in Dominica is now the last refuge of *Amazona imperialis* and *A. arausiaca* (60 to 100, and 300 individuals remaining, respectively). A small but critically important part of this forest, due for logging, was acquired by ICBP, RARE Center for Tropical Bird Conservation, and the government of Dominica in 1989. On St. Lucia and St. Vincent, the forest habitat of the amazons *A. versicolor* and *A. guildingii* is well protected by recent government initiatives (Butler 1991).

But because of their small populations it is prudent to regard these four species as still vulnerable to hurricanes, however well conserved their habitat may be. The smaller the area of forest becomes, the greater the risk must be of extermination by a direct hit from a storm. However, the case of *A. vittata*, a species which shares this seeming vulnerability (being confined to the Luquillo Forest in northeast Puerto Rico), suggests that the hurricane threat should not stampede conservation efforts toward exclusively ex-situ answers. This parrot appears to have survived moderately well the 1989 direct hit by Hurricane Hugo, the majority of the 50 or so wild birds weathering the disaster and breeding confidently in its wake. Similarly, the two Jamaican amazons, the Yellow-billed (*A. collaria*) and Black-billed (*A. agilis*), also survived the devastating 1988 Hurricane Gilbert quite well, and still do not merit threatened species status (Varty 1990). However, the region's sixth threatened amazon, *A. leucocephala*, provides a counterexample. In 1982, the population of *A. l. hesterna* living on Little Cayman was eliminated by a hurricane and this subspecies now persists only in small numbers (ca. 30) on Cayman Brac (J. W. Wiley pers. comm.). Birds on low flat islands may be far more at risk from storms than those in mountainous terrain where protected valleys can provide some shelter.

Unfortunately, an area of *A. l. hesterna*'s key breeding habitat is being fragmented by agricultural development (Bradley 1986). The other subspecies of *A. leucocephala* are faring better, but appear insufficiently secure to take the species as a whole out of danger. The race *caymanensis* on Grand Cayman is down to around 1,000 birds in the central and eastern part of the island, and is suffering in the wake of a major (and continuing) development boom. The subspecies *bahamensis* on Great Inagua and Abaco Islands, and formerly on four other islands in the Bahamas, has declined through habitat loss, shooting, and the pet trade. The avicultural press has declared *palmarum* extinct on Cuba's Isle of Pines (Isla de Juventud) (Noegel 1982), but the Cuban ornithological literature flatly contradicts this (Berovides 1986). Finally, the nominate race, *leucocephala*, by various reports in decline, maintains its major population in the Zapata Swamp, Cuba. Fuller information on these last two forms may alter the assessment of the species's overall prospects.

The Zapata Swamp is also the last stronghold of *Aratinga euops*, which has suffered a serious decline throughout Cuba.

Northern South American Lowlands

Two allopatric amazons occur in northern Venezuela. The range of the much-traded *Amazona barbadensis* of the central-north coastlands extends onto several Caribbean islands (Margarita, Blanquilla, and Bonaire). The apparently very uncommon *A. dufresniana* is restricted to heavy forest mainly on Venezuela's eastern border with Guyana, but it also extends into Surinam and French Guiana.

Guaruba guarouba (a.k.a. *Aratinga guarouba*) and the sympatric *Pyrrhura perlata* are confined to the humid forests south of the Amazon River in the states of Pará and Maranhão in northern Brazil. The recent discovery of a population of *G. guarouba* southwest of its previously known range somewhat ameliorates the species's conservation status (D. C. Oren pers. comm.). However, this part of Brazil is undergoing rapid development and effectively protected sites are urgently needed where both species occur, especially to account for all races of *P. perlata*.

Andes

An area of approximately 90,000 km² in Colombia that includes the departments of Cauca, Huila, Cundinamarca, Caldas, Santander, Risaralda, Quindío, Tolima, Chocó, and Valle contains 7 of the 11 threatened Andean species. These are *Leptopsittaca branickii*, *Ognorhynchus icterotis*, *Bolborhynchus ferrugineifrons*, *Touit stictoptera*, *Pyrrhura calliptera*, *Hapalopsittaca amazonina*, and *H. fuertesi*. The altitudinal preferences of all species except *T. stictoptera* overlap between 2,400 and 3,400 m.

All of these species (except for *H. fuertesi*) are thought to occur in protected areas, notably the Alto Quindío National Park in Quindío, Puracé National Park, Cerro Munchique, and the upper Magdalena valley in Cauca. *Ognorhynchus icterotis* is thought to occur in Munchique, Puracé, and Cueva de los Guácharos National Parks. Also, the Los Nevados National Park to the northeast of the main area is of some importance, particularly for *Bolborhynchus* and because it includes part of the possible range of *Hapalopsittaca fuertesi*, although this species may already be extinct.

An area of southern Ecuador including all or parts of the provinces of Loja, Zamora-Chinchipe, Morona-Santiago, Azuay, and El Oro covers all or part of the ranges of six threatened parrots. These are *Leptopsittaca branickii*,

Hapalopsittaca pyrrhops, Pyrrhura orcesi, P. albipectus, Touit stictoptera, and *Brotogeris pyrrhopterus*. The most likely altitude for sympatric occurrence is around 2,500 to 3,000 m, although both *P. albipectus* and *T. stictoptera* occur well below this. A priority area for the latter two species is the Cordillera Cutucú, an area which was designated as a Shuar Indian Reserve but has been settled as a result of Ecuadorean government initiatives. For *H. pyrrhops* and *L. branickii*, and possibly also for *P. albipectus*, the Podocarpus National Park in Loja province is thought to be of particular significance. This site is, however, also under threat, as is a neighboring unprotected site, from encroachment by agriculture (Poulsen et al. 1989).

Amazona tucumana was recently judged at risk by N. K. Krabbe working for ICBP. It has declined dramatically in numbers during the twentieth century as a consequence of habitat loss and trade, and is thought to be extinct in the Bolivian portion of its range. Protection of the remaining alder forests in northwest Argentina is essential for its survival.

Central South American Lowlands

This is the critical region for the macaws, whose exceptional vulnerability through naturally low rates of reproduction has recently been shown by Munn (1988, 1991). Currently most species of macaws remain sufficiently widespread that they are not threatened with overall extinction, but they are certainly at risk in some parts of their ranges. However, the blue macaws give the greatest cause for concern. *Anodorhynchus hyacinthinus* occupies, in a very fragmented fashion, a vast area fringing the southern reaches of the Amazon rainforest, but it has been massively reduced in numbers by trade. *A. leari* holds on at a single site in Bahia (60 birds). *A. glaucus* was last seen in 1951. *Cyanopsitta spixii* survives by the grace of less than 20 captive individuals and a single wild bird (Juniper and Yamashita 1990).

Habitat modification may threaten the survival of *Ara rubrogenys* through the removal of key tree species for industrial uses. Lanning (1982) reported that this species has a very limited range and that there is a need for protected areas. *A. glaucogularis* is another endemic Bolivian species that may suffer from the effects of habitat loss, but no information is available beyond its former prevalence in trade.

Southeast Brazil

In the central part of southeastern Brazil, the area encompassing the southern portion of the state of Bahia and the state of Espírito Santo (ES) contains populations of *Aratinga auricapilla*, *Pyrrhura cruentata*, *Touit melanonota*, *T. surda*, *Amazona rhodocorytha*, and *Trichlaria malachitacea*. Within these two states, the following sites (mostly already protected) are thought to be important: Monte Pascoal National Park, Bahia (*Touit surda* and *Amazona rhodocorytha*); Cumuruxatiba, Bahia (*Aratinga auricapilla*); Boraceia Ecological Reserve, ES (*Trichlaria malachitacea* and *A. rhodocorytha*); Sooretama Biological Reserve and contiguous Linhares Reserve, ES (*A. rhodocorytha* and *Pyrrhura cruentata*); Fazenda São Joaquim Biological Reserve, ES (*A. rhodocorytha*); Córrego do Veado Biological Reserve, ES (*P. cruentata*); and Nova Lombardia Reserve, ES (*Triclaria malachitacea*).

A second area of importance in the Atlantic Forest region includes the states of Rio de Janeiro (RJ), São Paulo (ESP), Paraná, Santa Catarina (SC), and Rio Grande do Sul (RGS). These states have populations of *Aratinga auricapilla*, *Pyrrhura cruentata*, *Touit melanonota*, *T. surda*, *Amazona pretrei*, *A. brasiliensis*, *A. rhodocorytha*, *A. vinacea*, and *Triclaria malachitacea*. Protected areas in this region that are thought to be of particular importance for the conservation of these psittacines include Tijuca National Park, RJ (*T. melanonota*); the southern coastal region of ESP and adjacent northern Paraná, i.e., the eastern part of the Serra do Mar (*Amazona brasiliensis*); Iguaçu National Park, Paraná (*A. pretrei* and *A. vinacea*); Aracuri-Esmarelda Ecological Station, RGS (*A. pretrei*); and Aparados da Serra National Park, RGS (*A. vinacea*).

The sites listed above are certainly important for the conservation of the threatened psittacines that occur in the Atlantic Forest. However, information on the occurrence of the above species in non-protected areas is urgently needed to guide the development of a more comprehensive network of key sites. This is especially urgent considering the absence of known protected areas for several of the species mentioned.

CAUSES OF THE CRISIS

Habitat loss

The majority of threatened parrots occur in regions where the destruction of natural vegetation has been and continues to be particularly severe (Fig. 1). These areas are the Atlantic Forest of southeast Brazil, the subtropical and temperate zones of the Andean valleys in Colombia and Ecuador, and the islands of the Caribbean. Together, these three broad regions contain the ranges of over 70% of the threatened species of New World parrots. Many of the threatened species in these regions are rendered especially vulnerable because of their naturally restricted ranges.

The Atlantic Forest originally extended from the state of Rio Grande do Norte to the southernmost borders of Brazil, into the northern Argentinian province of Misiones and parts of eastern Paraguay. In its natural state, the Atlantic Forest occupied about one million km², making it the third largest vegetation type in Brazil after the Amazonian rainforest and the *cerrado* (Mittermeier 1986). The region that includes the Atlantic Forest was the first to be settled by the Portuguese and today holds 43% of Brazil's population in 11% of its land area (da Fonseca 1985). As a consequence of various agricultural developments, charcoal production, logging, mining, and urbanization, the Atlantic Forest now constitutes the most endangered ecosystem in Brazil (da Fonseca 1985).

Threats to parrots in the Andean region stem mainly from the destruction of the subtropical and temperate forests. In many parts of the Andean valleys in Colombia and Ecuador, the destruction of natural vegetation is almost total. Forests in the tropical zone, particularly in Amazonia, have fared somewhat better. Ten years ago Colombia was losing an estimated 8,200 km² each year from a total of 464,000 km² (FAO/UNEP 1981—based on losses of all broad-leaved forests). Losses to natural vegetation cover have been severest in the Andes, where deforestation is more or less complete. Although it is estimated that 38% of Colombia is still under natural forest cover, most of this is lowland rainforest in Amazonia and Chocó (Gentry 1989). Massive deforestation has also taken place in Ecuador. In 1981, it was estimated that 3,400 km² from a total area of 142,300 km² of broadleaved forest was being cleared annually (FAO/UNEP 1981). The effects of such deforestation have been particularly severe in the Interandean valley, which runs roughly north-south the length of Ecuador, and little natural vegetation now remains in the subtropical and temperate zones (IUCN 1986). Agriculture has certainly taken up vast areas but even where the slopes are too steep for farming, wood is extracted for fuel and timber. Tropical forests at lower altitudes on the Pacific slope of the Andes have also suffered serious destruction.

Since their colonization by Europeans, the islands of the Caribbean have undergone extensive and as in the case of Puerto Rico, almost total deforestation. At the time of Columbus's discovery of these islands, the parrot fauna was very rich and included a minimum of 28 species, but in the subsequent 500 years, the number of psittacines in the region has been reduced by about half (Snyder et al. 1987, J. W. Wiley unpubl. MS). Of the 12 remaining species that are endemic to the Caribbean, 7 are threatened and the other 5 are "near-threatened." Although many of these birds were hunted in the past for food and trapped to supply pets for both the local population and overseas markets, today the main threat to their survival is posed by the scarcity of suitable habitat. A reduction in the area occupied by these birds also renders them more susceptible to the effects of catastrophic events like hurricanes. Logging for building materials, the extraction of timber for charcoal production, illegal shifting cultivation, subsistence agriculture, the replacement of native vegetation with cash crops, and the destruction of forests to make way for tourist developments continue to accelerate on most islands where native parrots survive.

Human Exploitation

The number of threatened species is much higher for parrots than for almost all other families of birds. This situation exists because the usual factor responsible for species endangerment, habitat destruction, is compounded by another major factor—direct human exploitation (hunting for food and feathers and, much more significantly, trapping for the pet trade). The only group of birds comparably threatened is the Galliformes, although in that case it is hunting, not trade, that is the dominant form of exploitation.

In the Neotropics, parrots are valued as pets and for ceremonial uses by a variety of indigenous peoples and were among the first goods to be traded with European explorers (Snyder et al. 1987). Thomsen and Brautigam (1991) reviewed the indigenous exploitation of Neotropical parrots and concluded that on the whole this was sustainable, and that the decline of almost all species occurred only after the arrival of Europeans. Instances since then of the extermination of populations, and even entire species as a result of excessive hunting, are few but cautionary. The Cuban Macaw, *Ara cubensis* (= *tricolor*), now extinct, was killed for food and trapped as pets (Greenway 1967), while *Guaruba guarouba* is still shot by colonists to the point where this is a serious threat (Oren and Novaes 1986). Snyder et al. (1987) discuss a number of other Caribbean parrots that may have been lost to hunting.

In general, under most conditions and for most species, hunting does not now pose a serious threat. However, where birds are naturally scarce or suffering from the effects of habitat loss or excessive exploitation for trade, hunting for subsistence and plumes can still be a significant factor affecting survival. Hunting for plumes may become a more serious threat when it is taken outside of its normal cultural context and conducted to supply tourist markets. The collection of plumes for products intended for the tourist trade is thought to be a factor adversely affecting the numbers of *Anodorhynchus hyacinthinus* present in the catchments of the Xingu, Araguaia, and Tocantins (Munn et al. 1989).

It is nevertheless trade, and in particular international trade, in parrots that is cardinally to blame for the plight of many species. This is ironic, given that the majority of threatened species are supposedly protected from trade by either national or international controls, or both (Thomsen and Mulliken 1991). Such controls have been introduced through CITES, through species-specific protection, and through the imposition of unilateral wildlife export bans. Appendix I to CITES includes species at risk of global extinction from trade and for which all commercial trading is prohibited (see Appendix in Thomsen and Mulliken 1991). Species listed in CITES Appendix II are those for which careful management is required to ensure that trade remains sustainable.

To some extent these instruments may work. In the five-year period from 1981 to 1985, the United States imported over 703,000 Neotropical parrots representing at least 96 (of a possible 140) different species (Jorgenson and Thomsen 1987). But since the majority of these birds were common species, the *legal* mass shipment of psittacine species to Europe and North America appears to threaten very few species with global extinction. Two exceptions include Peru's persistent export of *Brotogeris pyrrhopterus* in large numbers and Cuba's exportation of *Aratinga euops* to Eastern Europe.

In fact, few Neotropical countries currently allow the commercial export of their wildlife, although Argentina, Guyana, Surinam, and Peru still allow substantial commercial exports of parrots (Thomsen and Mulliken 1991). These countries are now trading under quotas. As a consequence, the *legal* trading of CITES Appendix II birds has not yet reduced the great majority of species' populations to a level where they are threatened. However, owing to the lack of good data on populations, density, and productivity of traded species, overexploitation can still be a problem. This is certainly happening with Blue-fronted Amazons (*Amazona aestiva*) in Argentina (Beissinger and Bucher 1991), and could lead to the local depletion of other species exported from that country.

The *illegal* trade is quite a different story. Specimens of CITES Appendix II species are sometimes captured in a country where a wildlife export ban exists and then moved to a country where documentation of local origin can be obtained, permitting their "legal" exportation (see Bucher's comments in James 1991, Thomsen and Mulliken 1991). For example, this is thought to occur in Venezuela where birds are taken illegally in the region of the Orinoco delta and introduced into international markets through Guyana (S. D. Strahl pers. comm.). Birds have also been captured in Brazil and exported from Bolivia. But since Bolivia introduced a wildlife export ban in 1986, Bolivian birds have sometimes been flown out of Argentina (Thomsen and Mulliken 1991).

The most intractable problems are presented by the clandestine dealing of the highly prized CITES Appendix I species. Most notable targets are the blue macaws and the Lesser Antillean amazons, because they combine great beauty with great rarity and prestige value in the eyes of those that collect them. *Anodorhynchus hyacinthinus*, which was formerly widespread from the Amazonian forest fringes in Brazil south to the Pantanal of Bolivia and Paraguay, is now scarce. Its three remaining population centers are becoming increasingly fragmented, mostly as a consequence of illegal capture for trade (Munn et al. 1989). *A. leari* is enviously sought after and will only survive through constant (and expensive) vigilance against trappers. The last known population of *Cyanopsitta spixii* (in the region of Curaçá, Bahia state, Brazil) was effectively wiped out by bird trappers: the only known nest was plundered and the chicks were offered for sale on the international market for $40,000 (Thomsen and Munn 1988). The situation of the Lesser Antillean amazons is considerably better owing to recent heightened national awareness of and pride in the birds in question (Butler 1991). Nevertheless, the price of these birds' freedom is eternal vigilance, and this is not without costs to the island states involved.

CONCLUSIONS

It is difficult to be precise about the degree of threat represented by trade compared to habitat loss in the 42 Neotropical parrots at risk. However, a general assessment suggests that without trade as a factor the number of species under consideration might be halved.

Thus there are 17 species for which habitat destruction is the primary cause of endangerment: *Leptopstittaca branickii, Ognorhynchus icterotis, Rhynchopsitta terrisi, Pyrrhura perlata, P. orcesi, P. albipectus, P. calliptera, Bolborhynchus ferrugineifrons, Touit melanonota, T. surda, T. stictoptera, Hapalopsitta amazonina, H. fuertesi, H. pyrrhops, Amazona pretrei, A. vinacea,* and *Triclaria malachitacea.* This is not to say that trade would not seriously harm them, but it has played no great part in their decline to date.

There are three species which face separate or unknown factors: *Aratinga brevipes, Amazona vittata,* and *A. dufresniana.* The first two are in small numbers on islands where habitat has diminished and introduced animals are a constraint; the third is too little known to be confident about the causes of its decline.

There are 11 species experiencing both habitat loss and the impact of trapping: *Ara rubrogenys, Guaruba guarouba, Aratinga euops, A. auricapilla, Rhynchopsitta pachyrhyncha, Pyrrhura cruentata, Brotogeris pyrrhopterus, Amazona leucocephala, A. viridigenalis, A. brasiliensis,* and *A. rhodocorytha.*

The four Lesser Antillean amazons, *Amazona versicolor, A. arausiaca, A. guildingii,* and *A. imperialis,* must be placed as a subgroup here, since they face some habitat loss and some trade. Both were major threats in the past but now are greatly moderated by strict new controls (Butler 1991).

Finally, seven species face extinction mainly from trade pressures, namely *Anodorhynchus hyacinthinus, A. glaucus* (if it still exists), *A. leari, Cyanopsitta spixii, Ara glaucogularis, Amazona tucumana,* and *A. barbadensis.*

As a very general rule, habitat destruction affects most Andean species, and trade affects the great majority of lowland mainland forms. It would appear straightforward to assume that species affected by both threats would be most at risk. However, none of these species, with the exception of *Amazona imperialis,* gives as great a cause for alarm as the four blue macaws at risk from trade, *A. vittata,* or the "missing" Andean parrots so urgently in need of attention (*Ognorhynchus icterotis* and *Hapalopsittaca fuertesi*). Present evidence clearly suggests that Neotropical parrot conservation has to proceed on many fronts and in many countries. Major initiatives in habitat conservation must be mounted for key sites in Colombia, Ecuador, and Brazil, and priority conservation measures must be aimed at controlling trade, concentrating on the protection of the most threatened and highly valued species.

Finally, it needs to be noted that the remaining 100-odd non- or near-threatened Neotropical parrots are still in need of monitoring. Most species must be in some sort of decline, given the ubiquitous problem of habitat loss in the Americas. The trade situation is always shifting, with new species becoming popular and new populations being exploited. If more species are not to enter the threatened listings, there has to be much more fieldwork and site protection throughout the Neotropical region.

ACKNOWLEDGMENTS

ICBP thanks the Commission of the European Communities for its financial support of work toward an action plan for the conservation of New World parrots, from which this paper is partly derived. We also acknowledge our use of drafts by L. A. P. Gonzaga and N. K. Krabbe for ICBP's forthcoming *Threatened birds of the Americas,* and thank T. P. Inskipp of the Wildlife

Trade Monitoring Unit (U.K.) for his comments on a draft of this paper. N.J.C.'s attendance at the AOU symposium was paid for by TRAFFIC International, and for this and much other support ICBP expresses warm thanks to J. B. Thomsen.

LITERATURE CITED

Berovides, A. V. 1986. Nidificación de la cotorra de Cuba (*Amazona leucocephala*) en la isla de la Juventud. Ciencias Biológicas 15:133–135.

Beissinger, S. R., & E. H. Bucher. 1991. Sustainable harvesting of parrots for conservation. This volume.

Beissinger, S. R., & J. R. Waltman. 1991. Extraordinary clutch size and hatching asynchrony of a Neotropical parrot. Auk 108: in press.

Bradley, P. E. 1986. A report of a census of *Amazona leucocephala caymenensis* and *Amazona leucocephala hesterna* in the Cayman Islands. George Town, Grand Cayman, Cayman Islands, Government Tech. Publ. No. 1.

Butler, P. J. 1991. Parrots, pressures, people, and pride. This volume.

Collar, N. J., & P. Andrew. 1988. Birds to watch: the ICBP world check-list of threatened birds. Cambridge, United Kingdom, International Council for Bird Preservation Tech. Publ. 8.

da Fonseca, G. A. B. 1985. The vanishing Brazilian Atlantic Forest. Biol. Conserv. 34:17–34.

Food and Agriculture Organization of the United Nations/United Nations Environment Program. 1981. Tropical forest resource assessment project (in the framework of the global environment monitoring system). Rome, Food and Agriculture Organization of the United Nations.

Forshaw, J. M. 1989. Parrots of the world, third revised edition. Willoughby, Australia, Lansdowne Editions.

Gentry, A. 1989. Northwest South America (Colombia, Ecuador and Peru). Pages 392–400 *in* Floristic inventory of tropical countries (D. G. Campbell & H. D. Hammon, Eds.). New York, New York Botanical Garden.

Greenway, J. C. 1967. Extinct and vanishing birds of the world, second edition. New York, Dover Publications.

Homberger, D. 1985. Parrot. Pages 437–439 *in* A dictionary of birds (B.

Campbell & E. Lack, Eds.). Calton, Staffordshire, United Kingdom, T. & A. D. Poyser.

International Union for Conservation of Nature and Natural Resources. 1986. Plants in danger: what do we know? Gland, Switzerland, International Union for Conservation of Nature and Natural Resources.

James, F. C. (Ed.) 1991. A round-table discussion of parrot trade problems and solutions. This volume.

Jorgenson, A., & J. B. Thomsen. 1987. Neotropical parrots imported by the United States, 1981 to 1985. TRAFFIC(USA) 2/3:3–8.

Juniper, T., & C. Yamashita. 1990. The conservation of Spix's Macaw. Oryx 24:224–228.

King, W. B. 1977–1979. Red data book, vol. 2: Aves, part 2. Morges, Switzerland, International Union for Conservation of Nature and Natural Resources.

Lanning, D. V. 1982. Survey of the Red-fronted Macaw (*Ara rubrogenys*) and Caninde Macaw (*Ara caninde*) in Bolivia, December 1981–March 1982. Unpublished report to International Council for Bird Preservation and New York Zoological Society.

Mittermeier, R. A. 1986. Atlantic forest: now for the good news. IUCN Bulletin 17:30.

Munn, C. A. 1988. Macaw biology in Manu National Park, Peru. Parrotletter 1: 18–21.

Munn, C. A. 1991. Macaw biology and ecotourism, or "when a bird in the bush is worth two in the hand." This volume.

Munn, C. A., J. B. Thomsen, & C. Yamashita. 1989. The Hyacinth Macaw. Pages 404–419 *in* Audubon wildlife report 1989/1990 (W. J. Chandler, Ed.). San Diego, Academic Press.

Noegel, R. 1982. Rare and endangered amazons. AFA Watchbird 9(2): 20–23.

Oren, D. C., & F. C. Novaes. 1986. Observations of the Golden Parakeet *Aratinga guarouba* in northern Brazil. Biol. Conserv. 36:329–337.

Poulsen, M. K., H. Bloch, C. Rahbek, & J. F. Rasmussen. 1989. Loja—garden of Ecuador. World Birdwatch 11(3):10.

Sick, H. 1990. Notes on the taxonomy of Brazilian parrots. Ararajuba 1:111–112.

Silva, T. 1989. A monograph of endangered parrots. Pickering, Ontario, Silvio Mattacchione.

Snyder, N. F. R., J. W. Wiley, & C. B. Kepler. 1987. The parrots of Luquillo: natural history and conservation of the Puerto Rican Parrot. Los Angeles, Western Foundation of Vertebrate Zoology.

Soulé, M. E. (Ed.) 1987. Viable populations for conservation. Cambridge, Cambridge University Press.

Stattersfield, A. 1988. A systematic list of birds presumed to have become extinct since 1600. Pages 241–244 and Appendix II *in* Rare birds of the world (by G. Mountfort). London, Collins.

Thomsen, J. B., & A. Brautigam. 1991. Sustainable use of Neotropical parrots. Pages 359–379 *in* Neotropical wildlife use and conservation (J. G. Robinson & K. H. Redford, Eds.). Chicago, University of Chicago Press.

Thomsen, J. B., & T. A. Mulliken. 1991. Trade in Neotropical psittacines and its conservation implications. This volume.

Thomsen, J. B., & C. A. Munn. 1988. *Cyanopsitta spixii*: a non-recovery report. Parrotletter 1:6–7.

Varty, N. 1990. Hurricane Gilbert—Jamaica counts the cost. World Birdwatch 12(1/2):6–7.

APPENDIX: THREATENED PARROTS OF THE NEOTROPICS

This list represents the current (June 1990) judgment of ICBP concerning parrots at risk in the Neotropics. It incorporates (except for the Rusty-faced Parrot, which is now split) the relevant texts from Collar and Andrew (1988), with sources omitted for the sake of space and with a few square-bracketed updated points. Entries have been made for several new species (marked *), which were mentioned in the section of this chapter entitled "Dimensions of the Crisis."

1. Hyacinth Macaw (*Anodorhynchus hyacinthinus*), the largest parrot in the world, inhabits dry forest and wet forest edge in central Brazil and the adjacent Pantanal regions of easternmost Bolivia and northeast Paraguay. It has greatly declined owing to trading and hunting, such that now only some 2,500 to 5,000 birds are estimated to remain, the vast majority of them in Brazil.

2. Glaucous Macaw (*Anodorhynchus glaucus*) of southeast Brazil, southeast Para-

guay, northeast Argentina, and possibly northern Uruguay is almost certainly now extinct.

3. Indigo (Lear's) Macaw (*Anodorhynchus leari*) is restricted to caatinga (thorn scrub) adjacent to a set of sandstone cliffs in one small part of Bahia state, northeast Brazil, where the total population is not known to be more than 60 birds.

4. Little Blue (Spix's) Macaw (*Cyanopsitta spixii*) stands now at the very brink of extinction in a small area of interior northeast Brazil, having declined mainly through hunting and trapping to a few individuals [one in 1990] in the wild. Initiatives to provide effective protection for these last wild birds have failed, as have endeavors to establish a captive-breeding program using the stock (perhaps no more than 20 in total) held in private collections around the world [but a new initiative is underway in 1990].

5. Blue-throated Macaw (*Ara glaucogularis*, formerly called Caninde or Wagler's Macaw, *A. caninde*) is known with certainty only from a very restricted part of Bolivia in Beni and Santa Cruz, where it numbers between 500 and 1,000 birds. It is still heavily exploited for the cage-bird trade.

6. Red-fronted Macaw (*Ara rubrogenys*) is restricted to a small area of east-central Bolivia with a total population not exceeding 5,000 birds. It is being heavily trapped for export and even persecuted for supposed crop damage.

7. Golden Conure [considered *Guaruba guarouba* by Sick (1990) but *Aratinga guarouba* by Forshaw (1989)] occurs in a small area of northern Brazil from western Pará to western Maranhão in terra firme (dryland forest), or adjacent várzea (seasonally flooded forest). It has declined considerably owing to habitat loss and trapping, mainly in the eastern part of its range where the creation of a secure reserve is the top priority.

8. Socorro Conure (*Aratinga brevipes*), considered distinct from the Green Parakeet (*A. holochlora*) based on voice, morphology, and plumage, is fairly common but vulnerable on Socorro, in the Revillagigedos Islands (Mexico).

9. Cuban Conure (*Aratinga euops*), although not considered in a recent review of the country's threatened birds, is restricted to and steeply declining in Cuba. It became extinct on the Isla de la Juventud (Isle of Pines), and is now possibly only fairly common in the woods of the Zapata Swamp.

10. Golden-capped Conure (*Aratinga auricapilla*) is restricted to forested parts of southeast Brazil. Although still common in a few places, it must be declining due to habitat fragmentation and trapping in numbers for the bird trade. There have apparently been no recent records of the species from the southern part of its range.

11. Golden-plumed Conure (*Leptosittaca branickii*) is a very poorly known bird with disjunct populations in the temperate-zone forests of Colombia, Ecuador, and southern Peru. Nowhere is it common.

12. Yellow-eared Conure (*Ognorhynchus icterotis*) is now confined to a small area of southwest Colombia and adjacent northern Ecuador, and has seriously declined due to extensive forest destruction. A flock of 25 on the northeast slope of Cerro Munchique, July 1978, apparently constitutes the most recent (Colombian) record.

13. Thick-billed Parrot (*Rhynchopsitta pachyrhyncha*) is endemic to the Sierra Madre Occidental, Mexico, where it is seriously declining due to trapping for the cage-bird trade, shooting, and destruction of its pine-forest habitat. A recent initiative to establish a breeding population in Arizona, U.S.A., has had some success.

14. Maroon-fronted Parrot (*Rhynchopsitta terrisi*) is endemic to the Sierra Madre Oriental, Mexico, where it numbers around 2,000 birds and suffers from considerable deforestation.

15. Blue-chested Parakeet (Blue-throated Conure) (*Pyrrhura cruentata*) is endemic to primary lowland forest in southeast Brazil, where its range is now highly fragmented and numbers have massively declined. It remains common locally in several areas, including some forest reserves, although most of these are under permanent pressure and are vulnerable to cutting and bird-trapping.

16. Pearly Parakeet (*Pyrrhura perlata* not including *P. perlata perlata* = *P. rhodogaster*) is endemic to a small part of north Brazil and has declined substantially owing to forest destruction.

17. *El Oro Parakeet (*Pyrrhura orcesi*) is a recently described species restricted to humid forest between 600 and 1,100 m on the west slope of the Andes in Azuay and El Oro in southwest Ecuador, where it is threatened by habitat destruction.

18. White-necked Parakeet (*Pyrrhura albipectus*) is restricted to a small region of southeast Ecuador in which it is uncommon and perpetually vulnerable to habitat loss. It probably breeds in the Cordillera Cutucú.

19. Flame-winged Parakeet (*Pyrrhura calliptera*) occupies both slopes of the eastern Andes of Colombia from southern Boyacá to southwestern Cundinamarca. Forest destruction has been extensive within its restricted range and, although still locally numerous, it is now clearly threatened.

20. Rufous-fronted Parakeet (*Bolborhynchus ferrugineifrons*) is endemic to high-elevation shrubland in the Central Cordillera of the Andes of Colombia. It had not been reported with certainty since 1955 until it was recently relocated at 3,280 to 4,000 m in the vicinity of Laguna de Otún and on Nevado del Ruiz, with an estimated population of 1,000 to 2,000.

21. Grey-cheeked Parakeet (*Brotogeris pyrrhopterus*) occurs in deciduous forest in southwest Ecuador and northwest Peru. It has declined considerably, apparently due to habitat loss and trapping. No fewer than 20,000 were exported from Peru in 1984.

22. Brown-backed Parrotlet (*Touit melanonota*) is endemic to southeast Brazil with a now fragmented range, within which it is rare though possibly much overlooked.

In 1987 there were records of one to seven birds in Rio de Janeiro state.

23. Golden-tailed Parrotlet (*Touit surda*) is endemic to mainly lowland forest in eastern Brazil. It is now probably rare, owing to extensive habitat loss, but it is certainly overlooked often. Recent records are from Ceará, Alagoas, southern Bahia, northern Espírito Santo, and Rio de Janeiro states.

24. Spot-winged Parrotlet (*Touit stictoptera*) inhabits Colombia (known definitely from only three localities in forested mountains), eastern Ecuador, and northern Peru. It is threatened by deforestation in Colombia.

25. Rusty-faced Parrot (*Hapalopsittaca amazonina*) occurs in humid forested highlands as three races in the Andes of Mérida, Venezuela, and Eastern and Central Andes of Colombia. It is now rare throughout its range.

26. *Fuertes's Parrot (*Hapalopsittaca fuertesi*) has not been seen for certain since 1911. It is known only from humid temperate forests on the west slope of the Central Andes of Colombia near the junction of Quindío, Risaralda, and Tolima, where it must be threatened by habitat destruction.

27. *Red-faced Parrot (*Hapalopsittaca pyrrhops*) is confined to the temperate forests at 2,500 to 3,500 m in the southern half of Ecuador and immediately adjacent to Peru. It is at risk from habitat destruction.

28. *White-headed (Cuban) Amazon (*Amazona leucocephala*) occurs in five subspecies, all likely to be threatened by either habitat destruction, trade, or introduced predators. It occurs on Cuba (nominate *leucocephala*), Isle of Pines (*palmarum*), Cayman Islands (*caymanensis* and *hesterna*), and Bahamas (*bahamensis*).

29. Puerto Rican Amazon (*Amazona vittata*) remains critically endangered in rainforest of the Luquillo Mountains of northeastern Puerto Rico owing to habitat destruction compounded by a scarcity of nest sites, and competition for nest sites and predation of nests by Pearly-eyed Thrashers (*Margarops fuscatus*). Intensive management has wrought a slow but steady improvement in the wild population from a low of 13 in 1975 to around 30 a decade later.

30. *Alder (or Tucuman) Amazon (*Amazona tucumana*) formerly ranged from Chuquisaca Department, Bolivia, south to Tucumán Province in northwest Argentina, but now seems to be found only in southern Salta and in Catamarca and Tucumán provinces, Argentina. Large numbers in trade from 1984 to 1986 have reduced it to a rare species.

31. Red-spectacled Amazon (*Amazona pretrei*) has a small range covering south Brazil and northeast Argentina, possibly also Uruguay and Paraguay. It is closely associated with *Araucaria*-dominated forest and is declining seriously.

32. Red-crowned (Green-cheeked) Amazon (*Amazona viridigenalis*) is endemic to a small area of northeast Mexico and has seriously declined, due to habitat destruction and trapping. Several thousands remain in the wild with thousands in captivity in the United States where some feral populations are established (e.g.,

Miami, Los Angeles, San Diego, and Brownsville, and on Puerto Rico).

33. Red-tailed Amazon (*Amazona brasiliensis*) is endemic to coastal forests of south Brazil where it is very rare. A population of no more than 4,000 is now confined to an area of approximately 600,000 ha in southeastern São Paulo and northeastern Paraná. This area is not yet fully protected from timber exploitation and bird trapping, although some parts of it have been given protected status.

34. *Blue-cheeked Amazon (*Amazona dufresniana*) occurs in rainforest in eastern Venezuela and adjacent Guyana, Surinam, and French Guiana, but seems everywhere very uncommon for reasons unknown.

35. Red-browed Amazon (*Amazona rhodocorytha*) is endemic to eastern Brazil where it has suffered a major decline as a result of forest clearance, trapping, and hunting. Recent records are from several areas in Minas Gerais, northern Espírito Santo, and Rio de Janeiro states.

36. Yellow-shouldered Amazon (*Amazona barbadensis*) has a disjunct and highly restricted distribution in northern Venezuela (plus Isla de Margarita and Isla la Blanquilla) and on Bonaire in the Netherlands Antilles. Still locally common on the mainland in the late 1970s, it is now easily found at only one locality, although it is still heavily traded. On Margarita Island it is confined to the center of the Macanao Peninsula and probably numbers 150 to 200 birds. On Bonaire numbers appear to be under 350, limited by nest predation by people, rats, and Pearly-eyed Thrashers.

37. Vinaceous Amazon (*Amazona vinacea*) occurs in southeast Brazil, southeast Paraguay, and northeast Argentina (Misiones). It has suffered a major decline mainly through widespread forest habitat loss. A relict population survives in Misiones but is gravely at risk there.

38. St. Lucia Amazon (*Amazona versicolor*) is restricted to the central mountain forests of St. Lucia. Its population was estimated to be 100 in 1977 but had risen to 250 in 1986, attributed to forest protection and the abolition of hunting.

39. Red-necked Amazon (*Amazona arausiaca*) was found in lowland forest in the northern two-thirds of Dominica, where hunting has been the major cause of its decline. Today it only occurs around Morne Diablotin and it is seriously threatened by the rapid clearance of its habitat for banana plantations. In 1987 the population was estimated at 300 birds.

40. St. Vincent Amazon (*Amazona guildingii*) is confined to several valleys along the mountainous backbone of St. Vincent, where it suffers from illegal hunting and loss of habitat. In 1979 a volcanic eruption and in 1980 a hurricane caused further habitat degradation. However, forest clearance for agriculture and charcoal-burning remains the greatest threat, with capture for the pet trade adding to the problems. The population was estimated to be about 420 in 1982.

41. Imperial Amazon (*Amazona imperialis*) is a mountain rainforest species from

Dominica and is very highly prized as a cage bird. Intense hunting for food and sport resulted in a range contraction by the 1970s to two areas. Serious hurricanes in 1979 and 1980 annihilated the southern population. The northern population, found on the slopes of Morne Diablotin, is threatened by habitat destruction and in 1987 was estimated to be only 60 birds [80 in May 1990].

42. Purple-bellied Parrot (*Triclaria malachitacea*) is endemic to and declining in southeast Brazil. Recent fieldwork has found it in only Rio de Janeiro, São Paulo, and Rio Grande do Sul states [but also Argentina (Misiones)].

Resumen.—El Nuevo Mundo alberga unas 140 especies de loros de las cuales no menos de 42 (30%) pueden ser consideradas en peligro de extinción. Esta proporción tan alta ha resultado principalmente por una combinación de la destrucción de hábitat y la explotación para satisfacer la demanda del comercio de mascotas. América Central (incluyendo a México) contiene 4 especies de loros en peligro; el Caribe 7; el norte de América del Sur 4; los Andes del noroeste de América del Sur 11; las sabanas del interior (principalmente Brazil y Bolivia) 6 (todos guacamayos); y la región de bosque costanera del atlántico de Brazil y Argentina 9 (estos números están sujetos a revisión constante). De estas 42 especies, 17 están en peligro únicamente por la pérdida de hábitat, 7 por el comercio, 15 por una combinación de ambos, y 3 por otros factores. De las 98 especies de loros que no están en peligro, casi todas están siendo reducidas en número y muchas requieren medidas de conservación para amortiguar los impactos actuales causados por la pérdida de habitat y la captura para el comercio.

2. Parrots, Pressures, People, and Pride

Paul J. Butler

RARE Center for Tropical Bird Conservation, 19th & The Parkway,
Philadelphia, Pennsylvania 19103

Abstract.—The parrots of the eastern Caribbean are unique symbols of nationhood. Despite being protected for nearly a century, most species are under threat of extinction from hunting, hurricanes, the pet trade, and habitat destruction. A decade ago there was little hope for their survival, but now they have a chance as the result of innovative conservation education programs taking place in Saint Lucia, Saint Vincent and the Grenadines, and Dominica. Through songs, dance, theater, and the mass media, forestry departments of these islands are using pride to promote species preservation. Local attitudes are changing and parrot populations are on the increase.

Most of the major islands of the Caribbean host *Amazona* parrots, usually a distinct species for each island. These species can be divided into two groups: the five medium-sized Greater Antillean species and the four larger Lesser Antillean species. This paper concentrates on the latter group.

Snyder et al. (1987) suggested that all parrots of the West Indies were derived originally from one or more separate invasions of continental forms arriving from Central or South America. They may have dispersed from Trinidad and Tobago, or from the Yucatan through Cuba, or through Jamaica from the Honduran-Nicaraguan bulge. However derived, two factors are certain: parrots have long been an integral part of the West Indian avifauna and they are, as a group, threatened with extinction. When Christopher Columbus "discovered" the West Indies in October 1492, they were inhabited by 26 or 27 species of macaws, parrots, and parakeets (Snyder et al. 1987). In the intervening 500 years, more than half of these psittacines have become extinct. All 7 species of macaws have vanished, as have 5 of the 8 species of parakeets and 3 of the 12 species of *Amazona* parrots. Today of the 14 parrot species that formerly existed in the Lesser Antilles only 4 remain (Table 1).

The Saint Lucia Parrot (*Amazona versicolor*)

This species is indigenous to Saint Lucia, where it inhabits the mountainous forests of the island's interior (Butler 1987). Although once common, its numbers have been seriously depleted and it is now confined to 37 km² of remnant forest surrounded by human habitation in the south-central part of the island (C. Nicholls pers. comm.). By 1976, only 150 ± 25 birds remained (Jeggo 1976).

During the decade that followed, an intensive conservation program was put into effect by Saint Lucia's Forestry Department. As a result of strengthened legislation, the establishment of reserves, and changing attitudes, the population of this species has slowly risen and today it numbers 200 to 250 individuals (Butler 1987). In 1982 the first successful breeding in captivity of this species occurred at the Jersey Zoo, where from an initial captive flock of 9 birds in 1975 there are now 22 birds. In late 1989 a captive-raised pair from Jersey Zoo were returned to the island accompanied by the Rt. Honourable Prime Minister of Saint Lucia, his Minister of Agriculture, and Chief Forest Officer. Since 1979 this species has been the National Bird of Saint Lucia.

The Saint Vincent Parrot (*Amazona guildingii*)

This parrot was probably never very common, at least in this century. A short time ago it was believed to be extinct (Knobel 1926). Most post-war accounts have estimated the population to be about 200 to 500 birds (Nichols 1980, Lambet 1983, Butler 1988).

In an attempt to conserve this endemic and endangered psittacine, Saint

Table 1. Species of psittacids in the Lesser Antilles at the time of the island's "discovery" by Columbus and their present status [adapted from Snyder et. al. (1987)].

Species	Island	Status	Comments
Ara guadeloupensis	Guadeloupe	Extinct	Described by Huttich (1534), Labat (1742); rare before 1760.
Ara atwoodi	Dominica	Extinct	Described by Labat (1742), Atwood (1791); rare before 1760.
Unnamed macaw	Martinique	Extinct	Clear that a distinctive species of *Ara* once existed; du Tertre (1654), Clark (1950a, 1908).
Amazona imperialis	Dominica	Endangered	Tiny population facing extinction.
Amazona arausiaca	Dominica	Endangered	Small population threatened with extinction.
Amazona violacea	Guadeloupe	Extinct	Described by du Tertre (1654) and Labat (1742); Buffon (1779) classed species as rare; formally described by Clark (1905b).
Amazona martinica	Martinique	Extinct	Common during Labat's (1742) visit; formally described by Clark (1905b).
Amazona versicolor	St. Lucia	Endangered	Small population, increasing due to recent conservation measures.
Amazona guildingii	St. Vincent	Endangered	Small population, probably stable.
Unnamed parrot	Grenada	Extinct	Described by du Tertre (1667).
Aratinga labati	Guadeloupe	Extinct	Described by du Tertre (1654), de Rochefort (1658), Labat (1742), and Clark (1905b); rare before 1760.
Unnamed parakeet	Martinique	Extinct	Clear that a distinct species of *Aratinga* once existed here; Clark (1905c).
Unnamed parakeet	Dominica	Extinct	Clear that a distinct species of *Aratinga* once existed here before 1878; Clark (1905c).
Unnamed parakeet	Barbados	Extinct	Described by Hughes (1750) and Schomburgk (1848); Clark (1905c).

Vincent's Forestry Division, under the direction of Calvin Nicholls and more recently under Brian Johnson, implemented a multi-faceted conservation program which is beginning to show signs of success. A reserve has been established, CITES (Convention on International Trade In Endangered Species) has been ratified and in 1988 the Saint Vincent Parrot was bred successfully in captivity for the first time on the island. This species is the National Bird of Saint Vincent and the Grenadines.

The Red-necked Parrot (*Amazona arausiaca*)

Early studies describe this parrot as being relatively common (Verrill 1892). Bond (1928) noted it to be "probably the most numerous of the four Lesser Antillean Amazons." However, by the mid-1960s its numbers had declined significantly, and Fisher et al. (1969) reported its population to have "suffered considerably as a result of forest destruction, shooting and trapping."

Further population declines can be attributed to the devastating effects of Hurricane David (Snyder and Snyder 1979). Evans (1988) recently estimated the population of *A. arausiaca* to be approximately 250 birds, all within the Northern Forest Reserve. The greatest density of parrots was in the Syndicate/ Picard Valley areas, near Morne Diablotin.

The Imperial Parrot (*Amazona imperialis*)

Because of its low reproductive potential (Forshaw 1989) and the limited amount of habitat available, this species has probably never been common on Dominica (Grieve 1906). Although Imperial Parrots have been protected by law since 1914, local people have shot them for food (Frost 1959). After the passage of Hurricane David in 1979, Snyder and Snyder (1979) estimated the population of *A. imperialis* had been reduced to fewer than 150 individuals. Evans (1988) recently estimated the parrot's population at about 60 individuals, mostly concentrated on the northwestern slope of Morne Diablotin. This species is the National Bird of Dominica.

NATURAL THREATS TO LESSER ANTILLEAN PARROTS

Populations of the Lesser Antillean parrots face a complex set of natural threats. Although they have few natural predators, it is possible that opossums (*Didelphis marsupialis*), rats (*Rattus* sp.), the semi-arboreal boa (*Constrictor constrictor*), and Broad-winged Hawks (*Buteo platypterus*) may take eggs and fledglings, but there is little supporting documentation (Nichols 1980). Pearly-eyed Thrashers (*Margarops fuscatus*) aggressively exclude parrots from nest cavities (Snyder et al. 1987). Thrashers may be an important competitor for nest holes with the parrots of Saint Lucia and Dominica, but they do not occur on Saint Vincent. Nichols (1976) noted competitive interactions at two *A. arausiaca* nest cavities in the Hampstead Valley and the thrashers ousted the parrots. It is also possible that honey bees (*Apis mellifera*) represent a threat to nesting parrots, since their nest site preferences overlap those of parrots (Snyder et al. 1987).

Catastrophic natural disasters, especially hurricanes and volcanic eruptions, may be the most significant sources of natural mortality for parrots on the islands of the Caribbean. After a severe hurricane on Saint Vincent, Clark (1905b) reported that the numbers of birds were "very sensibly diminished, those of the high woods, especially the parrots, appearing to have suffered the most. Hundreds, if not thousands of birds were killed on the island. . . ." Hurricane David struck Dominica in 1979 and its winds were especially severe. Afterwards Snyder and Snyder (1979) noted that "parrots (many of them weak and on the ground), were seen in a variety of unexpected lowland localities." They added, "Thus, although a large fraction of the parrot population must have been killed directly by the physical battering of the storm, the scarcity of food following the hurricane appears to have been an equally critical problem." In 1980 Hurricane Allen damaged an estimated 80% of Saint Lucia's forest, killing perhaps 40% of its trees, and presumably causing massive short-term food shortages and losses of nest sites (Jeggo 1980).

There have been five volcanic eruptions on Saint Vincent since 1717, with three occurring this century (1902, 1970, and 1979). Nichols (1980) reported that after the 1979 eruption parrots died as far south as the Buccament Valley.

Until recent times natural stresses probably represented largely insignificant threats to the survival of the Lesser Antillean *Amazona* because their numbers were large enough to be viable after population losses. However, during the last several decades, human activities have resulted in dramatic reductions in the numbers of parrots and the extent of their habitats. Today the passage of a hurricane, a volcanic eruption, an increase in competition, or other natural threats could easily spell the end of any one of these species.

HUMAN THREATS TO LESSER ANTILLEAN PARROTS

Parrots have been hunted for food on every West Indian island on which they have occurred. It was probably as a direct result of hunting that the endemic psittacines of Martinique and Guadeloupe became extinct. Clark (1905b), quoting de Rochefort in 1658, wrote: "The hunters place them in the rank of game birds, and do not think it is a waste of powder to shoot them, for they are good and fat as the best fowl. . . ." Knobel (1926) suggested that if the shooting of parrots in Saint Vincent was not prohibited it would ultimately lead to the extermination of the species. There are still reports of Red-necked Parrots on Dominica being shot, either for sport or food, or more likely in an attempt to wound them to allow their capture for sale (pers. obs.).

Parrots have always been popular as pets and were probably kept by the native peoples of all West Indian islands. With the decline in numbers of these parrots and because of the burgeoning international trade in endangered species, these birds have come under increasing demand. Gochfeld (1974), Andrle and Andrle (1975), Lambet (1983), and Snyder et al. (1987) document interviews with parrot trappers on the islands. Lambet (1983) reported "one villager, who had been involved in the parrot trade until 1978, told us that it was very easy to avoid customs officials by using yachts to remove birds. This particular trapper claimed to have caught 27 nestlings during a 2 to 3 year period, although 33% of them died before he was able to sell them." Fortunately, changes in legislation, higher levels of enforcement, and a greater level of local pride have recently reduced trade to negligible levels.

Today, deforestation for agricultural development and charcoal exploitation probably pose the most serious threat to the parrots of the Lesser Antilles. Lack et al. (1973), Gochfeld (1974), and Lambet (1983) all attributed the decline of *A. guildingii* to cutting forests. On Saint Lucia, primary rainforest, especially on private lands, is being destroyed at about 2% per year (G. L. Charles pers. comm.) to make way for agriculture. Deforestation destroys critical feeding and nesting habitat of parrots. A steep rise in banana prices experienced in the mid-1980s exacerbated deforestation on Saint Lucia, both directly through the felling of forest for land cultivation and indirectly through the expansion of the road system, which made the island's interior more accessible for agriculture.

Evans (1986) concluded that when rainforest was modified, the abundance of some species, such as Bananaquits (*Coereba flaveola*) and Lesser Antillean Bullfinches (*Loxigilla noctis*), increased but the overall number of species present decreased. Declines were particularly noticeable for species that require large expanses of undisturbed forest: Imperial Parrots, Red-necked Parrot, Ruddy Quail Doves (*Geotrygon montana*), and Forest Thrushes (*Cichlherminia lherminieri*). The effects of habitat modification vary depending on the size of intact rainforest nearby and the type of agriculture that replaces the forest. Continuing deforestation raises serious concerns not only for Caribbean parrots and other forest-dwelling species, but also for the water supplies of the islands.

LESSER ANTILLEAN PARROT CONSERVATION EFFORTS THROUGH LEGISLATION AND ENFORCEMENT

Saint Lucia, Saint Vincent, and Dominica have protected their parrots through the enactment of legislation dating back to the turn of the century. Such legislation includes the 1901 Birds and Fish Protection Ordinance of Saint Vincent and the 1914 Wild Birds Protection Ordinance of Dominica. These laws have been supplemented with the establishment of forest reserves, national parks, and conservation areas. Yet these actions failed to reverse declines of the populations of endemic psittacines.

A fundamental problem in using legislation to alter human behavior on small islands, like the Lesser Antilles, is that the majority of islanders are known to one another. Thus, forest officers and other law enforcement officials are reluctant to take their "neighbors" to court and, more often than not, a charge is never levied. Indeed for almost 90 years (1885 to 1975) no wildlife offenses were recorded in Saint Lucia. During this period it was estimated that over

40 parrots per year were being shot in attempts to catch them (Wingate 1969).

Even in those rare instances when offenders were taken before a magistrate, wildlife offenses were not perceived as being serious. The penalties handed down were often inadequate to serve as an effective deterrent, typically falling far short of the maximum penalty stated in the legislation. For example in 1984 an individual was fined EC$ 20 for killing a turtle in Saint Lucia, although the maximum possible fine for this offense was EC$ 250 (pers. obs.). Weak penalties demoralize forestry officers; they typically spend several days preparing for and attending court, facing community ostracism throughout, only to see the offender released with a token punishment.

Reserve establishment also has its limitations. While it is relatively easy for governments to set aside tracts of nationally owned land for reserves and national parks, in reality the land often has only "paper protection." Financial and manpower shortages preclude parks and reserves from being effectively patrolled, and seldom are boundaries well marked unless external financial support is obtained (e.g., on Saint Lucia). Even under those circumstances, a lack of continuing finances usually results in inadequate maintenance, especially in areas far from roads and other access points. Often these are the very areas under heaviest threat from illegal squatters.

In developing countries, particularly insular nations with a small land base, rapidly rising populations, increasing material expectations, and high unemployment place tremendous pressure on the physical environment. To reverse the loss of biological diversity and the destruction of habitat, there must be a fundamental change in people's perceptions and attitudes toward their natural heritage. Alternative forms of land use that have a minimum of negative effects on the environment must be promoted.

THE ROLE OF EDUCATION IN PARROT CONSERVATION

Education has a pivotal role to play by complementing the other "pillars" of a conservation program. The realization that wildlife is important and that threatened endemic species have national importance can help ensure that law enforcement agents view wildlife offenses with greater seriousness and that the fines imposed by magistrates reflect the gravity of the cases. Education in soil conservation, good land-use practices, and crop diversification reduces the scope and seriousness of squatting.

Environmental education programs initiated in developing, small island societies can be especially successful for several reasons: (1) These societies typically possess a youthful population with a high percentage attending some type of academic institution (23% in Dominica and 28% in Saint Vincent). Therefore, environmental education materials entering the school system will directly reach a considerable proportion of the populace; (2) Family size is large (Saint Vincent's averages 5) so that information disseminated to households can be extremely effective; (3) The communication media often guarantee the government air time each day, affording a good opportunity to direct environmental messages at a "captive audience"; (4) Although there is often a lack of locally produced educational materials of any sort, there is a desire on the part of parents and teachers to use information that relates to their own country. Materials produced which fulfill this need will be readily accepted and utilized; and (5) A strong sense of religious and community spirit exists on these islands. Most island villages have their own youth, social, or community groups through which education programs may be implemented.

Using their parrots as symbols of national pride, the islands of Saint Lucia, Saint Vincent and the Grenadines, and Dominica, with assistance from RARE Center for Tropical Bird Conservation, have undertaken a conservation education program that is achieving spectacular results. The general philosophy of this program is twofold. First, any conservation program that relies exclusively on foreign aid is often doomed to fail when the funds are exhausted. To ensure continued funding, local businesses must be encouraged to support the effort by financing conservation materials and activities that link the interests of local sponsors to a popular cause. Second, reliance on external technical assistance does not provide local conservationists with lasting tools to enact or continue their projects. Involving and training local personnel in every aspect of the work promotes greater local commitment long after foreign agency involvement has ended.

The strategy adopted on these islands was to run education programs like a corporate marketing campaign. Each island's colorful national birds (*A. versicolor, A. guildingii,* and *A. imperialis*) became a focus for promotion.

As in any marketing approach, the program commenced with a "consumer" research study. Approximately 1% of the population on each island was surveyed by a questionnaire (see Appendix for a sample). To cope with low literacy levels, the questionnaire was simple in format. While one of its functions was to gather data, it also played an important role in beginning the education component of the program. The questionnaire determined the existing levels of knowledge about the endemic parrot and its habitat, and people's attitudes toward parrot conservation. It also assisted in determining the percentage of the population that listened to the radio and read newspapers to ascertain the type and format of educational materials to be developed. Information concerning favorite radio programs was solicited so that these could be targeted in the education component of the project. Perhaps most important though, the questionnaire involved all forest officers, who acted as the agents for its distribution and whose responsibility it was to distribute them in the communities where they lived and worked. This enabled the public to familiarize themselves with the officers, developing personal contacts that were to become important in the future.

After respondents completed the questionnaire, they were informed of the correct responses and of the plight of the parrot. This began the process of stimulating an awareness and knowledge of the bird in question. Each respondent was given a colorful badge depicting the parrot as a token for his or her assistance (Fig. 1).

From the results of the questionnaire, each island's population was divided into a number of target groups and materials were produced specifically for each group (Fig. 2). Colorful posters depicting the parrot and linking its survival to island pride were distributed island-wide and displayed in store windows, bars, health centers, post offices, and police stations (Fig. 3).

The first audience to be addressed were the nation's children. In both Saint Vincent and Dominica every school was visited (87 in Saint Vincent) by forestry officers who spoke to over 90% of the island's children. Conservation songs were taught, badges were distributed, and parrot fan clubs were established.

Younger children participated in school programs by developing puppet shows, and in all three islands the school component was complemented by a monthly environmental newspaper which used the parrot to teach its readers

Fig. 1. A costumed "Vincie" the parrot hands a parrot badge to a school child on Saint Vincent (© Robert Rattner, 1989)

about other environmental problems facing their island home. Written, funded, and produced locally, these handouts also appeared as supplements in the region's newspapers.

School dropouts and teenagers were targeted through the use of music, dance, and theater. Local musicians and artists were encouraged to write lyrics and tunes promoting conservation and national pride. Recording studios and television stations supported the cause by providing assistance in producing audio and video tapes for public broadcast. In Dominica, six such songs were produced including a reggae dub entitled "Protect de Sisserou" by Daddy Cecil, a cadence entitled "Save the Sisserou" by Ophelia, and a gospel tune entitled "We're depending upon you" by Pastor Pascal. In addition, a 10-song, 45-minute children's musical depicting the plight of the island's national bird was produced by a local school of music.

Religious leaders were also invited to support the program. Some prepared

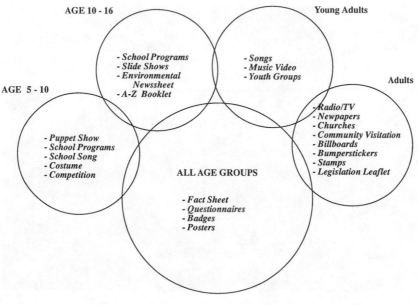

AGE 10 - 16   Young Adults

- *School Programs*   - *Songs*
- *Slide Shows*   - *Music Video*
- *Environmental*   - *Youth Groups*
  Newssheet   Adults
AGE 5 - 10   - *A-Z Booklet*

                                      - *Radio/TV*
                                      - *Newpapers*
                                      - *Churches*
                                      - *Community Visitation*
- *Puppet Show*   - *Billboards*
- *School Programs*   - *Bumperstickers*
- *School Song*   - *Stamps*
- *Costume*   - *Legislation Leaflet*
- *Competition*   ALL AGE GROUPS

                       - *Fact Sheet*
                       - *Questionnaires*
                       - *Badges*
                       - *Posters*

© RARE Center 1990

Fig. 2. Education materials and activities tailored to specific age group. (© RARE Center)

and delivered sermons on environmental themes in churches throughout the island. All farmers, youth, and community groups were visited to further spread the conservation message.

Finally, businesses were encouraged to link their products to parrot conservation. They sponsored booklets, bags, bumper stickers, and other educational materials. Large colorful billboards were also erected at prominent roadside intersections and in urban parks.

RESULTS OF THE PARROT EDUCATION PROGRAM

On each island at the end of the first year of the education campaign, the questionnaire survey was repeated using the same questions and again sampling 1% of the population (Table 2). Questions were phrased somewhat differently

Fig. 3. Saint Vincent parrot poster, used in public
education campaign, was placed in store windows,
bars, post offices, and other public areas.

on each island so a comparison between islands is not valid. Before the education
campaign began, most residents of Saint Vincent and the Grenadines, and
Dominica knew that the parrot was their national bird and that it was endemic
to their island, but were not familiar with the conservation problems threatening
the birds. On Saint Vincent, a significant increase in public awareness was
achieved for nearly all measures. Public knowledge of the parrots' status in the
wild and the penalty for killing parrots increased the most dramatically between
pre- and post-tests. Most important, 80% of the public rated it "very important"
and another 13% rated it "important" for the government to spend time and
money protecting the parrot and its forest home.

In response to this overwhelming support for conservation, the Government
of Saint Vincent and the Grenadines revised its wildlife legislation. It updated
fines, gave additional protection to the national bird, ratified CITES, designated
preserves including 13% of the island as a wildlife reserve for the parrot, and

Table 2. Summary of responses to questionnaires (n = number of respondents) before and after conservation education projects on two Lesser Antillean Islands.

Question: "Knowledge of"	Percent of respondents answering question correctly			
	Saint Vincent		Dominica	
	Pre-project	Post-project	Pre-project	Post-project
	n = 798	n = 743	n = 894	n = 808
Name of National Bird	95	94	88	94[a]
Status in wild	35	60[a]	49	54[a]
Endemic?	55	72[a]	78	86[a]
Penalty for hunting	1	24[a]	35	53[a]
Penalty for clearing forest	Not asked	Not asked	31	43[a]
Importance of protecting the National Bird[b]	69	80[a]	66	68

[a] X^2 test between pre-project and post-project, $P < 0.05$.
[b] Those answering "very important."

constructed a captive breeding complex for *A. guildingii* located in the Botanical Gardens where the island's first captive-bred parrot was raised. In addition, the 1990s were declared the "Decade Of The Environment." Today the national bird has also become a voice for a variety of other environmental issues. As a caricature on billboards and in the news sheet "Vincie's Nature Notes," the parrot continues to advocate water quality, a litter-free environment, and even the protection of marine resources.

Similar changes have occurred in Dominica. A significant increase in public awareness was achieved after a year of the education campaign for nearly all measures (Table 2). The greatest gain occurred in public awareness of the penalties for hunting parrots and clearing parrot habitat (forest lands). Although the percentage of respondents that rated it "very important" to protect the parrot did not increase, over 40% of the nation's school children contributed cash, and an additional 40% signed a petition saying that they would have contributed if they had any money.

These education programs are beginning to pay dividends for the target species. In Saint Lucia, the hunting and illegal trapping of *A. versicolor* has ceased. The government has allocated more resources toward forest protection and its sustainable use. In less than a decade, expenditures on forest management have increased almost ten-fold and harvesting of timber from the rainforest has been drastically reduced. Today Saint Lucia Parrots are increasing and they are beginning to re-populate areas of the island from which they vanished long ago (Butler 1987).

Reporting on aspects of Saint Lucia's conservation program, United States Federal agent Jeff Friend in 1981 (unpubl.) wrote: "Saint Lucia was a remarkable experience . . . they (the Forestry Department) have utilized their resources in the most efficient and expeditious manner. They have managed the most important element of successful support, they have made the protection of wildlife something that the public and thus the government officials have identified with. The incorporation of the conservation message, and even the Madison Avenue type marketing of the animals with their exaggeratedly-created human characteristics, has created a motivational variable not previously present in the populace." He concluded that "Saint Lucia is the prototype of a successful program for saving species threatened with extinction."

THE OVERALL POTENTIAL FOR USING NATIONAL PRIDE IN CONSERVATION EDUCATION

Can this type of program be replicated outside of small island nations? Perhaps not, but this has yet to be tested. The success of the Lesser Antillean programs has apparently depended on the close-knit composition of island societies, the accessibility of local politicians, and the acceptance of low levels of technology. If such programs were to be attempted in parts of Brazil for example, it is conceivable that the local population would endorse the efforts, but unlikely that decision makers in a far-away capital would respond as enthusiastically as Caribbean politicians have.

Such program achievements also depend on linking preservation to pride, an emotion common in small newly independent nations, as well as on using a colorful, easily recognizable animal. It would be far more difficult, perhaps impossible, to succeed with less charismatic species or with the concept of rainforest. Much depends upon the species selected as the focus for the conservation education program. Birds and certain mammals are recommended partly because they are proven environmental indicators and partly because they are highly visible, attractive, and often well known to local people. Many newly independent nations have declared birds as national symbols, and using national pride may be an ideal method to promote species preservation.

However, if the bird in danger is not the country's national bird, then perhaps consider if it lives in the same habitat or faces the same threats as the national bird. If the answer is yes, then it may be advisable to change the focus of the education program to the national bird and mention the "target species" when preparing press releases or visiting schools. Promoting the preservation of the national bird and its habitat will then help, by association, to conserve the target species. Alternatively the target species might be declared Parish or State bird or Bird of the Year, thereby giving a focus for the campaign.

Similar programs as those described earlier are shortly to commence elsewhere in the Caribbean, this time using local counterparts and a manual produced by RARE Center for Tropical Bird Conservation. This manual is directed at mid-level technical officers and educators who are actively involved in initiating and implementing species-related conservation programs. The manual guides its user through a step-by-step process of setting up a national cam-

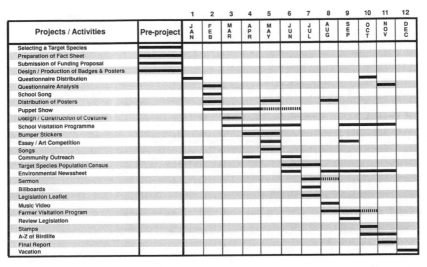

©RARE Center 1990

Fig. 4. Summary of major education activities by month for RARE Center's Caribbean Education Campaign. (© RARE Center)

paign to protect a target species. The core of the manual comprises a series of 12 monthly chapters that cover a total of 58 tasks, including running a questionnaire survey, bumper sticker production, puppet shows, music videos, etc. (Fig. 4). The pages of the manual are in different colors. Sample letters, press releases, and work sheets are in yellow, while designs for costumes and puppet shows are in blue. As the project coordinator progresses through the manual, these samples will be replaced with copies of his or her own work. At the end of the project, the manual should have no colored sheets and will serve as a comprehensive summary of the year's activities.

Included in the manual is information on census techniques, sample wildlife legislation, and copies of slides, tapes, and videos to illustrate similar work that has been carried out in the region. The user-friendly manual serves only as a guide and will hopefully be adapted to local conditions. To encourage this, RARE Center offers an annual monetary award for the best new idea, which will be incorporated in future editions of the manual.

Only when these projects get under way will we know the adaptability of this type of conservation program. Of one thing we can be sure—it has proven successful on the island paradises of Saint Lucia and her neighbors where the sight of parrots flying free over their forest home is living proof.

ACKNOWLEDGMENTS

A number of external agencies have assisted in the aforementioned programs including RARE Center for Tropical Bird Conservation, World Wildlife Fund, Jersey Wildlife Preservation Trust, Wildlife Preservation Trust International, and the International Council for Bird Preservation. Their role has been catalytic, but nothing could have been achieved without the dedicated efforts of the islands' Forestry Departments, and their Directors—Gabriel Charles, Brian Johnson, and Felix Gregoire—the true saviors of Caribbean Psittacines. Thanks also to Noel Snyder and Steve Beissinger for reviewing this paper, and James Wiley for help with Table 1.

LITERATURE CITED

Andrle, R. F., & P. R. Andrle. 1975. Report on the status and conservation of the Whistling Warbler on St. Vincent, West Indies. ICBP Bull. 12:245–251.

Atwood, T. 1791. The history of the island of Dominica. London, J. Johnson.

Bond, J. 1928. On the birds of Dominica, St. Lucia, St. Vincent and Barbados BWI. Proc. Acad. Nat. Sci. Phila. 80:523–545.

Buffon, G. L. L. 1779. Histoire naturelle des oiseaux. Vol. 6. Paris.

Butler, P. 1987. The Saint Lucia Parrot—recipe for success. Castries, Saint Lucia, Government of Saint Lucia.

Butler, P. 1988. The Saint Vincent Parrot (*Amazona guildingii*): the road to recovery. Philadelphia, Pennsylvania, RARE Center for Tropical Bird Conservation.

Clark, A. H. 1905a. The Lesser Antillean macaws. Auk 22:266–273.

Clark, A. H. 1905b. The West Indian Parrots. Auk 22:337–346.

Clark, A. H. 1905c. The genus *Conurus* in the West Indies. Auk 22:310–312.

Clark, A. H. 1908. The macaw of Dominica. Auk 25:309–311.

Evans, P. 1986. Dominica, West Indies. ICBP World Birdwatch 8:8–10.

Evans, P. 1988. The conservation status of Imperial and Red-necked Parrots on Dominica. Cambridge, International Council for Bird Preservation Report 27.

Fisher, J., N. Simon, & J. Vincent. 1969. Wildlife in danger. New York, Viking Press.

Forshaw, J. M. 1989. Parrots of the world, third revised edition. Willoughby, Australia, Lansdowne Editions.

Frost, K. D. 1959. Three amazon parrots. Avicult. Mag. 65:84–85.

Gochfield, M. 1974. Current status and threats to some parrots of the Lesser Antilles. Biol. Conserv. 6:184–187.

Grieve, S. 1906. Notes upon the island of Dominica. London, Adam & Charles Black.

Hughes, G. 1750. Natural history of Barbados. London.

Huttich, J. 1534. Die New Welt, der landschaften und Insulen, so bis hie her allen Altweltbeschrybern vnbekant, Jungst aber von der Portugalescrn vun Hispaniern jm Nidergcrglichen Meer herfunden. Strassburg (Strasbourg).

Jeggo, D. 1976. Lesser Antillean parrot programme: a progress report. Jersey Wildlife Preservation Trust XIII Annual Report 21–26.

Jeggo, D. 1980. The effects of Hurricane Allen on the status of the Saint Lucia Parrot. Jersey Wildlife Preservation Trust XVII Annual Report.

Knobel, E. M. 1926. Amazon parrots. Avicult. Mag. 4 (9):229–234.

Labat, J. B. 1742. Nouveau voyage aux isles de l'Amerique. New edition, 8 volumes. Paris.

Lack, D., E. Lack, P. Lack, & A. Lack. 1973. Birds on St. Vincent. Ibis 115: 46–52.

Lambet, F. 1983. Report of an expedition to survey the status of the Saint Vincent Parrot, *Amazona guildingii*. Cambridge, International Council for Bird Preservation Study Report No. 3.

Nichols, H. A. 1976. Parrot watching in the Caribbean. Save Animals From Extinction Newsletter 6:1–8.

Nichols, T. D. 1980. St. Vincent Amazon (*Amazona guildingii*) predators, clutch size, plumage polymorphism, effect of the volcanic eruption, and population estimate. Pages 197–208 *in* Conservation of New World parrots (R. F.

Pasquier, Ed.). Washington, District of Columbia, Smithsonian Institution Press.

de Rochefort, C. C. 1658. Histoire naturelle et morale des Isles Antilles de l' Amerique. Rotterdam, Chez Arnould Leers.

Schomburgk, R. H. 1848. History of Barbados.

Snyder, N. F. R., & H. A. Snyder. 1979. An assessment of the status of parrots on Dominica following Hurricane David. Unpubl. report to International Council for Bird Preservation.

Snyder, N. F. R., J. W. Wiley, & C. B. Kepler. 1987. The parrots of Luquillo: natural history and conservation of the Puerto Rican Parrot. Los Angeles, California, Western Foundation of Vertebrate Zoology.

du Tertre, R. P. J. 1654. Histoire generale des isles des Christophie, de la Guadeloupe, de la Martinique, et autres dans l' Amerique. Paris.

du Tertre, R. P. J. 1667. Histoire general des Antilles habitées par les François, 3 vols. Paris, Chez Thomas Iolly.

Verrill, G. E. 1892. Notes on the fauna of the island of Dominica, British West Indies, with lists of the species obtained and observed by D. E. and A. H. Verrill. Trans. Conn. Acad. Arts Sci. 8:315–355.

Wingate, D. 1969. Summary Report for International Council for Bird Preservation meeting. ICBP Newsletter.

APPENDIX: FORESTRY AND WILDLIFE DIVISION QUESTIONNAIRE

Sector: _____

To be completed by enumerator

Dear Friend:

As Dominicans we should cherish our natural environment and protect it. Symbolic of our island's natural beauty is its National Bird, and by answering the following questions you will help us to protect it and ensure that we never loose our National Pride.

(1) What is the National Bird of the Dominica?

_____ Don't Know ( )

(2) Is it only to be found on the Dominica?

     1. Yes ( )   2. No ( )   3. Don't Know ( )

(2a) If 'no' where else does it live? _____

(3) How scarce is our National Bird?

    1. Less than 100 remain ( )   4. 501–1000 remain ( )

    2. 101–250 remain ( )   5. More than 1000 remain ( )

    3. 251–500 remain ( )   6. Don't know ( )

(4) What is the main reason for our National Bird becoming scarce?

    _____ Don't Know ( )

(5) Do you think our National Bird is a good choice?

    1. Yes ( )   2. No ( )   3. Don't Know ( )

(6) What is the fine / penalty for hunting / shooting our National Bird?

    1. $48 ( )   2. $250 ( )   3. $2500 ( )   4. $5000 ( )

    Don't Know ( )

(7) What is the fine / penalty for illegally clearing lands in the Forest Reserve?

    1. $48 ( )   2. $240 ( )   3. $720 ( )   4. Don't Know ( )

(8) Protecting our National Bird is going to cost money. Money that could be used for other things. Do you think that it is important that your Government spend time and money on our National Bird?

    1. Not important ( )   2. Important ( )

    3. Very important ( )   4. Don't Know ( )

(9) Why? _____

BIO : DATA

(10) What is your age?

    1. 1–11 ( )   2. 12–16 ( )   3. 17–25 ( )   4. 26–35 ( )

    5. 36–45 ( )   6. 46–55 ( )   7. 56–65 ( )   8. 66+ ( )

(11) What is your job?

    1. Government employee ( )   2. Farmer / Laborer ( )

    3. Private sector ( )   4. Unemployed ( )   5. Housewife ( )

    6. Student ( )   7. Other ( )

(12) Do you listen to the radio?

    1. Every day ( )   2. Occasionally ( )   3. Never ( )

(13) What is your favorite program? _____

(14) Do you read the local newspaper?

    1. Yes ( )   2. No ( )

        YOU DO NOT NEED TO WRITE YOUR NAME ON THIS FORM

Return to:

Forestry & Wildlife Division, Ministry of Agriculture, Botanical Gardens, ROSEAU, Dominica

        THANK YOU FOR YOUR HELP

Resumen.—Los loros del Caribe oriental son símbolos únicos de nacionalidad. A pesar de ser protegidas por casi un siglo, la mayoría de las especies están en peligro de extinción por medio de la cacería, huracanes, el comercio de mascotas y destrucción de habitat. Hace una década habia poca esperanza de supervivencia para los loros pero ahora existen esperanzas como resultado de programas novedosos de educación conservacionista implementadas en Santa Lucía, San Vicente y las Granadinas, y Dominica. Por medio de canciones, danzas, obras de teatro, y medios de comunicación a las masas, los departamentos forestales de estas islas están usando el sentido del orgullo para promover la protección de especies. Las actitudes locales están cambiando y las poblaciones de loros están aumentando.

3. Macaw Biology and Ecotourism, or "When a Bird in the Bush Is Worth Two in the Hand"

Charles A. Munn

Wildlife Conservation International, New York Zoological Society, Bronx, New York 10460

Abstract.—In many cases, wild, free-ranging parrots can generate more foreign exchange for tropical countries and more local employment for forest people when exploited indirectly as tourist attractions than when exploited directly for the pet trade. Observations of hundreds of individually recognizable macaws at clay licks and studies of the fate of 38 macaw nests in Manu Biosphere Reserve, Peru, indicated that macaw density and productivity were low. Only 10% to 20% of the birds bred in a given year, pairs usually fledged only one young, and one-third of the nests failed. Estimates of revenues of Peruvian jungle lodges and data from tourist interviews show that each macaw potentially can generate between $750 and $4,700 annually in tourist receipts. Using a range of estimates for macaw longevity and ecotourism potentials, I calculate that each free-flying large macaw might generate $22,500 to $165,000 of tourist receipts in its lifetime. Indirect exploitation of parrots as tourist attractions is better understood, easier to manage, and less fraught with risks than direct exploitation of slow-reproducing adults and fragile nestlings for the pet trade. I also discuss difficulties in implementing ecotourism as a conservation method, how the lack of land tenure by local forest peoples makes any rational macaw management hard, and how to ensure that local people benefit from macaw ecotourism. Two promising new efforts to initiate macaw lick tourism in southeastern Peru are described, and I conclude with comments on the overall potentials of ecotourism in parrot conservation.

Recognition of the dangers of mechanized logging and agricultural development in fragile tropical wildlands has inspired considerable interest in sustainable development and conservation of the world's remaining tropical forests. Recent studies have demonstrated the potential conservation benefits of harvesting and marketing non-wood forest products such as Brazil nuts, rubber latex, palm fruits, essential oils, dyes and colorings, vegetable ivory (carved hard palm nut endosperm), and palm fronds for floral arrangements (Peters et al. 1989, Redford and Redford 1990, J. Nations pers. comm.). Most of the non-wood products discussed in this context are, like the list above, derived from plants.

Relatively little detailed analysis has been conducted on the animal products that can be exploited sustainably in rainforests. This omission is odd considering that the least destructive, and often the most lucrative, method of sustainable exploitation of some of the world's finest remaining tropical forests is through the use of wild animals as subjects for photo safaris and nature tours. This activity frequently is called "ecotourism" (Laarman and Durst 1987, Healy 1988, Boo 1990, Groom et al. 1991).

In this paper I integrate biological data from a long-term study of large macaws in the rainforests of Manu Biosphere Reserve with economic data from rainforest tourist lodges in the Peruvian Amazon. I demonstrate that wild macaws can serve as the basis for a profitable and sustainable ecotourism industry that can employ many local people, while simultaneously conserving macaws and the enormous expanses of forest on which they depend.

BIOLOGICAL CONSTRAINTS FOR MACAW CONSERVATION: MACAWS ARE SCARCE, REPRODUCE SLOWLY, AND ARE EASY TO EXTIRPATE

To estimate macaw density and reproductive rates in the unhunted, pristine forests of southeastern Peru, my colleagues and I studied macaw nests and a major riverbank macaw lick in the Manu Biosphere Reserve from 1985 through 1989. A macaw lick is an exposed riverbank or streambank clay deposit eaten on most clear days of the year by macaws and other species of parrots

Fig. 1. Scarlet Macaws (*Ara macao*) and Red-and-Green Macaws (*Ara chloroptera*) on a clay lick on the middle Manu River, Peru. (Photograph by Eduardo Nycander and Charles Munn)

(see Fig. 1). They probably eat the clay either to help detoxify defensive secondary compounds in their diet of seeds, unripe fruits, and leaves, or to supply essential mineral nutrients that are lacking in their entirely vegetarian fare (Emmons and Stark 1979, Munn 1988).

At the study lick we used 35-mm cameras with 400- to 1200-mm lenses to obtain close-up black and white photographs of the heads of several hundred Red-and-Green Macaws (*Ara chloroptera*). Photographs were processed using a gasoline-powered generator and an enlarger in a makeshift darkroom at the Totoracocha field station in Manu. By studying the lines of red facial feathers, and marks and irregularities on the large upper mandibles of the birds, we were able to recognize unambiguously 332 different face sides.

By examining all the face photos after each photo session from 24 July through 26 August 1989, we found by the last sessions that between 40% and 60% of the photos in each session were repeats or photographic "recaptures" of birds from previous sessions (Table 1). The sequence of photographs in

Table 1. Photographic recaptures of Red-and-Green Macaw faces in July and August 1989 at a macaw lick in middle Manu River, Peru.

Date and face side	Number of face sides photographed	Number of new faces photographed	Number of faces recaptured	Estimated population size[1]
Left face sides only (total of 178 sides)				
24 July	40	40	0	—
31 July	24	17	7	137
2 August	56	41	15	189
4 August	5	3	2	193
6 August	46	31	15	238
8 August	17	14	3	275
9 August	37	19	18	282
21 August	30	12	18	281
24 August	6	1	5	276
26 August	8	0	8	268
Right face sides only (total of 154 sides)				
24 July	31	31	0	—
31 July	17	12	5	105
2 August	56	44	12	173
4 August	7	2	5	161
6 August	31	24	7	217
8 August	19	15	4	256
9 August	25	13	12	259
21 August	28	10	18	248
24 August	8	3	5	247
26 August	5	0	5	241

[1]Based on Schnabel (Krumholz) formula (Davis and Winstead 1980).

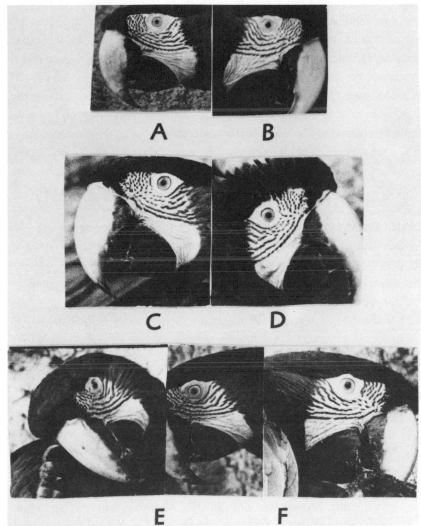

Fig. 2. Unsymmetrical left and right facial line patterns of three Red-and-Green Macaws.
A and B, C and D, and E and F represent the left and right sides of three different birds. Both
photographs that are combined in E are the left side of the same bird; they show how different
head positions typically change the appearance of a facial pattern, which nevertheless remains
distinctively recognizable.

contact prints made from the original negatives showed that 46 of the 332 face sides represented the left and right sides of 23 particular birds (the left and right sides were not the same on any bird; Fig. 2). The 286 remaining face sides (155 left sides and 131 right sides) were unmatched, and no doubt represent many fewer than 286 different birds. If we assume that the 178 left face sides photographed represent about 50% of all left face sides at the site (judging from a 50% recapture rate), then the total population of Red-and-Green Macaws using the lick was about 356 birds.

The Schnabel (Krumholz) formula (Davis and Winstead 1980), which conservatively estimates total population based on cumulative photographic captures and recaptures, yielded estimates of 268 to 282 birds (using only the left face sides) and of 241 to 259 (using only the right face sides). These estimates depend in part on the assumption that all the birds using the lick visit the lick with approximately the same frequency and are equally likely to be photographed. Since the next closest lick is at least 9 km away, a distance that seems to exceed the typical daily movements of the birds, it is unlikely that the birds visited other licks. The other assumptions of the recapture method (Davis and Winstead 1980) are probably reasonably well satisfied in the case of these macaws: (1) that there is no gain or loss of marks during the study period; (2) there is no substantial recruitment during the study; and (3) there is no difference in mortality of the "marked" and "unmarked" individuals.

The photographic information, together with visual resightings of individuals with distinctive face and wing markings, allowed us to determine that some individual birds came to eat clay every other or every third day. One particular macaw that we photographed during several different photo sessions in 1989 had identical facial line patterns to a bird filmed at the same lick 10 months earlier by the BBC Natural History Film Unit. Though it is impossible to state with certainty that these two birds are the same, in this case the precise match of the facial patterns and, in general, the apparent improbability that fixed feather follicles will migrate make it likely that facial patterns will remain stable and recognizable from year to year.

To gain information on the areas serviced by licks, we studied movements of individual birds. From treetop overlooks we used 10- and 15-power binoculars, a tripod-mounted Questar telescope, and a stop watch to record flight durations and distances of Red-and-Green, Scarlet (*Ara macao*), and Blue-and-Yellow Macaws (*Ara ararauna*) departing from licks in the Manu and in the upper Tambopata River of southeastern Peru. Though our data are still inconclusive, the birds seem not to fly more than 6 or 7 km at the most when they leave a lick. If we assume that the maximum distance they fly from the lick before landing gives a reasonable bound to the area serviced by the lick, and if we assume that all birds within this area use only the lick in question, then we can estimate crudely the absolute density of macaws in this area. Dividing the estimated 250 to 350 Red-and-Green Macaws coming to the lick by the 154 km² "pie" of forest lying within a 7-km radius of the Manu lick, the population density of this species in the upper Manu would range between 1.6 and 2.3 individuals per square km. These values accord well with our estimates for Red-and-Green Macaw density based on thousands of hours of walking on and off forest trails in this region.

Nevertheless, the assumption that all Red-and-Green Macaws within the 7-km radius come to the lick and to no other lick has not yet been substantiated, although it is a reasonable assumption. Also given that some habitat within 7 km of the lick is seasonally flooded, early successional forest that is not used by Red-and-Green Macaws, the density of the birds in their preferred habitats of upland (never flooded) forest and mature floodplain forest probably lies between 2.5 and 4.0 birds per km². This figure approaches Thiollay's (1989) estimate of 6 birds per km² for French Guiana. We have no face or wing covert photo dossiers for the Scarlet or Blue-and-Yellow Macaws, the other two large species of macaws found in the lowlands of southeastern Peru, but we believe they occur at similar or slightly higher densities.

To evaluate productivity, we studied the fates of nests of five species of macaws in Manu from the earliest stages of incubation. Of 35 large macaw nests, 34% failed completely, 40% fledged one young, and 26% fledged two young (Table 2). While these results suggest substantial nesting success, three types of evidence suggest that only 10% to 20% of the adult mated pairs in the population attempt to nest in any given year. First, of over 20 pairs of Blue-and-Yellow Macaws seen daily at one site in Manu near the end of the nesting season in 1986, only two pairs showed the very obvious dirty, tattered plumage that is typical of nesting birds of this species, whereas the rest were in resplendent, newly molted plumage. Second, of the mean number of 74

Table 2. Nesting success of five species of macaws from 1985 to 1989 in Manu Biosphere Reserve, Peru.

Macaw species	Number and percentage of nests that:			
	Failed	Fledged one young	Fledged two young	Fledged three young
Blue-and-Yellow	5(27.8)	8(44.4)	5(27.8)	0(0.0)
Scarlet	3(33.3)	4(44.4)	2(22.2)	0(0.0)
Red-and-Green	4(50.0)	2(25.0)	2(25.0)	0(0.0)
Chestnut-fronted[1]	0(0.0)	1(50.0)	1(50.0)	0(0.0)
Red-bellied[2]	0(0.0)	0(0.0)	0(0.0)	1(100.0)
Total for large species	12(34.3)	14(40.0)	9(25.7)	0(0.0)
Total for all species	12(31.6)	15(39.5)	10(26.3)	1(3.6)

[1]*Ara severa*
[2]*Ara manilata*

Red-and-Green Macaws seen on 31 days from August through October 1988 at the Manu macaw lick, an average of only 6.8% or 4.9 birds per day possessed the very dark iris color which indicated they were young that had fledged earlier in the year. Interestingly, of 95 sightings of Red-and-Green Macaw pairs with young at that lick (many of which no doubt were repeated sightings of the same families), 57 were of two parents with one young and 38 were of two parents with two young. This result suggests that successfully nesting Red-and-Green Macaws more frequently fledge one young than two.

The third kind of evidence that only 10% to 20% of the adult birds attempt to breed in any given year is that only 22 (15%) of 147 apparent family groups of large macaws seen flying over the Manu River in the 4 months immediately following the end of the nesting season contained more than 2 birds. Most groups (71%) were pairs and 21 (14%) were singletons. Since in all 40 observations of trios or quartets of large macaws at the Manu lick, the third and fourth birds had the very dark irises typical of macaws younger than one year of age, we assume that the trios and quartets flying over the Manu represented mated pairs with young fledged in the previous breeding season.

What are the factors that apparently prevent the vast majority of adult macaws from attempting to reproduce in a given year? First, a substantial number of the apparent adult birds may in fact be between one and five years of age and may still be sexually immature. Second, it is possible that many sexually mature birds are not in physiological condition to reproduce due to poor nutrition or high parasite loads. But perhaps the most severe bottleneck preventing pairs from attempting to breed may be a scarcity of adequate nesting cavities. The plausibility of nest site scarcity is suggested by a number of observations. In 1988 we observed a non-nesting pair of Blue-and-Yellow Macaws mutilate and eject a nearly-fledged conspecific from a nest in the top of a dead palm trunk. The ejected bird subsequently died. A second nestling in the same nest managed to fledge despite further attacks from the marauding pair, who immediately took over the cavity after the second nestling left. At this same site at the beginning of the 1988 nesting season we observed 20 pairs of Blue-and-Yellow Macaws searching a group of dead palm trunks for cavities. Only five of the palms actually had cavities suitable for nesting. After two weeks of daily examination of the dead palms, only five pairs persisted and managed to nest.

Strong competition for nesting cavities has also been apparent at other locations. One especially roomy and dry nest cavity 25 m above the ground in the bole of a 55-m-tall live hardwood tree has been the nesting site for Red-and-Green Macaws each year since we found the cavity in 1987. In the 1988, 1989, and 1990 nesting seasons, the breeding pair spent an enormous amount of time and energy defending the hole from other pairs, at times falling nearly to the ground while viciously fighting beak to beak and feet to feet. The great height of the nest hole so far has made it impossible to photograph the face patterns of the nesting birds, so we do not know if the same pair or different pairs of birds have been using the cavity in different years. We suspect that this nest hole may be used by Red-and-Green Macaws for decades or even centuries if the tree continues to stand.

To understand better the apparent shortage of nest cavities, we thoroughly examined 52 ha of mature floodplain forest for cavity availability. In this area, we scrutinized every large tree of the two hardwood species that produce almost all the best nest cavities for large macaws, *Dipteryx alata* and *Cal-*

licophyllum spruceanum. We also examined all of the 35-m-tall palms (*Iriartea ventricosa*), since these palms also frequently produce good nest cavities after they die. We chose this particular 52-ha patch because we knew that it contained among the highest densities of large specimens of these tree species of any forest in the entire Manu Biosphere Reserve. To assess cavity availability, we used binoculars to examine from the ground all sides of the trunks and branches of all large specimens of these tree species. We found only three potentially acceptable cavities, two of which were traditional Red-and-Green Macaw nests. The third was already well known to us because macaws frequently landed on it and vocalized loudly while examining it as a potential nest site. Thus, it appears that the macaws had located all the potential nest sites in this large tract of forest.

To further test the hypothesis that macaw productivity was limited by nest site availability, we mounted 9 crude nest boxes made from 1.7-m-tall sections of *Iriartea ventricosa* palm trunks at various sites in the forest near the Manu River. These boxes were installed from October 1989 through early January 1990 (egg-laying takes place mostly in December). For logistical reasons, we were only able to hang three boxes high enough in the trees (at heights >13 m on the boles of 35-m-tall *Mauritia flexuosa* palms) that they could be expected to interest macaws. All three boxes attracted nesting pairs immediately. One of the boxes fledged Blue-and-Yellow Macaw young in April 1990, while the other two boxes had design flaws that prevented successful nesting.

Between October 1990 and April 1991, we plan further experiments with 25 improved nest boxes hung in the forest near the Tambopata Macaw Lick. These experiments will be carried out by the personnel of the Tambopata Research Center and have the potential to demonstrate that in southeastern Peru, where there is no timber harvesting or felling of nest trees by bird-catchers, one of the principal factors limiting the number of breeding pairs is a severe shortage of good cavities.

Since large macaws naturally occur at low densities and have low reproductive rates, they can be easily extirpated from large areas of forested land by meat and feather hunters, and birdcatchers. Seventeen macaw counts from moving boats on the Manu River, where there has been no hunting of macaws for decades, yielded totals ranging from 0.8 to 18.9 macaws per hour, with a mean of 6.2 per hour. Similar values for large macaws were obtained from high, concealed lookout points on a hill above the mature floodplain forest of the Manu River. In contrast, counts in areas that are subject to moderate to intense meat hunting (such as on the Alto Madre de Dios River adjacent to Manu, on the Madre de Dios River from the mouth of the Inambari River to the Bolivian border, and from Villa Verde, Bolivia, all the way to Manaus, Brazil) nearly always yielded no large macaws. In a comparison of macaw counts on hunted and unhunted rivers in southeastern Peru, only 3 out of 37 hours of counts on hunted rivers yielded 1 or more large macaws, whereas 69 of 83 hours of counts on unhunted rivers yielded 1 or more large macaws, an obviously significant difference ($\chi^2 = 60.0$, $P < 0.001$). Apparently moderate hunting is sufficient to extirpate large macaws from large regions of the Amazon where the forest cover is still mostly intact. In southeastern Peru there is no substantial harvest of birds for the pet trade, and almost all destruction of macaw populations is due to subsistence and market hunting for meat. In many other parts of the Amazon, however, harvest of macaw nestlings by people who climb or fell nest trees may be a significant factor in the disappearance of these birds.

RAINFOREST TOURISM IS BIG BUSINESS AND IS GROWING FAST

Over the last ten years, nature tourism, or "ecotourism," has grown explosively—more than 25% per year (Boo 1990). Some of the most extraordinary growth in the past five years has been in companies providing tours in the Amazon rainforest. In the 8 August 1989 *New York Times*, Rómulo José de Paula Nuñes, President of the Tourism Agency of the Brazilian State of Amazonas stated, "The number of foreign tourists arriving in Manaus [in the heart of the Brazilian Amazon] increased to 70,000 in 1988 from 12,000 in 1983. In a decade, the number should hit 200,000." Further evidence of the mushrooming interest in rainforests, the Amazon in particular, is provided by the number of cruise ships visiting Manaus, Brazil: 21 ships in the 1988–1989 winter season as compared with only 1 ship in the 1982–1983 season.

Although the Peruvian Amazon has also been the scene of enormous growth in rainforest tourism in the last 10 years, only 2 or 3 of the 30 or more lodges in the Peruvian Amazon offer access to pristine wilderness filled with large, photographable animals. In February 1988, Alfredo Salcedo R., the Peruvian Vice Minister of Tourism, reported (pers. comm.) that 60,000 tourists per year visited the jungle city of Iquitos on the banks of the Upper Amazon in northern Peru. Tour lodges were the fastest growing and most lucrative businesses in Iquitos, and these lodges often repaid government loans in less than one tourist season. Even if only half of the 60,000 visitors went on jungle trips near Iquitos, and the average trip was 3 nights at about $60 per person per night, the gross revenues generated would have been 5.4 million dollars. The actual tourist revenues in Iquitos might have been double or triple that amount.

Rainforest tourism in the Iquitos region grew fast during the past 15 years, even though wildlife viewing in the Iquitos region is poor compared to that available at some easily accessible lodges in pristine southeastern Peru. Furthermore, the boom in jungle tourism across the Amazon of Brazil, Ecuador, and Peru has brought so many tourists into contact with largely animal-poor Amazon forest that, paradoxically, the entire Amazon now has an undeservedly bad reputation as a wildlife viewing destination. What most tourists never realize is that, with the exception of southeastern Peru and a few other remote, virgin parts of the Amazon basin, wildlife density and accessibility is very low across almost the entire region due to heavy exploitation of wildlife resources. Those who wish to see the extraordinary wildlife that used to be common throughout the Amazon now must seek out the few undisturbed parts of the basin.

As a demonstration of the rate of growth that is possible in tour companies that offer excellent wildlife viewing in pristine Amazon forest, I examine the case of one small company in southeastern Peru operating in the Manu Biosphere Reserve (Table 3; B. Gomez pers. comm.). This company is owned entirely by local Peruvian conservationists who live in the forest adjacent to Manu and in the city of Cusco to the southwest of the Reserve. It has grown from 2.5 full-time employees and $7,000 of gross revenues in 1985 to 18 full-time employees and a gross of $240,000 in 1989. Since each employee tends to be the head of a family, and the average family size in Peru is 5 individuals, the lodge directly supported about 90 people in 1989. Each direct job in tourism is estimated to create an additional two jobs in other industries that support the tourism industry. Thus, adding all the direct and indirect jobs

Table 3.   The growth and economic impact of a small Peruvian ecotourism company, Manu Nature Tours and Lodge, composed of a 25-bed lodge, a 26-seat bus, and four 12-passenger, motorized canoes.

Economic benefit	Year				
	1985	1986	1987	1988	1989
Gross income ($)	7,000	24,000	48,000	90,000	240,000
Number of jobs generated in Manu Nature Tours and Lodge	2.5	4.0	10.5	15.0	18.0
Number of jobs generated in supporting companies	5	8	21	30	36
Total number of employees and dependent family members supported	37.5	60.0	157.5	225.0	270.0

created by this one company and multiplying by the average family size of 5, this lodge currently supports approximately 270 people. Since social and economic problems tend to greatly overshadow environmental problems in Latin America, it is important to understand the potential economic and social benefits of properly designed and executed ecotourism.

Further insight into the economic and employment potentials of rainforest ecotourism can be gained by an examination of the Tambopata-Candamo Reserved Zone. Like Manu, this zone is located in the largely pristine forests of southeastern Peru. Daily jet service from Lima and Cusco, Peru makes this region more accessible and less expensive to visit than Manu. In 1989, Tambopata's 3 lodges (by 1990 there were 2 more) with a total of 250 beds had more than doubled the capacity of Manu's 4 lodges (100 beds total), and were grossing many hundreds of thousands of dollars annually (Table 4). Their revenues, and the small amount grossed by independent jungle tour guides in Tambopata, added up to nearly $1.2 million of foreign exchange in 1989. Together with the $380,000 of tourist revenues from Manu, $435,000 gener-

Table 4.   Estimated 1989 revenues from tourism in the Tambopata region of Peru.

Lodge	Number of beds	Number of clients/yr.	Length of stay (days)	Fee ($) per day	Gross income ($)
Cusco-Amazonico	110	5,000	3	48	720,000
Explorer's Inn	70	2,550	3	50	382,500
Tambo Lodge	70	800	3	25	60,000
Independent Guides	–	350	4	20	28,000
Total	250	8,700	–	–	1,190,000

ated in tourist airfares between Cusco and the Tambopata region, and an estimated $262,000 spent elsewhere in Peru by people coming principally to visit the rainforests of Manu and Tambopata, I estimate a total of 2.3 million dollars generated by tourism in southeastern Peru in 1989. An additional $556,000 of revenues were provided by scientific research projects, conservation funding, and sustained capture and utilization of floating trunks of "tropical cedar" (*Cedrela odorata*, a species of mahogany) during annual floods on the Manu River, adding up to a grand total of over $2.8 million (Munn unpubl. data). Considered together as indirect uses of the tropical forest, tourism, research, conservation work, and floating mahogany represent the third most important generator of foreign exchange in all of southeastern Peru, a region of approximately 100,000 km² (a New York State's worth) of intact rainforest.

The most important generator of foreign exchange in southeastern Peru is placer gold mining in the rivers that originate in the nearby Andes. This activity, which generates about $30 million of revenues annually (Rios et al. 1983), consumes large quantities of wildlife to feed some 10,000 to 20,000 employees. It also dumps large amounts of mercury into the rivers, contaminating the fish that are the major source of animal protein for much of the populace. The second largest revenue generator in the region is the more or less sustainable extraction of wild Brazil nuts and rubber latex, which together generated about $4 million in 1989 (Rios et al. 1983, Ministry of Agriculture unpubl. data). Like ecotourism, these nut and latex industries depend entirely on wild trees in intact primary forest. Unlike ecotourism, however, it is not yet clear how indefinitely sustainable these harvests really are, since it is not known how well young Brazil nut and rubber trees are recruited into groves subject to intensive harvesting.

Perhaps more important than the dollar value of ecotourism is the number of jobs involved. Peru is a country where the unemployment rate now exceeds 40%. In 1989 about 9,000 foreigners visited southeastern Peru to see the rainforest. If tourism to the rainforest of southeastern Peru were to grow to 30,000 people per year, each staying for an average of 5 nights instead of the current 2, the demand for jungle lodge beds would rise from the 1989 total of 325 beds to between 2,000 and 2,500. If the ratio of full-time employees to beds is 1:2 (it currently varies from near 1:1 to near 1:4 in the lodges in southeastern Peru), and if 2 indirect jobs were created for every direct job in tourism, then about 18,000 to 19,000 people (including families of employees), or 25% to 30% of the entire population of southeastern Peru, could be supported directly or indirectly by ecotourism. It is reasonable to project that within 5 to 10 years at least 5,000 and possibly as many as 20,000 people in southeastern Peru will be living from rainforest tourism alone.

IMPORTANCE OF MACAW LICKS TO TOURISM POTENTIALS

Tourists Want to See Big Rainforest Birds and Mammals, but are Unsuccessful in Most Places in the Tropics

Interviews I have conducted with over 300 people in the airports of Lima, Cusco, and Puerto Maldonado over the past 11 years indicate that approximately 75% of the foreign visitors to Peru would go to a jungle lodge in the Amazonian rainforest if they knew of a good site to visit. When asked why they would go, or what would they would want to see, 60% to 70% answered wildlife, while only 10% to 20% indicated an interest in seeing Indians, and only 10% to 15% wanted to see trees or the whole ecosystem. When asked what kind of wildlife they would want to see, about 80% to 95% responded birds and monkeys. When asked what kind of birds they would like to see, about 50% indicated parrots and toucans, and few were able to think of other kinds of tropical birds.

About 80% to 95% of the tourists leaving existing lodges in the Tambopata region in 1989 were unsatisfied with wildlife viewing there. This dissatisfaction may have resulted principally from depressed animal densities due to hunting by local people, sometimes even by lodge employees. The implications of lack of good wildlife viewing are obvious: the "word of mouth" about most Amazon jungle lodges is not very good. This bad reputation, which leads to direct losses of referred clients in the future, in turn slows the growth of ecotourism in the Amazon. Furthermore, unsatisfied ecotourists returning home from an uninspiring Amazonian experience are unlikely to make substantial donations to local and international conservation organizations. By comparison, 30% to 50% of wealthy North American and European ecotourists who have visited Manu subsequently made donations of $50 to $100 annually to the local conservation group, the Conservation Association for the Southern Rainforest of Peru (ACSS) based in Cusco.

Macaw Licks Are Major Predictable Amazon Wildlife Spectacles

Even the finest regions of the Amazon offer few opportunities for tourists to see large concentrations of wildlife. In a few pristine sites, ecotourists can see up to 6 species of monkeys in large numbers each day for up to 2 weeks in a large fruiting tree, or a herd of 100 to 200 white-lipped peccaries (*Tayassu pecari*) scouring the forest floor for fallen nuts and fruits. But neither of these phenomena can compare with a large macaw and parrot lick in terms of the color, noise, photo opportunities, and predictability. This last factor, predictability, cannot be overstated in its importance for ecotourism, because a tour company lives or dies based on its ability to deliver a consistently high-quality product. Many ecotourism companies in North America and Europe will avoid a local rainforest tour operator if the quality of the local operator's product varies too much from one trip to the next.

Major macaw licks (which can be defined as those that are visited daily for much of the year by at least 30 large macaws) used to occur in rainforest regions of most or all of the Amazonian countries (Brazil, Peru, Bolivia,

Colombia, and Ecuador). Now reports suggest that most or all of the major macaw licks remaining in the Amazon are confined to the 100,000 km² of largely pristine rainforest of southeastern Peru. My Peruvian colleagues and I have confirmed the existence of at least 26 major macaw licks in southeastern Peru. Furthermore, we have received reliable reports of at least another 10 major licks. Probably there are a score or more of unreported major licks in southeastern Peru.

DIFFICULTIES IN IMPLEMENTING ECOTOURISM AS A CONSERVATION METHOD

Lack of Land Tenure Makes Rational Management Hard

In most tropical countries of Latin America, the local people living in forested habitats have no land titles or legal land tenure. Instead, the forest and its renewable resources belong to a nebulous, sometimes oppressive government or a wealthy, absentee landlord. This situation inexorably leads to overexploitation of forest resources. There is no incentive for the poor forest dwellers to manage the forest for medium and long-term gain. Rather, their best strategy is usually "grab it before my neighbor does," which is simply a restatement of the "tragedy of the commons"—predictable overexploitation of resources that are held in common and not owned by one person or family (Hardin 1968). The conservation crisis of large parrots such as macaws is likely to continue until means are found to counter this basic problem.

I suggest that the lack of land tenure and absence of legal control of harvesting activities in the Amazon mean that the capture and sale of fragile nestlings is presently not a viable strategy for managing macaw populations. In comparison, titling large areas of intact forest to local rainforest peoples and helping them to set up macaw lick ecotourism, as well as other forms of sustainable exploitation of non-wood forest products, represents a relatively easy, fast, and profitable development strategy that may simultaneously protect macaws and the rainforests on which they depend.

Giving local rainforest peoples a stake in managing their own resources, and thus their own future, is the best conservation strategy that one can devise.

The great strength of this strategy is that it depends only on one very robust assumption: that people generally are selfish and only take care of what is theirs while usually abusing that which belongs to others. It is time that conservation strategies be founded on the principles of selfishness and greed, human traits that are difficult to overestimate.

It is important not to underestimate the potential tourist income that forest people could receive by showing off their large macaws. Each male lion living free in the national parks of Kenya currently is worth approximately two to three million dollars in its lifetime as a tourist attraction (Western and Henry 1979). Likewise, each major macaw lick that is accessible and properly displayed by locally owned ecotourism companies might easily be worth as much as or more than the two biggest grossing lodges of Tambopata, Peru, which currently take in $300,000 and $700,000 per year. If each major macaw lick is used by a total of 150 to 400 macaws, then each free-flying, wild macaw would be worth between $750 and $4700 per year as a tourist attraction. If large macaws live an average of at least 30 or 35 years, which is not unlikely, then each bird might be worth $22,500 to $165,000 in its lifetime.

Ensuring that Financial Benefits of Ecotourism Wind up with Local Inhabitants and not with Rich Promoters

It is not sufficient for conservationists simply to tell rainforest peoples to protect and manage their forests through ecotourism. Initially these people will need our help in setting up and learning how to operate ecotourism companies. The first step to ensure that the financial benefits of macaw lick and rainforest tourism stay in the hands of a wide number of local people is for conservationists to help groups of local people to obtain the land title or rights to key macaw licks and other rainforest attractions. Subsequently, conservationists need to provide technical assistance and arrange inexpensive financing for these local peoples so they can learn how to set up, operate, and sell proper tours. On occasion, it may be necessary for conservationists to intervene politically at the highest levels to ensure that rich, experienced companies from tropical capitals, or from North America and Europe, do not take unfair advantage of fledgling local rainforest tour companies. The goal always should be for conservationists to transfer the technology and know-how to the local forest companies so local companies can fight their own battles in the punishing business arena. But inevitably this transfer of technology and know-how takes a few years. Conservationists will need to be aware of threats to these locally owned companies, which often will be the first and best line of defense of the forest and its macaws.

The details of the best ownership and management structure for a local ecotourism company are impossible to define in general, since social and historical factors vary so much from site to site in the Neotropics. Nevertheless, one should try to ensure that at least 51% of the company is owned by people who share a long-term commitment to proper rainforest management. It is also desirable to try to structure companies such that it is difficult for one or a few potentially greedy owners to concentrate wealth and power excessively, while stifling the advancement of other members of the community.

CURRENT STATUS OF EFFORTS TO INITIATE MACAW LICK TOURISM

As of November 1990, there were three new efforts underway to protect macaw licks for ecotourism and research. These efforts include (1) my Wildlife Conservation International (WCI) project (which is exclusively research) at the lick in the middle Manu River, (2) a rustic 20-bed lodge at Blanquillo lick 2 hours by boat downstream from the mouth of the Manu River, and (3) another nearly identical lodge at the huge Tambopata lick 7 hours upstream from Puerto Maldonado. The Blanquillo lick, which is just now being protected for the first time (thanks to five owners who live at the site and are trained conservationists), is the most accessible and photogenic large macaw and parrot lick in the Manu region. The lick on the upper Tambopata, which first came under protection in January 1990, thanks to three other resident owner/conservationists, is the largest and most photogenic macaw lick in South America. The lick, lodge, trails, and photographic blinds at the latter site collectively are called the Tambopata Research Center (TRC). In 1990 and 1991 two of the three Peruvian owners of TRC were actively engaged in WCI-sponsored macaw nest box and face photo dossier research at the site.

Besides these projects, the owners of TRC have been advising the Native Community of Infierno (two hours up the Tambopata River from Puerto Maldonado) to build their own photographic and observation blinds and their own small, rustic lodge near a small lick that lies on the banks of the Tambopata River within 9,000 ha of community land. In anticipation of possible tourism benefits, the president of the Community issued orders in May 1989 that no one should shoot parrots at their lick. Yet, despite continuous advice from the owners of TRC and a general show of enthusiasm from the Community, as of November 1990 the Community had taken no concrete actions to install their own facilities at their Community parrot lick. Probably the Community will take action, but new ideas such as lick tourism take a long time to become accepted by Indians who have been systematically abused for centuries by outsiders.

With regard to Indian attitudes toward macaw hunting, it is clear from our experience at the lick in the middle Manu, as well as from the experience of the owners of the Blanquillo and upper Tambopata lick facilities, that individual Indians very easily change their views toward hunting once they receive concrete benefits from protecting the birds. It remains to be seen, however, how successfully and rapidly such a change in attitudes and behavior is accepted in an entire community of lowland Indians who traditionally have hunted macaws (Redford et al. in press). I suspect that such an attitude change is possible, but, once again, only after most families in the community materially benefit from protecting the birds.

In the case of the Native Community of Infierno, the owners of TRC have suggested that the Community's parrot lick would be best protected and exploited by forming a Community Tourism Cooperative which any member of the Community could join at any time. Each Coop member would contribute materials or labor to the lick project and be paid based on his or her share of the Coop's revenues. Members would also be subject to penalty or expulsion from the Coop if they hunted or captured parrots within a determined distance of the lick. Effectively each Coop member would be like a stockholder in a company, with his or her return commensurate to the amount of capital or labor they contributed.

OVERALL POTENTIALS OF ECOTOURISM IN
PARROT CONSERVATION

Ecotourism will only work as a conservation strategy where at least some attractive, easy-to-see wildlife can be guaranteed to tourists. Amazonian sites that have been heavily hunted and have few attractive medium- or large-sized animals will have difficulty attracting a substantial number of ecotourists, though it is possible that tourism which concentrates on cultures of forest peoples might succeed. Nevertheless, my interviews with tourists suggested that the strongest growth in Amazonian tourism probably would be at sites that had both abundant wildlife and some forest cultures. Though data are few, I estimate that between 20% and 50% of the Peruvian Amazon still has enough wildlife to be viable for ecotourism. But as far as ecotourism potential is concerned, accessible yet pristine regions like Manu and Tambopata are in the top few percent of the Peruvian Amazon and of the entire Amazon Basin.

There are two additional factors that come into play when designing viable ecotourism programs. First, the amount of existing tourism to a region can affect the viability of new ecotourism projects. For instance, if there is an existing heavy flow of tourists to sites near a potential ecotourism site, then to develop a new ecotourism site one needs only to convince a small percentage of the tourists to include a new site in their itineraries. This logic might apply, for instance, to ecotourism sites designed to display nesting or roosting sites of endangered amazon parrots (*Amazona* spp.) of the Caribbean. Many millions of people visit the Caribbean region each winter. The flow of only a few thousand tourists to new Amazon parrot ecotourism sites might justify modest investments, and generate employment and revenues in the impoverished island interiors.

Of course, the reverse situation may also occur. An animal may be spectacular, but may either be too inaccessible (due to distance or travel discomfort) or too unwatchable (due to dense vegetation, exclusively nocturnal habits, or excessive and unremediable timidity) to be an effective subject for ecotourism.

Fortunately parrots thoroughly qualify as superb subjects for ecotourism programs. They are diurnal, colorful, easy to observe, easy to tame, and, among birds, uniquely loved by humans. I believe that with appropriate interpretation and marketing, almost any parrot species in the world could become a good subject for a successful ecotourism program. Obviously some species, such as the large, colorful macaws and amazons, are intrinsically better subjects for ecotourism programs than are others, for example parrotlets of the genera *Forpus* or *Touit*. But even some of the smallest parrots could probably be used successfully in ecotourism programs if promoters were clever and aggressive, and there was a substantial existing flow of tourists to adjacent sites. As spectacular as licks are, I do not believe they are the only way to make parrots attractive for ecotourism. Any active parrot nest can be made into an ecotourism attraction with the use of appropriate blinds, spotting scopes, interpretation, and maybe eventually even photo opportunities, cut-away nests, or closed-circuit television (for viewing inside the nest cavity).

A second factor that can strongly affect the viability of a particular ecotourism program might seem obvious, but it is surprisingly neglected in practice: the quality of field presentations and interpretations given by ecotourism guides. It is equally as possible for bad interpretation to make a fascinating and spectacular animal seem boring, as it is for good interpretation to make a relatively subtle, obscure animal seem riveting. For instance, only three ecotourism guides in the entire Amazon use tripod-mounted 20-power telescopes to show toucans, parrots, monkeys, and other animals to tourists. Experience has shown that most tourists do not bring appropriate binoculars for rainforest use, and often are inexpert in using those they do have. With any hand-held binoculars, a beautiful toucan 55 m up in a tree is too small to appreciate, but when viewed in a spotting scope, the same bird becomes a visual treat. The tiny wasps that pollinate and lay eggs in rainforest fig fruits are easily overlooked by most tourists. But a truly proficient guide can point out these wasps and be able to explain clearly the amazingly intricate symbiosis between figs and wasps, and how that symbiosis produces massive crops of figs that keep the forest's most attractive birds and monkeys alive during the annual fruit shortage. In short, the quality of interpretation by guides can either promote or kill potentially viable ecotourism projects.

How many parrot licks could be protected by ecotourism? I estimate that 10 to 20 licks could be protected and exploited by ecotourism programs in southeastern Peru alone in the next 5 to 7 years. Given that each lick probably requires a minimum of about 150 km² of intact, protected forest to guarantee macaws and other parrots for the lick, approximately 1500 to 3000 km² of forest could be directly protected and exploited in macaw lick ecotourism in southeastern Peru. This amount may not seem impressive when compared with the approximately 100,000 km² of southeastern Peru. But remember that for each 14 km (twice a radius of 7 km) of riverbank protected by an officially declared macaw lick ecotourism site, much more than the 154 km² of forest will be protected, because controlling river frontage keeps colonists and loggers out of the forest behind the tourism concession.

The new 1.5-million-ha Tambopata-Candamo Reserved Zone of southeastern Peru was declared in part to allow macaw lick ecotourism to be implemented without the interference of destructive development activities. Thus, the large lick in the upper Tambopata already has shown that in the short term, at least, licks can protect huge areas of land. A widely traveled ecotourism expert recently stated that the lick on the Upper Tambopata at TRC is the most beautiful sight he has ever seen (D. Rand pers. comm.), which bodes well for the amount of tourists that can be attracted to the site.

Finally, lick ecotourism should not prevent the utilization of other, nondestructive rainforest products, such as the sustainable extraction of Brazil nuts, rubber, vegetable ivory, palm fronds, orchids, turtle eggs, and fish. Fortunately, parrots quickly become accustomed to high levels of noise and disturbance created by humans. They easily coexist with humans as long as humans do not hunt and capture them, or cut down their food and nest trees. Hyacinth Macaws (*Anodorhynchus hyacinthinus*) in Brazil copulate, preen, sleep, and eat within a few meters of the world's largest iron mine and iron-ore railroad, and sit on ranch buildings and drink out of cattle troughs in the middle of cattle ranches (Munn et al. 1989). Thus, parrot ecotourism easily can be combined with other sorts of human economic activity.

A potential limitation to the growth of ecotourism in Peru, and other tropical countries, is that North Americans and Europeans shy away from destinations that are perceived as politically unstable. In the last 10 years, activity by leftist insurgents in Peru has given the country a bad image in the international press, despite the fact that no tourists on recommended itineraries have been killed. Most of Peru, including the southeastern rainforest, has remained calm and safe to visit throughout this period. But the cumulative effect of years of bad press has reduced the tourist flow to Peru by 60% over the last 18 months. Even during this slump in conventional tourism, ecotourism to Manu has actually increased substantially. Apparently the high quality of the rainforest tourism experience in Manu more than compensates for the difficulty in selling Peru to the general tourist. Finally, experience in Africa and South America demonstrates that even bad press is forgotten quickly by tourists, and tourism recovers within a matter of a year or two. There is currently such great interest in North America and Europe concerning the Amazon rainforest that companies operating in the best Amazonian sites will have little difficulty riding out this slump and will probably continue to grow rapidly.

CONCLUSIONS

Wild macaws and other parrots may only survive if they can pay for themselves. Therefore, it is fortunate that these birds have so much to offer as natural attractions to the world's increasingly nature-starved urban professionals. If two new model projects of locally owned macaw ecotourism can succeed in south-eastern Peru, then macaws and other parrots may still have a chance for survival in this region and, perhaps by extension of these strategies, in other regions where macaws still occur in the wild.

ACKNOWLEDGMENTS

I would like to thank D. Blanco, A. Huaman, E. Nycander, E. Raez, K. Renton, B. Ribeiro, D. Ricalde, D. Shoobridge, M. Valqui, B. Gomez, E. Huaman, and scores of other Peruvian and foreign assistants and volunteers who have worked so hard on the macaw project from 1985 until the present. I also am grateful to the Peruvian National Parks Program for authorization to work in Manu and Tambopata, and to Martha Brecht and my children, Charlotte and

Alex, for cheerfully enduring my long absences in the field. This research has been generously supported by Wildlife Conservation International, a division of New York Zoological Society.

LITERATURE CITED

Boo, E. 1990. Ecotourism: the potentials and pitfalls. Washington, District of Columbia, World Wildlife Fund.

Davis, D. E., & R. L. Winstead. 1980. Estimating the numbers of wildlife populations. Pages 221–245 *in* Wildlife management techniques manual, fourth edition (S. D. Schemnitz, Ed.). Washington, District of Columbia, The Wildlife Society.

Emmons, L. H., & N. M. Stark. 1981. Elemental composition of a natural mineral lick in Amazonia. Biotropica 11:311–313.

Groom, M., R. Podolsky, & C. P. Munn. 1991. Tourism as a sustained use of wildlife: a case study of Madre de Dios, southeastern Peru. Pages 393–412 *in* Neotropical wildlife use and conservation (J. G. Robinson & K. H. Redford, Eds.). Chicago, University of Chicago Press.

Hardin, G. 1968. The tragedy of the commons. Science 162:1245–1248.

Healy, R. 1988. Economic considerations in nature oriented tourism. Research Triangle Park, North Carolina, S.E. Center for Forest Economics Research, FPEI Working Paper No. 34, pp. 1–35.

Laarman, J. G., & P. B. Durst. 1987. Nature travel and tropical forests. Research Triangle Park, North Carolina, S.E. Center for Forest Economics Research, FPEI Working Paper No. 23, pp. 1–16.

Munn, C. A. 1988. The real macaws. Animal Kingdom 91:20–33.

Munn, C. A., J. B. Thomsen, & C. Yamashita. 1989. The Hyacinth Macaw. Pages 404–419 *in* Audubon wildlife report 1989/1990 (W. J. Chandler & L. Labate, Eds.). New York, Academic Press.

Peters, C. M., A. H. Gentry, & R. O. Mendelsohn. 1989. Economic valuation of an Amazonian rainforest. Nature 339:655–656.

Redford, K. H., A. M. Stearman, & C. J. Lagueux. In press. Eating macaws—

the paradox of consuming $2,000 birds. Proceedings of the second world conference on parrots, Curitiba, Brazil. International Council for Bird Preservation.

Redford, P., & K. Redford. 1990. Can a bunch of nuts save the rainforest? Zoogoer 19:9–17.

Rios, M. A., P. G. Vasquez, C. F. Ponce, A. Tovar, & M. J. Dourojeanni. 1983. Plan maestro Parque Nacional del Manu. Lima, Peru, National Agrarian University.

Thiollay, J. M. 1989. Estimates of population densities of raptors and game birds in the rainforest of French Guiana. Conserv. Biol. 3:128–137.

Western, D., & W. Henry. 1979. Economics and conservation in third world national parks. BioScience 29:414–418.

Resumen.—En muchos casos los loros silvestres, en estado libre, generan más divisas para paises tropicales, y proveen más empleo local para gente ubicadas en la selva, cuando son explotados indirectamente como fuentes de turismo en vez de directamente para el comercio de mascotas. Observaciones sobre cienes de guacamayos, que se pueden distinguir individualmente en lamederos de arcilla, y estudios sobre la suerte de 38 nidos de guacamayos en la Reserva de la Biósfera del Manú, Perú, demostraron que la densidad y productividad de los guacamayos es baja. Solo el 10% al 20% de las aves reprodujeron al año, parejas solo criaron un pichón, y una tercera parte de los nidos no lograron producir pichónes. Cálculos de los ingresos generados por albergues Peruanos ubicados en la selva y datos de encuestas hechos a los turistas, señalan que cada guacamayo tiene el potencial de generar entre $750 y $4,700 en ingresos turísticos anuales. Usando una variedad de cálculos para determinar la edad máxima de los guacamayos y el potencial del ecoturismo, yo calculo que cada guacamayo grande, en estado libre, puede generar de $22,500 a $165,000 en ingresos turísticos durante su vida. La explotación indirecta de los loros como fuentes de turismo tiene mayor comprensión, es más facil para manejar, y es menos arriesgado que la explotación directa de los adultos, con su tasa baja de reproducción y pichónes frágiles para el comercio de mascotas. También discuto las dificultades de implementar el ecoturismo como método de conservación, de como la falta de tenencia de tierras por los habitantes locales de la selva hace dificil cualquier manejo racional de los guacamayos, y de como asegurar que la gente local se beneficien del ecoturismo generado por los guacamayos. Se describen dos esfuerzos nuevos para iniciar turismo alrededor de lamederos de guacamayos en el sureste del Perú y concluyo con comentarios sobre el potencial general del ecoturismo en la conservación de loros.

4. Sustainable Harvesting of Parrots for Conservation

Steven R. Beissinger and Enrique H. Bucher

School of Forestry & Environmental Studies, Yale University, New Haven, Connecticut 06511; and Centro de Zoología Aplicada, Universidad de Córdoba, Casilla de Correos 122, Córdoba 5000, Argentina

Abstract.—We explore the applicability of sustainable harvesting of parrots as a conservation technique. Biological knowledge needed for a comprehensive sustained harvest program for any animal species includes (1) population size and range, (2) habitat requirements, (3) resilience to human disturbance and habitat changes, (4) mortality and productivity rates, (5) key factors regulating populations, and (6) the effects of environmental variation on demography. In parrots, nestlings are preferable to adults for harvesting because they make better pets, their harvest has a relatively low impact on wild populations, and they can be harvested in greater numbers. A harvestable surplus of parrots can theoretically be maximized by maximizing the number of occupied nest sites and their success. Potentially this can be accomplished by adding nest sites (especially in the form of nest boxes), increasing food supply, protecting nests from predators, deliberate multiple-clutching of wild pairs, or decreasing hatching asynchrony. Unfortunately, it takes many years to accumulate enough demographic information to set comprehensive harvest levels. In the absence of complete demographic information to set harvest levels, we propose the *Conservative Nestling Harvest Model*: if there is evidence that wild populations are stable or increasing, any increase in productivity resulting from management programs can be harvested. Estimates of annual sustainable harvests for Green-rumped Parrotlets in a study population in Venezuela range from 105 to 298 birds from 100 nest boxes. Commercial operations could be started following the conservative harvest approach, adjusting harvest rates on the basis of population size. A consistent decline in population size or in nest site occupancy should always be a signal to decrease harvesting levels. We detail the substantial social, political, and economic problems inherent in sustained harvesting programs and make some suggestions for avoiding pitfalls where possible. The utility of sustained harvesting as a means of conserving species and habitats is discussed. If some substantial difficulties in implementation can be overcome, sustained harvesting could be advantageous for conservationists, aviculturists, and local peoples. On the other hand, failure to achieve success in sustained harvesting programs may exacerbate conservation problems by stimulating harvest of parrots in an unsustainable manner.

In the face of development pressures, conservationists are exploring ways to conserve resources by utilizing them. Large-scale preservation efforts lock land away, sometimes in an economically unproductive manner. In developing countries with growing populations and economic needs, effective land preservation is becoming increasingly difficult. Strategies that can integrate conservation and development in a sustainable manner (I.U.C.N. 1980, Reid 1989), such as extractive reserves where latex and other plant products are harvested from primary forest instead of timber (Fearnside 1989, Peters et al. 1989), deserve consideration as alternative conservation strategies.

Sustainability refers to the continued persistence and replenishment of a resource despite utilization. In the case of wild populations of animals, sustainable populations are harvested at a rate equivalent to the productivity of the population, so that overall numbers remain more or less stable (Caughley 1977). Sustainable management schemes have played an important role in traditional American and European wild game management. The goal of game management is to provide large numbers of animals for harvest by hunters on a continuing basis (Leopold 1933, Caughley 1977, Robinson and Bolen 1984). In developing countries, sustainable harvest programs with wild animals may take the form of "ranching." For example, game ranches in Africa (Bothma and Du Toit 1989) and iguana (*Iguana iguana*) ranches in Central America (Cohn 1989, Werner 1991) provide wild meat for food. Biologists working with endangered species have applied the principles of sustained harvesting for short periods as last-resort efforts to build captive flocks by taking animals from wild populations with minimal effects on the overall productivity of these populations (Snyder et al. 1987, Snyder and Snyder 1989).

Neotropical parrots are being harvested from the wild by the pet trade at alarming rates (Nilsson 1989, 1990; Thomsen and Mulliken 1991). For example, 920,000 parrots were exported from Argentina between 1982 and 1988 (Thomsen and Mulliken 1991), with a peak of 176,481 birds shipped in 1986. One species, the Blue-fronted Amazon (*Amazona aestiva*), composed about 25% of all exports during this period. Blue-fronted Amazons were trapped for the pet trade in relatively small numbers until the 1980s, when the demand increased dramatically; annual exports from Argentina rose from about 5,000 in 1981 to over 30,000 after 1984, totaling over 204,000 between 1981 and 1987. Both the range and number of wild Blue-fronted Amazons have been decreasing in recent years due to habitat destruction and overexploitation. Blue-fronted Amazons nest in mature forests with large trees and forage in the crowns of trees, mostly on fruits, berries, and leaf buds (Forshaw 1989). These forests are disappearing at a rate of at least 50,000 ha/yr in the western Chaco, and the historical average was as high as 300,000 ha/yr (C. S. Toledo pers. comm.). This trend explains the local extinctions that occurred in the species' southern range, particularly in the provinces of Córdoba and southern and central Santiago del Estero. In areas where the forest has been cut, no nests occur (Bucher and Martella 1988). The impact of habitat destruction is also exacerbated by the current method of collecting nestlings: to obtain nestlings, campesinos usually open a hole in the trunk or even cut the entire tree, which leaves 95% of the cavities unusable for future nesting by parrots. Harvesting pressure on young presently is very high. According to interviews conducted with traders in northern Argentina, approximately 3,000 young parrots have been taken annually from a forested area of 90,000 ha in Salta.

Clearly, exploitation of the Blue-fronted Amazon is occurring in an unsustainable manner and, unless the rates of harvesting and habitat destruction can be slowed, its numbers will continue to dwindle. This is also likely for many other species in the trade but few data exist to allow an evaluation of sustainable harvest levels.

In this paper, we explore the application of sustainable harvesting as a tool to conserve parrots in the wild based on our field studies of species that are agricultural pests (Monk parakeets; *Myiopsitta monachus*), are heavily exploited (Blue-fronted Amazons), or are common and capable of intensive ranching (Green-rumped Parrotlets; *Forpus passerinus*). We detail the specific biological knowledge needed to develop sustainable harvesting programs, propose models for setting harvesting regimes, and delineate management techniques for maximizing productivity. Finally we examine the social, cultural, and political conditions favoring or inhibiting the successful implementation of sustained harvest approaches.

BIOLOGICAL KNOWLEDGE NEEDED FOR SUSTAINABLE HARVESTING

Before harvesting of any population can be implemented in a sustainable manner, a detailed understanding of the biological machinery that limits and regulates the population is needed. Much of this information should be obtained during a several-year period before harvesting commences; other information can be gathered later in conjunction with limited harvesting. In this section we cover the general types of knowledge that are needed for site-specific harvesting programs with any animal, and apply the principles to harvesting parrots in particular.

Population Size and Range

Basic information on population size is needed to monitor the effects of a harvesting program on the population. Minimally, we must be able to detect population trends. Ideally, we would like to assess population densities. Optimally, these densities would be measured for different habitat types or land uses so that the effects of land conversion can be evaluated.

But measuring population size of parrots has been a difficult problem because many species range widely in their daily activities. For example, Blue-fronted Amazons frequently fly up to 50 km in daily foraging flights (Bucher pers. obs.). Also, most Neotropical parrots live in the canopy of forests where they may be difficult to detect and enumerate.

A preliminary understanding of population trends can emerge from a comparison of a species' present distribution with its historical range. A detectable decrease in range probably signals that the species has already declined greatly. For example, the range of the Patagonian Conure (*Cyanoliseus patagonus*) has been reduced severely since 1950. Although this species is still sold in considerable numbers in the pet trade, it is clearly declining in the wild (Bucher and Rinaldi 1986). Changes in range are easier to detect than changes in population density, and are useful for identifying species in trouble. But they are much too crude as indices of population changes to be useful in setting harvesting quotas.

Several techniques have been employed successfully to census parrots. Counts can be made from fixed points above the forest canopy (Snyder et al. 1987) or in open habitats (Pérez and Eguiarte 1989, S. D. Strahl and P. A. Desenne pers. comm.). Monk Parakeet numbers have been censused by trapping all birds in communal nests at night (Bucher et al. in press). Green-rumped Parrotlet numbers potentially can be assessed by using resightings of color-banded birds in statistical models designed to estimate densities from mark and resighting data (Caughley 1977, Eberhardt 1978). Some species roost communally (e.g., Chapman et al. 1989) and counts at roosts may provide an accurate estimate of population trends, if all roosts in a study area can be found. Caution must be exercised in assessing population trends by using nest occupancy rates because there often are large nonbreeding components of parrot populations that are ready to occupy nest sites when they become available (see the section *Increasing Productivity* later in this chapter). The nonbreeding component may compose a significant proportion of a parrot population and can vary quite independently of the breeding components.

Finally, any estimate of population trends must include some understanding of the roles of immigration and emigration. These factors are especially important when considering managed populations that are delineated by land-ownership and not by biological characteristics of populations. Information from color-marked or telemetered birds may yield some insights into the importance of these processes in parrot populations.

Habitat Requirements

Breeding and feeding requirements interact to determine habitat needs for a species. Each must be assessed seasonally because changes may occur (Verner et al. 1986). Understanding diet, habitat requirements, and ranging behavior is critically important to assess the effects of landscape-level processes on population viability (Soulé 1987).

Habitat use by parrots can be quantified in respect to the most important resources utilized by a species. Because breeding habitat may differ substantially from foraging habitat, requirements for each must be known. For both breeding and feeding habitats, measurements of the vertical structure and composition of vegetation are needed, including the availability of snags or tall trees for canopy-nesting species. But the horizontal configuration of habitats can also be important for species, such as amazons, that require patches of mature trees for nesting near early successional habitats containing fruit-bearing trees for food. It is important to bear in mind that many parrot species are associated with mature forests, sometimes in ways that are not always apparent or detected using traditional census techniques. As mature forests are disappearing at high rates, special attention must be devoted to understanding the requirements of species that use these habitats.

Diet should be determined by direct observation. Observations should be made in a systematic manner and throughout the year to detect seasonal shifts in diet.

An understanding of ranging behavior is important for defining management areas and habitat requirements. Because many species of parrots make landscape-level movements (> a few km daily), telemetry studies may be required for good estimates of home range. Also, little is known about seasonal or local migration of parrots. If large-scale movements take parrots out of a management area, then control of the effects of habitat changes on population viability is limited. In this situation the opportunity for sustainable management is greatly decreased.

Resilience to Human Disturbance and Habitat Changes

Human activities may have both direct and indirect effects on productivity. Direct effects may occur if a species is likely to abandon its nest if disturbed too frequently by human visitation. With proper knowledge of a bird's behavior, disturbance from observations and nest checks can usually be kept at tolerable levels. Occasionally human visitation can attract predators to the nests of birds (Bart 1977, Livezey 1980, MacIvor et al. 1990, Sedinger 1990). Sometimes, these effects can be minimized by protecting nests from predators (see next section).

More significant are the impacts of indirect disturbance that result from changes in land use. Such changes can affect species in different ways. Changes in land use often dramatically alter the natural vegetation and consequently habitat quality, which can result in changes in parrot population size and productivity (Saunders 1977). One obvious example is the decrease in parrot numbers that can result from deforestation (Bucher and Martella 1988). Other more subtle alterations of habitat suitability can result from the introduction of domestic cattle and overgrazing, which may also have a profound impact on vegetation. Changes in regional agricultural practices can increase or decrease the abundance of food (Saunders 1977). Finally, introduced tree species may provide high quality breeding or feeding habitat, as in a recent range expansion of the Monk Parakeet following *Eucalyptus* planting in the Pampas (Ridgely 1980, Forshaw 1989). These types of land use changes may decrease or increase the carrying capacity of a species. Information on the resilience of a managed population to habitat loss and land-use conversion is also needed to plan for the effects of future changes on population trends.

Another aspect of habitat alteration that is generally neglected in current evaluation methods is habitat changes at the landscape level. Dispersal, colonization, and migratory movements of animals can be greatly affected by habitat fragmentation, lack of corridors between habitats, and the erection of barriers to movement (Noss and Harris, 1986, Wilcove et al. 1986). Landscape changes may particularly impact migratory and nomadic species, which need an adequate network of habitats preserved throughout the year (Myers et al. 1987, Takekawa and Beissinger 1989).

Demography

Demographic information provides the basis for determining the harvesting potential of a species. Ideally, age-specific schedules of natality and mortality rates, including age of first breeding and senescence, are required to provide a measure of r (the intrinsic rate of natural increase of a population). The minimum duration of demographic studies depends on the lifespan of the species. Studies should ideally last for at least the lifespan of one cohort. Because parrots are often long lived (Forshaw 1989), this period requires 7 to 20 years.

However, some shortcut methods may be scientifically acceptable. For instance, stage-based demographic models (Caswell 1989, Getz and Haight 1989) that lump age classes into fewer groups can be used in longer-lived species where age-specific information is usually lacking. Productivity data are often easier to obtain in sufficient sample sizes in three to four years of study than survivorship data, which usually require a minimum of five years to accumulate. Because many parrot species are long-lived, at least 10 years of data are often advisable.

Few reliable demographic data currently exist for parrots. In part, this is due to the difficulties inherent in working with this group of birds. Demography is hard to establish when the sexes are not dimorphic. In addition, ratios of juveniles to adults cannot be used to estimate productivity for most species because juveniles cannot be distinguished from adults (for exceptions see Snyder et al. 1989 and Munn 1991).

Marking studies can provide direct estimates of demography, but marking parrots can be problematic. First, the number of usable band combinations may be limited because many species are unable to carry more than one band per leg on their short tibias (e.g., *Forpus* sp.; Beissinger pers. obs.). The strong beaks of most species necessitate that hard materials be used for bands (i.e., anodized aluminum rather than colored plastic bands) to minimize band loss and injuries caused by birds trying to remove their bands. Second, because of the hourglass shape of parrot tibias, foot injuries or infections may result from the rubbing of flattened aluminum or plastic bands (e.g., *Amazona ventralis*; J. W. Wiley pers. comm.). Instead, small cylindrical wire-like bands are often used as permanent markers in captivity. These are useless for field identification without recapturing the bird. Tropical rainforest birds, especially understory species, have developed foot infections leading to death from bands (C. A. Munn pers. comm.). Third, patagial tags have been used but with mixed success (Rowley and Saunders 1980, Saunders 1988) and we do not recommend their use.

In our own work with parrots, we have had partial success with banding programs. Beissinger and his colleagues have used combinations of a single colored plastic band on one leg and a numbered anodized aluminum band on the other leg to band over 1,000 *Forpus passerinus*. No foot injuries have been noted. Loss of plastic bands appears to be low in nestlings, but as many as 35% of the adults remove their plastic bands annually. Bucher and his colleagues (in press) have used numbered and colored aluminum bands without injury in marking 753 Monk Parakeets.

Because few reliable life tables for parrots currently exist, demographic parameters might be estimated from data available for species that are similar in size and ecological requirements to create models to estimate the feasibility of harvesting programs (see later section). But these models should not be used to set harvesting levels because demography can vary considerably between species and even between populations of a species.

Key Factors

Key factors regulate populations, determining their tendency to increase or decline (Varley and Gradwell 1960, Murton and Westwood 1977). Using several annual life tables, the demographic traits that control population numbers can be determined through correlation analyses. This technique is also useful to investigate demographic trends in relation to environmental variation. Once identified, key factors can be managed to increase productivity. In the case of most parrots, it is not clear what factors regulate populations (e.g., food, predation, nest sites, social behavior, human predation, or weather), or whether population regulation occurs as a function of population density.

Effects of Environmental Variation on Demography

Year-to-year variations in rainfall and temperature can strongly affect productivity and survivorship in some birds (e.g., Beissinger 1986, Bayliss 1989). In these species, average demographic traits may lead to faulty harvesting decisions (Bayliss 1989) because averages are less meaningful than the extremes. Sometimes, environmental extremes occur cyclically, particularly rainfall-related phenomena (Beissinger 1986). Relationships between productivity or population trends and environmental variation should be examined. Frequently it is possible to obtain long-term data on rainfall or temperature from stations

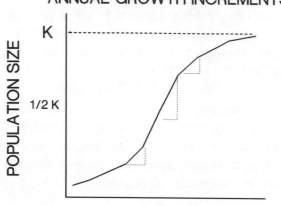

Fig. 1. Stylized logistic curve of the growth of a population. The carrying capacity (K) for a particular environment is shown. Annual growth increments, or recruitment of young into the population, are illustrated by the finely dotted lines. Note that the largest annual recruitment occurs at population densities near ½ K.

relatively near a management area. Such long-term data can then be analyzed for predictability and cyclic trends (Colwell 1974, Low 1978, Beissinger 1986) to begin to understand how populations may be expected to fluctuate.

How to Set Sustainable Harvesting Regimes to Maximize Productivity Safely

Setting harvesting regimes has been the subject of much study and debate (Larkin 1977). Wildlife ecologists and fisheries biologists have developed population models based on the concepts of maximum sustained yield or optimum sustained yield to determine harvest levels of intensively harvested species (Caughley 1977, Getz and Haight 1989). These models have been only partially successful in maximizing productivity and allowing populations to replenish

TRADITIONAL SUSTAINED YIELD MODEL

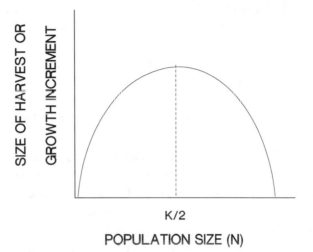

Fig. 2. The traditional sustained yield model of harvest size versus population size. Individuals harvested could come from any age class but would be adults primarily. Note that the maximum sustained yield occurs at approximately ½ K.

numbers, although no commercially managed species has yet been driven to extinction.

What Should Be Harvested?

Most managed species are harvested as adults: for example, hunted wildlife (e.g., deer and game birds), commercial fisheries, and shellfish. Theories of harvesting often assume that population growth is logistic with some maximum number of individuals or a carrying capacity (K) for any habitat (Fig. 1). Traditionally, harvesting regimes have concentrated first on setting population density at levels where annual recruitment will be maximized and then determining the appropriate number of individuals to harvest to remain at that density (Caughley 1977). When harvesting is apportioned across all ages of animals, the greatest annual growth increment occurs where the logistic growth curve rises most steeply, which is near intermediate densities or approximately ½ K (Fig. 1). This results in the traditional parabolic sustained yield model (Fig. 2), which shows the population size capable of yielding the greatest harvests is near ½ K.

While adult parrots can be harvested, they frequently make poor pets because they are difficult to tame and may have trouble adapting to captivity. Also they often bring a lower market price than hand-tamed birds (Carter and Curry 1987, Thomsen and Brautigam 1991). In contrast, young parrots removed from nest sites and hand-reared or tamed generally make good pets, and consequently are more valuable in the trade.

Harvesting nestlings instead of adults can have less impact on a wild population because nestling parrots generally have relatively low survival rates and hence a low reproductive value (Fisher 1930). Therefore, nestlings can probably be harvested in greater numbers than adults from the same population. Furthermore, if recruitment of young birds into a population (e.g., juvenile survivorship) is density-dependent and the population is near K, then many young produced are unlikely to survive. A compensatory mechanism following nestling harvest may occur which can result in reduced juvenile mortality from other sources, as has been demonstrated for the Gray Partridge (*Perdix perdix*) of Europe (Potts 1986). In other words, in some species it is in principle possible to harvest the surplus of juveniles that would die anyhow before reaching breeding age because of competition. Whether any parrots fall into this category is unknown.

Because nestlings are preferable to adults for harvesting, maximizing parrot sustained harvests operates on a completely different model than traditional game harvesting regimes (Fig. 3). *When harvesting nestlings, productivity and yield are maximized by maximizing the number of occupied nest sites. Therefore, a parrot population would not have to be reduced to ½ K to maximize productivity and yield, but instead productivity and yield may be maximized at or close to K.* Thus, sustained harvesting of parrot nestlings, if properly done, would result in robust wild parrot populations.

Increasing Productivity

Productivity can be maximized by intensive management of the factors that limit population growth. Although little is known about the key factors that limit parrot populations, potential ways to increase productivity (Fig. 4) in-

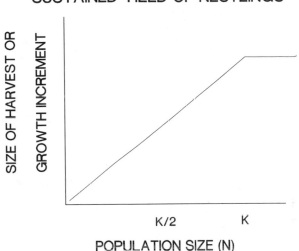

Fig. 3. A hypothetical sustained yield model for harvesting parrot nestlings. Note that the maximum sustained yield occurs near *K*.

clude increasing the number or proportion of adults breeding (e.g., the number of active nests), the percentage of nests fledging young (nesting success), and the number of young fledged per nest (fledging success).

Productivity may be increased significantly by increasing the proportion or number of adults nesting (Figs. 4, 5). Limited abundance or access to nest sites or food can restrain adults from breeding or select for delayed maturity. Either effect would result in a population of nonbreeders of significant size.

Several studies have found a significant proportion of nonbreeding adults in parrot societies: (1) From 1973 to 1979, 57% of the Puerto Rican Parrots (*Amazona vittata*) observed annually did not breed, including many pairs defending territories (Snyder et al. 1987); (2) In *F. passerinus* 41% of the males > 1 year of age did not breed but only 8% of same-aged females were nonbreeders. Of first-year birds, 44% of the females and 91% of the males did not breed (Beissinger unpubl. data). These results were found despite the addition of numerous nest sites in the form of boxes, most of which were occupied; (3) The percent of chambers in communal nests occupied by Monk Parakeets that did not receive eggs varied from 9% to 47% between years (Navarro and Bucher

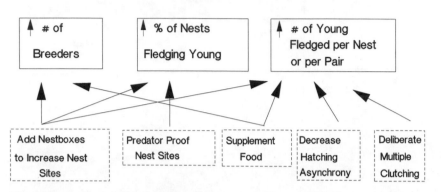

Fig. 4. Methods to increase the productivity of parrot populations. Arrows indicate the particular breeding attribute that management activities would affect.

unpubl. MS); (4) In Hispaniolan Parrots 20% to 23% of wild pairs defended territories but did not nest (Snyder et al. 1987); and (5) Munn (1991) has noted many pairs of nonbreeding macaws (*Ara ararauna* and *A. chloroptera*) visiting active nest sites and estimated that only 10% to 20% of pairs attempted breeding in any year.

The availability of nesting cavities can limit breeding opportunities for many parrot species. If additional nest sites (e.g., boxes) are added and utilized by a population, then a significant increase in the number of birds nesting, and in turn the number of nestlings that could be harvested, should be expected (Fig. 5). When the number of nest sites has been increased in experiments with other cavity-nesting birds, a higher proportion of adults bred as well as more first- or second-year birds (e.g., von Haartman 1971, Eriksson 1982, Brawn 1987).

The best evidence for increasing the number of breeding parrots through increasing the number of nest sites comes from studies of *F. passerinus*. Nests of the Green-rumped Parrotlet have been recorded in holes in tree boles or limbs, termitoriums, and also in a clothesline support (Friedman and Smith 1955, Forshaw 1989). Recent studies in Venezuela found parrotlets nesting most commonly in hollowed fenceposts (Beissinger unpubl. data). An artificial nest box, designed from the dimensions of fencepost cavities (Fig. 6), replaced

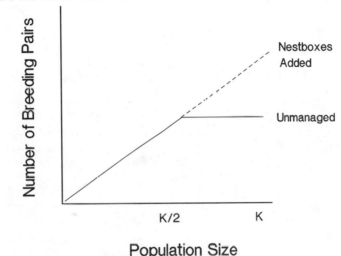

Fig. 5. The effects of adding nest sites on the number of breeding pairs assuming that nest sites limit population growth.

fenceposts in 1988 as the most frequently used nest site at Hato Masagural in Venezuela. Nearly every nest box was visited at least once by parrotlets during 1988 and 1989 (Table 1), and an average of 1.45 and 1.19 nesting attempts per box were recorded during those years, respectively. Only eight parrotlet nests in fenceposts were found in the study area during the same period.

In the absence of carefully constructed experiments, it is difficult to estimate directly a change in the number of birds breeding with the addition of nest boxes. Instead we can examine several forms of evidence to assess the magnitude of change in the number of nesting birds after nest boxes were provided. The study area that contained 100 nest boxes in 1989 contained 10 known seminatural nest sites in fence posts from 1985 to 1987. Beissinger and colleagues (unpubl. data) probably did not find all nests in the area. But even if twice as many sites existed, the area would have contained only one-quarter of the number of nests currently occupied (Table 2). A survey on 7 July 1989 of the density of parrotlets nesting in boxes versus those nesting outside of the study area in the most frequently used nest sites, fenceposts, illustrates the potential for

Fig. 6. The nest box designed for use by Green-rumped Parrotlets (*Forpus passerinus*) at Hato Masagural in the llanos of Venezuela. The nest box was constructed from plastic polyvinylchloride pipe (PVC) with a removable inner sleeve made of hardware cloth that the parrotlet can use to climb. Sawdust is placed at the bottom for nesting material. Both the top and bottom are removable.

Table 1. Use and success of nest boxes by *Forpus passerinus* in the llanos of Venezuela.

	Year	
Nest use characteristic	1988	1989
Number of nest boxes	40	100
Number of boxes visited at least once	39	96
Number of nesting attempts in boxes	58	119
Number of attempts with fate known	53	117
Number of attempts fledging young	33	56

increasing the number of breeding adults. Only 0.77 nests/km were found along 7.8 km of fence line, whereas 16.3 nests/km occurred in nest boxes located along 3 km of fence line. Part of the 21-fold increase in nesting birds may have been the result of parrotlets attracted to the nest boxes from the fence line area that was censused. But the survey found only 4.5 potential nest sites per km of fence line. So even if all of these sites were occupied, the boxes would represent a 3- to 4-fold increase in nesting birds.

Potentially nest boxes could be used to increase the number of nesting pairs with a variety of hole-nesting parrots. Nest boxes have been used on a limited basis by other small species like the Blue-winged Parrotlet (*Forpus xanthopterygius*; G. H. Kattan pers. comm.) and by larger ones like the Blue-and-Yellow Macaw (*Ara ararauna*; C. A. Munn 1991). On the other hand, nest boxes had very limited use by Puerto Rican Parrots (Snyder et al. 1987), and three other amazons in Mexico (Pérez and Eguiarte 1989). For various reasons, nest sites may not have limited these populations. Or the design or placement of the nest boxes might not have been attractive to the parrots. In any case, not all species may accept nest boxes, and few may accept them as frequently as the Green-rumped Parrotlet. Still we suspect that nest boxes may be adopted to some extent by many parrot species.

Nest boxes may also be more productive than natural nesting cavities

(Møller 1989). Clutch size, fledging success, and nesting success often tend to be higher in boxes than in natural cavities (Karlsson and Nilsson 1977, Korpimaki 1984, Nilsson 1984). For example, *F. passerinus* nests in boxes that were not affected by investigators checking nests during egg-laying were approximately 1.4 times as likely to fledge at least some young as nests in seminatural cavities (Beissinger unpubl. data). Also, nest boxes fledged significantly more young per nest, averaging 4.7 young per successful nest, compared to 3.5 young per successful nest in seminatural sites (fenceposts).

Not only may nest sites be limiting in some populations of parrots, but often current harvesting practices result in the loss of nest sites. Frequently nestlings are removed from a cavity in a tree by cutting the tree down, as was already mentioned for Blue-fronted Amazons. This results in both the loss of productivity from the nesting pair in the current year and the loss of the nest site itself, which may lead to the loss of productivity from that pair in the future if it cannot find another cavity. Young could be removed from a tree cavity without damaging the site, if harvesters would climb to the cavity and cut a small wedge from the trunk near the bottom of the cavity. The wedge can be replaced and sealed with wood putty at the conclusion of the nest visit. This technique has been used successfully with macaws (C. A. Munn pers. comm.), amazons (J. W. Wiley pers. comm), and other cavity-nesting birds (W. D. Koenig pers. comm.). Of course, the use of nest boxes would eliminate this problem altogether in those species that accept them.

Both the number of adults breeding and fledging success could also potentially be increased by augmenting the food supply (Fig. 4). Restraint from breeding by many Monk Parakeet pairs may be related to dominance relations that reduce food availability, but the evidence is unclear (Bucher et al. in press). Studies of other birds have shown that often birds respond to increased food supply by laying more eggs and fledging more young (Martin 1987). To our knowledge, no good information currently exists that demonstrates increased productivity in parrots resulting from controlled increases in food supplies. Food abundance could be supplemented for parrots by planting preferred fruit trees, seed crops (e.g., sorghum, corn, and millet), or managing natural forests to increase the proportion of food-bearing plants.

The success rate of nests in natural sites can be increased by protecting nests from predators. This may be done by placing 1–2 m of greased aluminum flashing around the boles of nest trees to inhibit mammalian or reptilian predators from reaching the nest. (See Snyder et al. 1987:101 for an example of a metal guard in place.) Although nest protection did not result in significantly increased productivity for Snail Kites (*Rostrhamus sociabilis*) in Venezuela (Beissinger unpubl. data), increased fledging success was found at Bicolored Wren (*Campylorhynchus griseus*) nests protected in the same manner at the same study site (Austad and Rabenold 1985). Snail Kites have open nests and a substantial proportion of nest failures appeared to be due to aerial rather than terrestrial predators. Because Bicolored Wrens nest in domed nests, nest failure due to avian predators is unusual and aluminum flashing was effective in preventing terrestrial predators from reaching wren nests. Since most parrot nests in cavities are vulnerable to terrestrial rather than aerial predators (Forshaw 1989; but see Snyder et al. 1987 for exceptions), we suspect that their nest success may often be increased by preventing terrestrial predators from reaching nests.

Productivity may also be increased in many parrots by decreasing hatching asynchrony (Fig. 4). Most parrots hatch their eggs very asynchronously over a period of 2 to 14 days (Smith 1975, Snyder et al. 1987, Beissinger and Waltman 1991). Last- and penultimately-laid eggs can have a low probability of hatching (e.g., only 50% compared to about 90% for earlier laid eggs in large clutches of *F. passerinus*). Brood reduction (death of younger chicks due to starvation or from other causes) also commonly occurs during the first two weeks after hatching. In some species of birds, brood reduction occurs disproportionately more often in larger broods, whereas in other species brood reduction may occur in almost every brood ("obligate brood reducers"; O'Connor 1978, Mock 1984, Beissinger and Waltman 1991). Eggs or chicks that would otherwise be expected to die from this cause could be harvested from nests, and incubated or hand-reared successfully. Instead of artificial incubation and hand-rearing, which is labor and time intensive, last-laid eggs or chicks could be transferred into foster nests that either contained a smaller brood (Snyder et al. 1987) or that would result in a more synchronously hatched brood with a higher chance of raising all young (Beissinger and Stoleson in press). Harvesting later-hatching young that would ordinarily be likely to die in the nest results in no net loss of productivity to the natural population, but may provide significant numbers of young for harvesting.

Finally, productivity of wild bird populations can often be greatly increased by deliberate multiple-clutching, if pairs will readily lay replacement clutches for clutches taken into artificial incubation. Though deliberate multiple-clutching has rarely been tried with wild parrot populations, it was successfully employed in management of the endangered Puerto Rican Parrot (Snyder et al. 1987). Outstanding success was also gained with the remnant wild population of California Condors (*Gymnogyps californianus*) through deliberate multiple-clutching (Snyder and Hamber 1985). Utilization of multiple-clutching necessitates facilities and personnel for artificial incubation of eggs and hand-rearing of young. Thus, it is a relatively capital- and labor-intensive technique, increasing the costs of production significantly. How widely applicable the technique may be for parrots is as yet unknown, as there have been few studies assessing tendencies of wild parrots to lay replacement clutches or the extent to which pairs of various species may abandon nest sites as a result of egg removals.

Setting Harvest Levels

Defining a level of sustainable use of a resource depends on the political scale at which management occurs. Setting sustainable harvesting regimes at the national or international level, such as export quotas, requires much of the same information as setting sustainable limits to utilization at the regional or local level, such as at a particular ranch. But because of the difference in scale, estimates of the biological data that are required for setting sustainable harvests will be much harder to obtain for a region than at particular sites. Regional estimates of sustainability will be constantly in need of revision because of the rapidity with which habitat destruction can proceed across terrestrial ecosystems. Local estimates of sustainability can be site-specific and, as we describe below, can depend upon site-specific increases in productivity from management operations and small-scale changes in habitat quality. Thus, we restrict ourselves to defining site-specific estimates of sustainable harvests.

Frequently, all of the information needed to set harvesting regimes may not be available. In the absence of information, we propose following the *Conservative Nestling Harvest Model* to allow a harvesting regime to be initiated. *If it can be demonstrated that a local population is stable or growing, any increase in reproductive output by management programs (e.g., nest boxes, predator pro-*

tection, removal of last young, etc.) would lead to increased productivity, which is harvestable. Managers would need to document natural nesting success patterns before or during the start of intensive management programs to define natural productivity per nest. Once management began, the number of nestlings fledging into the wild could be managed to achieve natural levels of recruitment, and the excess young produced could be harvested. At the same time, population sizes or trends must also be monitored on a continuing basis. Only with both sets of information can the nesting population be managed to ensure population stability while harvesting an excess of young produced.

The *Conservative Nestling Harvest Model* may be useful for setting harvesting regimes when initiating a sustained harvesting program. This model would permit some harvesting to be done while gathering data to obtain better estimates of demographic parameters and population regulation to develop more sophisticated harvest models (Bothma and Du Toit 1989). It is unlikely that the *Conservative Nestling Harvest Model* would lead to overexploitation unless initial population densities were low. In this case, managers should first attempt to increase population size by increasing productivity and/or decreasing mortality. Harvesting should not be contemplated until healthy population sizes are achieved.

Estimates of the magnitude of excess production for sustainable harvesting under the *Conservative Nestling Harvest Model* are derived from data for *F. passerinus* (Table 2). The most conservative estimate of harvestable young assumes that all birds nesting in boxes would otherwise have nested in natural nest sites if nest boxes were not available. Even using this unrealistically high estimate of the number of natural nests (Table 1, Fig. 5), nest boxes would produce an annual excess of 105 young, based on differences between nest cavities and nest boxes in nest success and fledging success rates (Table 2). If, however, we assume that the density of nest boxes (16.3/km) has increased the availability of nest sites over that normally found along fenceposts (4.5/km), nest boxes would produce a whopping 277 young annually in excess of natural production. Actually, only 10 natural nest sites were found in the study area from 1985 to 1987. If we assume production only from these sites, or if we estimate production based on 0.75 active nests per km as was found in surveys outside of the nest box management area, harvestable annual production would be estimated at 284 to 298 young (Table 2). While the latter figures

Table 2. Estimates of population and sustainable harvest levels for *Forpus passerinus* from a population of 100 nest boxes.

| Conditions | Key assumptions | Reproductive characteristics | | | | | Sustainable yield[1] |
		No. nests	No. attempts	Percent success	No. young/nest	No. young produced	
Managed	Nest boxes only	100	130[2]	50[2]	4.7	305	–
Natural	Nest sites = no. nest boxes	100	130	44	3.5	200	105
	Nest sites = 4.5 nests/km	14	18	44	3.5	28	277
	Known nest sites (1985–1987)	10	13	44	3.5	21	284
	Nest sites = 0.75 nests/km	4	5	44	3.5	7	298

[1]Sustainable yield = (No. young produced under managed conditions) – (No. young produced under natural conditions).
[2]Conservatively estimated from Table 1.

may be estimates in excess of what the population can support, it seems likely that the number of young that could be harvested sustainably from this nest box population may be somewhere between the 105 and 298 figures.

More sophisticated estimates of harvest rates can be derived from life table calculations (Caughley 1977, Getz and Haight 1989). However, long time periods (at least 4 to 10 years) are required to generate the information needed to derive adequate survivorship and fecundity estimates. Any estimate of harvest rates based on life table calculations must be considered with caution because parameter estimates may change in a density-dependent manner. Also, emigration and immigration may greatly affect the results. Frequently, the age distribution of a population is not stable, an important assumption of life table models. Finally, differences in productivity between habitats may alter the predicted recruitment dramatically.

For instance, in a five-year study of Monk Parakeets in central Argentina where they are considered to be agricultural pests (Navarro and Bucher unpubl. MS), an average population increase of 12% was predicted from life table calculations. This was consistent with observed population changes in a study area where the population was recovering from previous control campaigns. However, observed increases in some years were much higher than predicted by the model due to immigration, which probably resulted when nests in adjacent areas were destroyed as part of control campaigns. Such effects may occur commonly in species inhabiting regions undergoing habitat destruction and could lead to overestimates of harvestable surpluses.

Biological Monitoring of Harvesting Programs

Once a harvesting regime has been implemented, regular population monitoring is required to determine how harvesting levels are affecting population densities. The effects of harvesting can be evaluated from samples over time of population counts or indices of population change. In regions undergoing extensive habitat destruction, immigration rates must also be estimated. Population change may then be taken into account in resetting harvesting levels, either up or down, to achieve desired results.

Population censuses provide the most direct means of assessing changes in density. A number of techniques have been used to estimate parrot density, presented earlier in this chapter in the section *Population Size and Range.* One or more of these techniques should be used once or twice a year to assess populations in the study area. Minimally, trends in population growth or decline should be detected. This would enable managers to set harvest levels based on the number of individuals or pairs entering the breeding season. This approach to harvest management is known as "tracking" (Caughley 1977) because it allows managers to flexibly set harvest levels in relation to current conditions.

Change in the percentages of nest sites or boxes occupied may also give an indication of the population trends. For instance, if occupancy declines, harvest levels should be lowered. However, as noted earlier, in some parrots there appears to be a substantial nonbreeding population. Under such circumstances, it might be possible to remove a large proportion of nestlings (i.e., unsustainable harvest levels) for several years without seeing a substantial decline in nest site occupancy, because the breeders that died would be replaced by nonbreeders in the population. Only after the proportion of nonbreeders is exhausted would we see a decline in the overall breeding population and nest site occupancy. Unfortunately, this poses some risks, since inexperienced managers may accept higher exploitation rates if they do not perceive a decline in the nesting population.

If resources other than nest sites limit populations in a density-dependent fashion, then a modest decline in population size might not lower overall productivity. Assuming nonbreeders take the place of lost breeders, productivity might not decline until the supply of nonbreeders was exhausted. The result is a lower population density that may be just as productive as the original. However, if recruitment of young into the population is not density-dependent, then harvesting rates may need to be reduced to keep the same level of adults (and productivity) in the population. Thus, *under any circumstances, a consistent decline in nest box occupancy or population size should be a signal to begin decreasing harvesting levels.*

We caution against schemes that propose to harvest a large proportion of nonbreeding individuals. Although we know little about the role of nonbreeders in parrot populations, there are several indications that nonbreeders play important roles in parrot society. First, Snyder et al. (1987) suggest that nonbreeders may play an important role in social facilitation of breeding. As many parrots forage in flocks, perhaps a threshold number of nonbreeding individuals is required to compose foraging flocks. Foraging in groups can reduce the chance of being surprised by a predator while foraging or during flights to food sources, and can increase the chance of finding food (Pulliam 1973, Powell 1974, Clark and Mangel 1984, Brown 1988). Moreover, as the size of a parrot flock increases, individuals can spend more time feeding and less time watching for predators (Wescott and Cockburn 1988). Second, nonbreeders may act as a population buffer against the effects of environmental variation. Extreme over-harvesting that depletes this buffer may increase the chance that a population will be vulnerable to a large decline. Finally, it is not clear in many parrots whether individuals breed annually or only every other year. In species where breeders do not breed every year, nonbreeders in one year may be breeders in the following year. Thus, the role of nonbreeders in parrot society could be more important than otherwise might be suspected in regulating population density.

PROBLEMS AND ADVANTAGES OF THE SUSTAINED MANAGEMENT APPROACH

The preceding sections have concentrated on demonstrating the biological potential for sustained harvesting of parrots and defining a methodology for implementation. Yet we recognize that solving the biological problems may be far easier than solving some of the social, economic, and political problems that are inherent to sustained harvest programs.

Sustained harvest programs fall under the rubric of conservation by imparting economic value to wild animals. Critics of the market approach have long pointed out the difficulties of conservation attempts to raise wild meat for market through ranching schemes (Geist 1988), or by farming sea turtles (Dodd 1979, Ehrenfeld 1979). These problems include: (1) the difficulty of regulating harvesting and trade; (2) stimulating the market economy past the limits of sustainable production; (3) the lack of important scientific information; and (4) the difficulty in setting harvesting quotas. Some of these problems are inherent to utilization of all wildlife products, whereas others apply to specific systems. In the following section, we discuss ways to avoid or ameliorate, where possible, the human-related problems associated with sustained harvesting of parrots based on our experiences and those of other programs of marketed wildlife.

Are There Ways to Avoid Implementation Problems?

Successful implementation of sustainable harvesting schemes requires that harvesting rules be based on the best science available, be adhered to, and be enforced. Strong regulation has helped make successful programs with butterflies and crocodiles in Papua New Guinea (National Research Council 1983a, 1983b). Butterfly farming is regulated by the Insect Farming and Trading Agency. This government organization provides the market, fixes fair prices, ensures quality control of the specimens, provides extension services to landowners, and promotes research to conserve species. The Government of Papua New Guinea also regulates licenses of commercial crocodile farms and tanneries. These operations have been successful in part because protective legislation was passed that banned unlicensed commercial operations that harvested and traded crocodilians, or exported butterflies. Similar prohibitive legislation in neighboring countries also assists this effort (National Research Council 1983b).

The Papua New Guinea experience implies that some regulatory commission or body should take responsibility for monitoring parrot ranching. Each ranching program must be registered with this commission if it is to harvest birds. Representatives of the commission, trained biologists, must visit each site and conduct the surveys to help set harvesting levels. Nest sites should be registered and mapped. Parrot populations on the managed area should be monitored in accordance with the regulations established by the commission. The survey information may then be used so that individual harvesting regimes can be set for each program.

But government regulations may be susceptible to corruption without some recourse for input into decision-making from other parties with no economic interests in regulating parrot ranching, like nongovernmental conservation organizations and scientists. These groups can act as watchdogs and help to ensure that the program is implemented in the best possible manner. Their representatives could be part of an independent policy committee with the ability to appeal government decisions. For instance, appeals by ranchers to change harvest limits can be made through representatives to the independent policy board. A diverse power structure, open to public inspection, could help decrease the possibility of corruption.

Initially some modest financial assistance from international conservation organizations may be needed to help organize the political structure, and to train commission members and their field representatives in parrot biology. Thereafter, a small tax on each bird harvested could support the program, as is the case for caiman harvesting in Venezuela (Thorbjarnarson 1991). Care should be taken to ensure that government bureaucracies do not benefit from the tax on harvested birds to such an extent that they might permit overharvesting. Support should also be used to educate ranchers on the best techniques for intensive management of nests to maximize productivity. Managers and workers will also need to learn how to maximize the survival of parrot chicks, and how to hand-train young birds to increase their worth in the pet trade.

One of the most serious potential problems with maintaining a sustainable market for parrots is the harvesting of animals from the wild by individuals who are not part of the established program. These birds could be sneaked into the trade by being incorporated into part of an established ranching program or sold to a black market. Regulations could be enacted that required all chicks harvested to be marked and identified (e.g., banded with closed stainless steel rings). But no identification system would be completely free from cheating. Determining the source of nestlings may be difficult and cheating of this nature may be hard to detect. Genetic, isotope, and mineral markers have been used to determine source locations of ivory (Cherfas 1989, van der Merwe et al. 1990, Vogel et al. 1990) and bird feathers (Hanson and Jones 1968, Parrish 1989). So far these techniques appear to be applicable only in specific circumstances and we do not know if they would work with parrots.

Nevertheless, strict but flexible harvest limits based on monitoring population changes and the number of active nest sites should set a limit on the number of nestlings to be harvested. If a nestling that is sold in a sustained harvest program did not come from the managed population (i.e., was laundered into the sustained harvest program), it would take the place of one that would have. For ranching programs on private lands the net result should be the same, based on the harvesting quota. Sooner or later overharvesting of this type should be detected through population monitoring and then harvest limits could be lowered.

Can nest sites in a managed program be protected from harvesting by poachers? Ranching schemes on public land may be expected to have this problem more often than programs on private lands. Legislation that outlawed commercial trade of psittacines would help to reduce the black market but probably would not eliminate it completely, especially if birds could be transported across borders to countries that allowed trade (Thomsen and Mulliken 1991). On public lands, nests may require guarding from after hatching until harvesting, which would increase the costs to producers. In small, frontier villages, people live in such close contact with their neighbors that it is unlikely that cheating would go undetected for long (C. A. Munn pers. comm.). But the chances for cheating are higher if campesinos do not expect to live in the same place for more than a few months or perhaps years.

Therefore, land tenure may well be one of the main bottlenecks for rational wildlife exploitation in Latin America and may be a critical problem in managing parrot harvests sustainably. If the exploiters do not own the land, they may be unlikely to make investments for the future (e.g., allowing some young to fledge) that are required to sustain parrot populations. Thus, campesinos on public land are affected by the "tragedy of the commons" (Hardin 1968). Nest box schemes may be the most vulnerable to exploitation by thieves because of the ease of finding and entering nests, although boxes grouped in clumps relatively near each other may be the easiest sites to protect.

Overharvesting has often been cited as a problem in sustained harvest programs (e.g., Dodd 1979, Vasquez and Gentry 1989). Accurate censuses must be conducted by trained biologists in cooperation with land managers. Furthermore, safeguards must be taken to avoid corruption in the reporting of census results by including monitors from other organizations.

Education programs targeted at people living in the management area could help to ease some of these conflicts. But it is unlikely that campesinos living on the edge of survival will be convinced that the economic returns of foregoing the harvest of a portion of nestlings so as to increase future breeding productivity is superior to maximizing immediate returns by harvesting all nestlings. There may be no way of helping campesinos unless their quality of life can be improved beyond the threshold of survival. This implies some kind of land ownership, although this may not be the only requirement (Schofield and Bucher 1986).

Can Sustained Harvesting Be Economically Competitive?

The economics of sustained harvesting of birds from the wild will be critical to the success of such programs. Birds harvested from sustained management programs will have to compete in the market place with birds bred in captivity and those harvested illegally. Unfortunately, we have very little information on the economics of parrot ranching and can only assess the situation in general terms.

We suspect that the economics of sustained harvesting can compete favorably with captive-bred birds. Birds reared in the wild and harvested when nearly full grown only need to be kept in captivity for a short time until being sold, whereas captive-bred birds are in captivity for much longer periods. Moreover, during the first month of life young chicks in captivity usually require very intensive care. Captive-bred young also have parents which must be cared for throughout the year and throughout periods without successful reproduction which may last several years. These are sizeable expenses (Clubb 1991) not incurred in sustained harvest programs. Thus, birds produced in captive situations will probably cost more to house and feed than birds produced from sustained harvest programs.

Sustained harvest programs will have some expenses that aviary businesses do not incur, but many other costs are common to both. Nest boxes must be constructed for both captive breeding and sustained harvest business, but these need not be expensive (US$5.00 per box for materials used for parrotlet boxes in Venezuela). Costs associated with transporting and exporting birds (e.g., shipping, quarantine, and veterinarian fees), if they are exported, are likely to be significant for sustained harvest businesses. But similar costs are incurred by captive breeding. It may be more practical for sustained harvest operations to sell their birds directly to exporters or to an exporting agency, since the exporter then assumes the risks of losing birds to disease or death during the importation process. Of course, this would mean lower prices for the producer. Alternatively, parrot ranchers could be organized into cooperatives that could arrange for transportation or exportation simultaneously of all parrots from sustained harvest programs to reduce costs on a per-head basis.

Obtaining field information, guarding nests, and harvesting the young may be the largest, unique expenses incurred in sustained harvest operations. Several years of study are needed to set site-specific harvest levels. Additional years of follow-up studies are strongly recommended until ecological patterns begin to emerge across several sites. Thereafter, populations will need to be monitored at least annually and perhaps more often.

Differences in the scale of sustained harvest and captive breeding operations also affect economic feasibility. Landowners with large holdings that are part of sustained harvesting programs can probably produce more young than most captive breeding facilities. For instance, the sustainable harvest of 105 to 298 Green-rumped Parrotlets from a very small portion of Hato Masagural in Venezuela (Table 2) is probably more than one to three times the annual production of *F. passerinus* breeders in the United States (R. Conser pers. comm.). We are less certain of how economically competitive sustained harvesting programs can be on small parcels of land, especially if large species are being harvested.

We are less optimistic about sustained harvest operations competing well with birds harvested in an unsustainable manner or harvested illegally for black market smuggling. This problem also plagues captive breeding programs (Clubb 1991). It may always be less costly to take birds from the wild in an unsustainable manner and sell them, or to export them through illegal channels, unless laws or enforcement efforts make smuggling much more difficult and costly. Successful sustained harvest operations may require truly effective control over illegal harvests, and achieving such control may take large investments in law enforcement and education.

What Conditions Favor Sustained Parrot Harvesting?

Sustained harvesting of parrots is most likely to be successful if it is part of a diversified set of products being managed sustainably (e.g., cattle, latex, brazil nuts, selective logging, ecotourism, or other harvested wildlife). Under such circumstances, parrot ranching might provide extra income during years when other products are being produced, and could play an important role in subsistence living during less profitable times. Diversification of income may be necessary for sustainable management to compete with schemes that simply maximize immediate returns (Bucher 1987).

A diverse, multispecific production system may also be important because the future of a market for sustainably harvested parrots is full of uncertainty (e.g., changes in demand and prices) for parrot ranchers. First, captive breeding is likely to increase in scope and efficiency. Second, the possibility exists for a partial or complete ban of parrot importation to many developed countries within five years. As part of this campaign, changes in public attitudes could render parrots less desirable as pets. Third, many species of parrots are long lived and the possibility exists for some degree of market saturation. This uncertainty in future prospects may tempt some managers and traders to maximize immediate returns instead of harvesting in a sustainable manner.

However, sustained harvesting could benefit from a ban on parrot importation by developed countries (if the ban allowed for imports of ranched birds). First, a ban on importation, especially in the United States, would likely cause an initial increase in the price of parrots because the costs associated with captive rearing of birds are higher than costs for import operations with wild birds (Clubb 1991). Second, an import ban will help to establish trade bans in parrot-producing countries which could make enforcement of sustained harvesting rules easier (National Research Council 1983b). Thus, an import ban may help, at least initially, to make sustained harvesting of parrots more feasible.

Based on the previous presentation of the biological and sociological considerations of sustainable use of wildlife, we present some criteria to judge the applicability of wildlife for sustainable use. It may be easier to implement the sustainable use of wildlife in systems with the following characteristics: (1) Age classes with a low reproductive value (Fisher 1930) are harvested. This would allow both productivity and population density to remain high (Fig. 3); (2) Products are marketed shortly after harvesting so that long periods (e.g., years) in captivity can be avoided. This would act to minimize losses and expenses during captive husbandry; (3) The potential to increase productivity through management is high. Under such circumstances, sustainable harvests can be larger; (4) Species are ranched that require only a small or moderate amount of land that is under the control of one owner. Usually social species will require less land than territorial species because individuals group closer together and often occur in higher densities (Emmons 1987). Species requiring less land to farm allow more people to participate in the ranching program, spreading the economic benefits to more and needier people. However, both goals could be

Table 3. Similarities and differences between sustained harvesting of parrots and other types of harvested wildlife (C = captive breeding, F = food added, H = habitat management, K = predator control, N = nest boxes, P = protect nests, RV = reproductive value [Fisher 1930]).

Animals ranched	Stage harvested	Primary product	Target market	When marketed	Productivity increasable	Habitat requirements	Life cycle completed in management area	Age classes harvested	Fecundity per bout	References
Parrots	Nestling	Live pet	Both	Soon	N, H, P	Moderate areas	Sometimes	Low RV	Low	This chapter
Sea turtles	Egg	Meat	Both	Years later	P	Beaches	No – need open ocean	Low RV	High	Dodd 1979
Game ranches	Adults	Meat	Local	Soon	H, K	Large land areas	Yes	High RV	Low	Bothma & Du Toit 1989
Butterflies	Adults	Specimen	Export	Soon	F	Small land areas	Yes	High RV	High	National Research Council 1983a
Iguanas	Adults	Meat	Local	Soon	C, H	Small land areas	No – captive bred	High RV	High	Cohn 1989, Werner 1991
Crocodilians	Adults	Hide	Export	Soon	C, H	Small to moderate	Yes	High RV	High	National Research Council 1983b
Capybara	Adults	Meat	Local	Soon	H	Moderate areas	Yes	High RV	Low	Ojaste 1991

accomplished by well-structured programs on large land holdings. The latter may be preferred since a wealthier landowner might be more willing to sustain wild populations under economic stress; (5) Species that complete their life cycle within the management area will be easier to monitor and manage for sustainability; (6) Species that are fecund and adapted to earlier successional stages will be easier to sustain and be less susceptible to overharvesting than species with low rates of reproduction or requiring mature forests, which are disappearing rapidly.

Table 3 compares the similarities and difference between sustained harvesting of parrots and ranching schemes implemented with other wildlife species. Sustained harvesting of parrots fit these criteria as well as most other species of wildlife currently being marketed. Parrots are harvested as nestlings, and do not have to be kept in captivity for years before being marketed. In the case of some species, parrots are capable of greatly increased productivity through intensive management, and may spend their complete life cycle within a management area. The potential for death in captivity (Carter and Currey 1987; Nilsson 1989, 1990), especially due to disease, may be the major disadvantage of harvesting parrots compared to other wildlife systems (Table 3). Also many parrots have a relatively low reproductive potential (Table 3) and may be more susceptible to overharvesting than more fecund species (Bucher 1991).

We do not, however, advocate launching hundreds of parrot ranching efforts. Quite to the contrary, we believe that there is still much methodology to be perfected, parrot biology to be learned, and sociological research to be conducted before a generic recipe for sustained harvesting of parrots can be developed. Several small demonstration projects should help determine the feasibility and scale of sustained harvesting of parrots. These projects must include both biological and sociological expertise if mechanisms can be developed to avoid some of the inherent difficulties of the market approach to conservation of parrots.

Advantages and Disadvantages of Sustainable Harvesting as a Means of Conservation

Sustainable harvesting programs offer several advantages for conservation of parrots that some other approaches discussed in this book do not. Funds generated from a sustained harvesting program can go directly to support local people. Currently the "middle men," buyers and importers, make the largest profits from the sale of parrots (Thomsen and Brautigam 1991). As mentioned earlier, landowners that ranch parrots in a region could be organized into cooperatives which could either demand higher prices for birds from buyers or arrange to market their birds themselves.

Most importantly, marketing parrots imparts value to the habitats in which they live. For example, if parrots can be sustainably harvested from tropical rainforests, this would provide another commodity, which in addition to brazil nuts, latex, and assorted fruits (Fearnside 1989) might make extractive reserves more economically valuable than forest land cleared for timber harvest or cattle production (Peters et al. 1989). Ranching many species of parrots will require substantial areas of land maintained as mature forest. Thus, sustained harvesting of parrots can be a means to protect natural habitats.

There is an inherent risk, perhaps even a contradiction, in attempting to conserve some parrots by exploiting them in trade and attempting at the same time to conserve other parrots by making their private ownership unacceptable (Butler 1991, Thomsen and Mulliken 1991). Stimulating demand for certain parrots may encourage demand for others. And considering that rare parrots can be artificially colored to look like species legal in the trade, preventing exploitation of rare species will be a problem so long as trade exists in common species. The costs of effectively regulating such problems may be substantial and beyond the available resources of many developing countries (Thomsen and Mulliken 1991). Unfortunately, many of the most highly endangered (and prized) parrots are large species with low reproductive rates, delayed breeding, and a dependence on primary forests (e.g., many amazons and macaws). These are the most dangerous species with which to attempt a legal trade in the face of ongoing illegal trade. Laundering illegal birds through a legal harvesting operation can be expected to be an overwhelming temptation.

Finally, attempts at sustained harvesting, ranging from timber harvests to waterfowl hunting, have had problems in preventing overharvesting, even in highly developed countries like the United States. The benefits of short-term exploitation have a strong tendency to overwhelm the benefits of sustainability, making successful sustained harvesting difficult to achieve in the long term. This is especially true when illegal trade already exists. The temptation to overexploit when prices are favorable will always be strong, even though such exploitation may jeopardize the very existence of the market in the long run.

CONCLUSIONS

In conclusion, biological data suggest that there is a good potential to harvest parrots in a sustainable manner. However, substantial social, political, and economic difficulties lie in the way of implementing sustainable harvest schemes. If these obstacles can be overcome, sustainable harvesting of parrots may provide advantages for conservationists, aviculturists, the pet industry, and local peoples. Conservationists could gain by having wild parrot populations that are near carrying capacity, and by transmitting economic value to habitats to help conserve them in their natural states. Aviculturists would be able to obtain new genetic stock for their breeding programs. The pet industry would have a steady inflow of legally imported birds that would be conditioned to captivity. And finally, the profits from these programs could be directed to the local people who are most in need of ways to support themselves.

Unfortunately, actually realizing the benefits will require a degree of control over trade that may be difficult to achieve. In the absence of effective controls, attempts at sustained harvesting could prove counterproductive and exacerbate conservation problems.

The keys to making sustainable harvesting of parrots work are good scientific information, a strong organization to control and enforce harvesting and trade regulations, and the incorporation of parrot ranching within a diverse set of products being managed sustainably. It remains to be demonstrated if the sustainable use of wildlife products, like parrots, can provide an avenue for development and conservation to coexist together.

ACKNOWLEDGMENTS

This paper benefited greatly from comments by Noel Snyder. Scott Stoleson and James Waltman kindly contributed unpublished data from their studies of Green-rumped Parrotlets. Beissinger's fieldwork was supported by grants from the Smithsonian Institution's International Environmental Sciences Program in Venezuela and the National Geographic Society. Bucher's field studies were supported by the World Wildlife Fund. Support from Yale University's Seminar in Sustainable Systems in the School of Forestry and Environmental Studies made our collaboration possible.

LITERATURE CITED

Austad, S. N., & K. N. Rabenold. 1985. Reproductive enhancement and an experimental inquiry into its mechanism in the Bicolored Wren. Behav. Ecol. Sociobiol. 17:19–27.

Bart, J. 1977. Impact of human visitations on avian nesting success. Living Bird 16:187–192.

Bayliss, P. 1989. Population dynamics of Magpie Geese in relation to rainfall and density: implications for harvest models in a fluctuating environment. J. Appl. Ecol. 26:913–924.

Beissinger, S. R. 1986. Demography, environmental uncertainty, and the evolution of mate desertion in the Snail Kite. Ecology 67:1445–1459.

Beissinger, S. R., & S. H. Stoleson. In press. Nestling mortality patterns in relation to brood size and hatching asynchrony in Green-rumped Parrotlets. Christchurch, New Zealand, Proceeedings of the XX International Ornithological Congress.

Beissinger, S. R., & J. W. Waltman. 1991. Extraordinary clutch size and hatching asynchrony of a Neotropical parrot. Auk 108: in press.

Bothma, J. du P., & J. G. Du Toit. 1989. The harvesting or cropping of game. Pages 255–289 *in* Game ranch management: a practical guide on all aspects of purchasing, planning, development, management and utilisation of a modern game ranch in southern Africa (J. du P. Bothma, Ed.). Pretoria, J.L. van Schaik.

Brawn, J. D. 1987. Density effects on reproduction of cavity nesters in northern Arizona. Auk 104:783–787.

Brown, C. R. 1988. Social foraging in cliff swallows: local enhancement, risk sensitivity, competition and the avoidance of predators. Anim. Behav. 36: 780–792.

Bucher, E. H. 1987. Fauna silvestre chaqueña: como manejarla? Santiago de Chile, FAO-PNUMA. Flora, Fauna, y Areas Silvestres 1:21–24.

Bucher, E. H. 1991. Neotropical parrots as agricultural pests. This volume.

Bucher, E. H., & M. B. Martella. 1988. Preliminary report on the current status of *Amazona aestiva* in the western Chaco, Argentina. Parrot Newslettter 1: 9–10.

Bucher, E. H., L. F. Martin, M. B. Martella, & J. L. Navarro. In press. Social behavior and population dynamics of the Monk Parakeet. Christchurch, New Zealand, Proceeedings of the XX International Ornithological Congress.

Bucher, E. H., & S. Rinaldi. 1986. Distribucion y situacion actual del loro barranquero (*Cyanoliseus patagonus*) en la Argentina. Vida Silvestre Neotropical 1:55–61.

Butler, P. J. 1991. Parrots, pressures, people, and pride. This volume.

Carter, N., & D. Currey. 1987. The trade in live wildlife: mortality and transport conditions. London, Environmental Investigation Agency.

Caswell, H. 1989. Matrix population models. Sunderland, Massachusetts, Sinauer.

Caughley, G. 1977. Analysis of vertebrate populations. New York, Wiley & Sons.

Chapman, C. A., L. J. Chapman, & L. Lefebvre. 1989. Variability in parrot flock size: possible functions of communal roosts. Condor 91:842–847.

Cherfas, J. 1989. Science gives ivory a sense of identity. Science 246:1120–1121.

Clark, C. W., & M. Mangel. 1984. Foraging and flocking strategies: information in an uncertain environment. Am. Nat. 123:626–641.

Clubb, S. L. 1991. The role of private aviculture in the conservation of Neotropical psittacines. This volume.

Cohn, J. P. 1989. Iguana conservation and economic development. BioScience 39:359–363.

Colwell, R. K. 1974. Predictability, constancy and contingency of periodic phenomena. Ecology 55:1148–1153.

Dodd, C. K., Jr. 1979. Does sea turtle aquaculture benefit conservation? Pages 473–480 *in* Biology and conservation of sea turtles (K. A. Bjorndal, Ed.). Washington, District of Columbia, Smithsonian Institution Press.

Eberhardt, L. L. 1978. Appraising variability in population studies. J. Wildl. Manage. 42:207–238.

Ehrenfeld, D. 1979. Options and limitations in the conservation of sea turtles. Pages 457–463 *in* Biology and conservation of sea turtles (K.A. Bjorndal, Ed.). Washington, District of Columbia, Smithsonian Institution Press.

Emmons, L. H. 1987. Ecological considerations on the farming of game animals: capybaras yes, pacas no. Vida Silvestre Neotropical 1(2):54–55.

Eriksson, M. O. G. 1982. Differences between old and newly established Goldeneye (*Bucephala clangula*) populations. Ornis Fenn. 59:13–19.

Fearnside, P. M. 1989. Extractive reserves in Brazilian Amazonia. BioScience 39:387–393.

Fisher, R. A. 1930. The genetical theory of natural selection. New York, Dover.

Forshaw, J. M. 1989. Parrots of the world, third revised edition. Willoughby, Australia, Lansdowne Editions.

Friedmann, H., & F. D. Smith. 1955. A further contribution to the ornithology of north-eastern Venezuela. Proc. U.S. Natl. Mus. 104:463–524.

Geist, V. 1988. How markets in wildlife meat and parts, and the sale of hunting privileges, jeopardize wildlife conservation. Conserv. Biol. 2:15–26.

Getz, W. M., & R. G. Haight. 1989. Population harvesting. Princeton, New Jersey, Princeton University Press.

von Haartman, L. 1971. Population dynamics. Pages 391–459 *in* Avian biology, vol. 1 (D. S. Farner & J. R. King, Eds.). New York, Academic Press.

Hanson, H. C., & R. L. Jones. 1968. Use of feather minerals as biological tracers to determine the breeding and molting grounds of wild geese. Biol. Notes Ill. Nat. Hist. Surv. 60:1–8.

Hardin, G. 1968. The tragedy of the commons. Science 162:1245–1248.

International Union for Conservation of Nature and Natural Resources (I.U.C.N.). 1980. World Conservation Strategy. Gland, Switzerland.

Karlsson, J., & S. G. Nilsson. 1977. The influence of nest-box area on clutch size in some hole-nesting passerines. Ibis 119:207–211.

Korpimaki, E. 1984. Clutch size and breeding success of Tengmalm's Owl *Aegolius funereus* in natural cavities and nest boxes. Ornis Fenn. 61:80–83.

Larkin, P. A. 1977. An epitaph for the concept of maximum sustained yield. Trans. Am. Fish. Soc. 106:1–11.

Leopold, A. 1933. Game management. New York, Charles Scribner's Sons.

Livezey, B. C. 1980. Effects of selected observer-related factors on fates of duck nests. Wildl. Soc. Bull. 8:123–128.

Low, B. S. 1978. Environmental uncertainty and the parental strategies of marsupials and placentals. Am. Nat. 112:197–213.

MacIvor, L. H., S. M. Melvin, & C. R. Griffin. 1990. Effects of research activity on Piping Plover nest predation. J. Wildl. Manage. 54:443–447.

Martin, T. 1987. Food as a limit on breeding birds: a life-history perspective. Annu. Rev. Ecol. Syst. 18:453–487.

van der Merwe, N. J., J. A. Lee-Thorp, J. F. Thackeray, A. Hall-Martin, F. J. Kruger, H. Coetzee, R. H. V. Bell, & M. Lindeque. 1990. Source-area determination of elephant ivory by isotopic analysis. Nature 346:744–746.

Mock, D. 1984. Infanticide, siblicide, and avian nestling mortality. Pages 3–30 *in* Infanticide: comparative and evolutionary approaches (G. Hausfater & S. Hrdy, Eds.). New York, Aldine.

Møller, A. P. 1989. Parasites, predators, and nest boxes: facts and artefacts in nest box studies of birds? Oikos 56:421–423.

Munn, C. A. 1991. Macaw biology and ecotourism, or "when a bird in the bush is worth two in the hand." This volume.

Murton, R. K., & N. J. Westwood. 1977. Avian breeding cycles. Oxford, Clarendon Press.

Myers, J. P., R. I. Morrison, P. Z. Antas, B. A. Harrington, T. E. Lovejoy, M. Sallaberry, S. E. Senner, & A. Tarak. 1987. Conservation strategy for migratory species. Am. Sci. 75:19–26.

National Research Council. 1983a. Butterfly farming in Papua New Guinea. Washington, District of Columbia, National Academy Press.

National Research Council. 1983b. Crocodiles as a resource for the tropics. Washington, District of Columbia, National Academy Press.

Nilsson, G. 1989. Importation of birds into the United States in 1985. Washington, District of Columbia, Animal Welfare Institute.

Nilsson, G. 1990. Importation of birds into the United States in 1986–1988. Washington, District of Columbia, Animal Welfare Institute.

Nilsson, S. G. 1984. Clutch size and breeding success of the Pied Flycatcher *Ficedula hypoleuca* in natural tree-holes. Ibis 126:407–410.

Noss, R. F., & L. D. Harris. 1986. Nodes, networks, and MUMs: preserving diversity at all scales. Environ. Manage. 10:299–309.

O'Connor, R. J. 1978. Brood reduction in birds: selection for fratricide, infanticide and suicide? Anim. Behav. 26:79–96.

Ojaste, J. 1991. Human exploitation of capybara. Pages 236–252 *in* Neotropical wildlife use and conservation (J. G. Robinson & K. H. Redford, Eds.). Chicago, University of Chicago Press.

Parrish, J. R. 1989. The biogeochemistry of Neartic Peregrine Falcons. Provo, Utah, Brigham Young University, Ph.D. Dissertation.

Pérez, J. J., & L. E. Eguiarte. 1989. Situacion actual de tres especies del genero *Amazona* (*A. ochrocephala, A. viridigenalis,* y *A. autumnalis*) en el noreste de Mexico. Vida Silvestre Neotropical 2(1):63–67.

Peters, C. M., A. H. Gentry, & R. O. Mendelsohn. 1989. Valuation of an Amazonian rainforest. Nature 339:655–656.

Potts, G. R. 1986. The partridge. London, Collins.

Powell, G. V. N. 1974. Experimental analysis of the social value of flocking by Starlings (*Sturnus vulgaris*) in relation to predation and foraging. Anim. Behav. 22:501–505.

Pulliam, H. R. 1973. On the advantage of flocking. J. Theor. Biol. 38:419–422.

Reid, W. V. C. 1989. Sustainable development: lessons from success. Environment 31:7–35.

Ridgely, R. S. 1980. The current distribution and status of mainland Neotropical parrots. Pages 233–384 *in* Conservation of New World parrots (R. F. Pasqier, Ed.). Washington, District of Columbia, Smithsonian Institution Press/International Council for Bird Preservation Tech. Publ. No. 1.

Robinson, W. L., & E. G. Bolen. 1984. Wildlife ecology and management. New York, Macmillan Publishing Co.

Rowley, I., & D. A. Saunders. 1980. Rigid wing tags for cockatoos. Corella 4:1–7.

Saunders, D. A. 1977. The effect of agricultural clearing on the breeding success of the White-tailed Black Cockatoo. Emu 77:180–184.

Saunders, D. A. 1988. Patagial tags: do benefits outweigh risks to the animal. Aust. Wildl. Res. 15:565–569.

Schofield, C. J., & E. H. Bucher. 1986. Industrial contributions to desertification in South America. TREE 1:78–80.

Sedinger, J. S. 1990. Effects of visiting Black Brant nests on egg and nest survival. J. Wildl. Manage. 54:437–443.

Smith, G. A. 1975. Systematics of parrots. Ibis 117:18–117.

Snyder, N. F. R., & J. A. Hamber. 1985. Replacement-clutching and annual nesting of California Condors. Condor 87:374–378.

Snyder, N. F. R., & H. A. Snyder. 1989. Biology and conservation of the California Condor. Current Ornithology 6:175–267.

Snyder, N. F. R., H. Snyder, & T. Johnson. 1989. Parrots return to the Arizona skies. Birds International 1:40–52.

Snyder, N. F. R., J. W. Wiley, & C. B. Kepler. 1987. The parrots of Luquillo: natural history and conservation of the Puerto Rican Parrot. Los Angeles, California, Western Foundation of Vertebrate Zoology.

Soulé, M. E. (Ed.). 1987. Viable populations for conservation. Cambridge, Cambridge University Press.

Takekawa, J. E., & S. R. Beissinger. 1989. Cyclic drought, dispersal, and the conservation of the Snail Kite in Florida: lessons in critical habitat. Conserv. Biol. 3:302–311.

Thomsen, J. B., & A. Brautigam. 1991. Sustainable use of Neotropical parrots. Pages 359–379 *in* Neotropical wildlife use and conservation (J. G. Robinson & K. H. Redford, Eds.). Chicago, University of Chicago Press.

Thomsen, J. B., & T. A. Mulliken. 1991. Trade in Neotropical psittacines and its conservation implications. This volume.

Thorbjarnarson, J. B. 1991. An analysis of the spectacled caiman (*Caiman crocodilus*) harvest program in Venezuela. Pages 217–235 *in* Neotropical wildlife use and conservation (J. G. Robinson & K. H. Redford, Eds.). Chicago, University of Chicago Press.

Varley, G. C., & G. R. Gradwell. 1960. Key factors in population studies. J. Anim. Ecol. 29:399–401.

Vasquez, R., & A. H. Gentry. 1989. Use and misuse of forest-harvested fruits in the Iquitos area. Conserv. Biol. 3:350–361.

Verner, J., M. L. Morrison, & C. J. Ralph. 1986. Wildlife 2000: modeling habitat relationships of terrestrial vertebrates. Madison, Wisconsin, University of Wisconsin Press.

Vogel, J. C., B. Eglington, & J. M. Avret. 1990. Isotope fingerprints in elephant bone and ivory. Nature 346:747–749.

Werner, D. I. 1991. Research for the rational use of green iguanas. Pages 181–201 *in* Neotropical wildlife use and conservation (J. G. Robinson & K. H. Redford, Eds.). Chicago, University of Chicago Press.

Westcott, D. A., & A. Cockburn. 1988. Flock size and vigilance in parrots. Aust. J. Zool. 36:335–349.

Wilcove, D. S., C. H. Mclellan, & A. P. Dobson. 1986. Habitat fragmentation in the temperate zone. Pages 237–256 *in* Conservation biology (M. E. Soulé, Ed.). Sunderland, Massachusetts, Sinauer.

Resumen.—Nosotros exploramos la factibilidad de la explotación sostenible de loros como una técnica de conservación. Los conocimientos biológicos requeridos para programas de explotación sostenible de cualquier especie de animal incluyen (1) tamaño de la población y su distribución, (2) requisitos de habitat, (3) la capacidad de recuperar después de disturbios humanos y alteraciones de habitat, (4) tasas de mortalidad y productividad, (5) factores claves que regulan las poblaciones, y (6) los efectos de la variación ambiental sobre la demografía. En los loros, se prefiere la explotación de pichónes en vez de adultos ya que producen mejores mascotas, su explotación tiene un impacto relativamente bajo sobre las poblaciones silvestres, y pueden ser explotados en mayor número. Teóricamente, se puede lograr la sobretasa explotable de loros máxima con mantener activos al número máximo de nidos y con asegurar su éxito. Esto tiene el potencial de lograrse agregando más sitios de anidación (especialmente en forma de nidos artificiales), incrementando la provisión de alimento, protegiendo los nidos de depredadores, produciendo nidadas múltiples en parejas silvestres, o reduciendo el nacimiento asíncrona. Desafortunadamente, se requieren muchos años para acumular suficiente información demográfica para establecer tasas de explotación comprensivas. Cuando faltan datos demográficos suficientes para establecer niveles de explotación, nosotros proponemos el *Modelo Conservador de Explotación de Pichónes*: si hay pruebas de que una población silvestre es estable o se está incrementando, cualquier aumento en productividad que resulta por medio de programas de manejo puede ser explotada. Cálculos de la explotación anual sostenible para periquitos (*Forpus passerinus*) en una población bajo investigación en Venezuela varían entre 105 y 298 pichónes de 100 nidos artificiales. Se pudieran iniciar operaciones comerciales siguiendo el método de explotación conservador, ajustando las tasas de explotación según el tamaño de la población. Una reducción consistente en el tamaño de la población o en el uso de sitios de anidar siempre se debe tomar como seña de que se deben reducir las tasas de explotación. Nosotros detallamos los problemas sociales, políticos, y económicos, que son substanciales e inherentes en programas de explotación sostenible, y hacemos algunas sugerencias de como evitar estos problemas donde sea posible. Discutimos la utilidad de la explotación sostenible como medio de conservar especies y habitat. Si se pueden sobrepasar algunas dificultades de implementación substanciales, la explotación sostenible pudiera ser ventajosa para conservacionistas, avicultores, y poblados locales. Viéndolo de manera contraria, la falta de obtener resultados positivos en programas de explotación sostenible puede agravar problemas de conservación con estimular la explotación de loros de modo que no es sostenible.

5. The Role of Private Aviculture in the Conservation of Neotropical Psittacines

Susan L. Clubb

Avicultural Breeding and Research Center, 1471 Folson Road, Loxahatchee, Florida 33470

Abstract.—The potentials of private aviculture to contribute to conservation are great but have been little realized. The principal avenues by which aviculture might aid conservation include supplying the pet trade with significant numbers of common species at competitive prices, developing avicultural techniques that can be used with endangered parrots, advancing the state of knowledge in avian medicine, maintaining viable captive gene pools of some species, and breeding birds for reintroduction programs. Unfortunately, mutual distrust and fear between conservationists and aviculturists, and among aviculturists have inhibited positive progress in achieving many of these goals. Organized species preservation plans demand a level of commitment and cooperation that many aviculturists have been reluctant to offer. Zoos have generally shown higher levels of inter-institutional cooperation, but have exhibited little overall interest in breeding psittacines. Perhaps the most significant future contributions of aviculture may lie with private foundations patterned on the model of the Peregrine Fund. Resolving conflicts over ownership and control of birds, overcoming traditional attitudes of independence and secrecy, and achieving good control over disease threats are among the most important challenges to be overcome in integrating private aviculture with conservation efforts.

"Aviculture is conservation too." This slogan is often used by private aviculturists (Clinton-Eitniear 1989, Desborough 1989, Marshall 1989, Low 1989b), but is it accurate? Some observers are skeptical, but others feel that private aviculture could play a role in coordinated conservation efforts for Neotropical psittacines.

Ideally, the role of aviculturists in conservation could include: (1) supplying the pet trade with common species in high demand at a reasonable cost; (2) developing avicultural techniques with common species which could be applied to endangered species; (3) contributing to the body of knowledge in avian medicine; (4) striving for improved husbandry techniques that would make captive birds healthier and more productive; (5) cooperating in studbooks, registries, or species survival programs to maintain populations of known genetic diversity as safeguards against the decline or loss of species in the wild; and (6) breeding birds for present or future reintroduction projects.

Many aviculturists consider themselves conservationists and would like to participate in organized conservation efforts. However, opportunities to participate have not been readily available. Providing a means for aviculturists to become involved in conservation may be all that is necessary. But fear and independence may prevent many aviculturists from becoming involved in cooperative efforts. Perceptions of aviculturists as consumers rather than producers of avifauna, and a general distaste of conservationists for commercialism in aviculture stand between conservationists and aviculturists.

If conservation efforts are to utilize the tremendous potential of avicultural collections, prejudice and misconceptions on both sides must be put aside. Doors must be opened to establish a dialogue. These initial efforts, followed by education, encouragement to participate, and mutual respect, could lead to a beneficial alliance between conservation and aviculture (Toft 1990).

WHO ARE AVICULTURISTS?

By definition an aviculturist is one who cares for and raises birds in captivity. For practical purposes aviculturists may be divided into six categories: pet owners who happen to breed a few birds, serious hobbyists, exhibition breeders, commercial aviculturists, zoos, and non-profit foundations or conservation-oriented aviculturists. While joined by a common fascination with birds, the roles that these groups could play in conservation efforts are quite different.

Pet Owners

Pet owners are the ultimate consumer group for vast numbers of birds. Educated consumers could play a role in conservation, by preferentially buying captive-bred birds of species that can be maintained in captivity. Most pet owners are not inclined to purchase rare or expensive birds. But they are a prime market for inexpensive imported birds, especially common or readily available species. They also unintentionally buy smuggled birds.

Most aviculturists begin as pet owners and become so enamored of these pets that they continue to obtain additional individuals. This often leads to breeding on a small scale, typically utilizing common or semi-domesticated species such as cockatiels (*Nymphicus hollandicus*). Early success with these species encourages the acquisition of larger and more difficult avicultural subjects.

Today's pet owners will be the next generation of aviculturists, making education of this vast group of consumers of primary importance to conservation efforts.

Exhibition Breeders

As with any hobby, many aviculturists breed primarily or exclusively for exhibition and competition, striving for the best type, color, mutation, song, or ability (e.g., racing pigeons). These aviculturists work primarily with highly domesticated species. While this type of aviculture does not directly benefit conservation, many birds which are unsuitable for exhibition are utilized as pets. Such birds may be promoted as making superior pets to birds of wild origin.

Hobbyists and Collectors

Commercial aviculturists may have the greatest potential for supplying the pet trade but the role of hobbyists must not be discounted. The trend among serious hobbyists is to specialize and many restrict their efforts to a genus or group of closely allied species (Desborough 1989). These breeders are more likely to maintain good pedigree information and to retain offspring for future breeding. Many hobbyists are concerned about conservation efforts involving their special interest groups. Given the proper direction, and a desire to work cooperatively, they could maintain genetically diverse, self-sustaining populations in case of future destruction of wild populations.

Unfortunately hobbyists and collectors have been implicated in the extinction or near extinction of rare species, such as Spix's Macaw (*Cyanopsitta spixii*), from the wild (Collar and Juniper 1991). In their desire to possess a representative pair of rare species, collectors have been willing to pay very high prices.

Conservation efforts involving hobbyists will require a great deal of cooperation and coordination. Removal of rare birds from the wild for collections cannot be considered conservation unless such efforts are part of officially sanctioned conservation programs. Some specialty groups of aviculturists have begun this task and are attempting to establish studbooks for some species or genera (e.g., *Pionus* and *Amazona*). Some aviculturists also participate in studbooks established by the American Association of Zoological Parks and Aquariums (AAZPA). For example, of 67 institutions participating in the Golden Conure (*Aratinga guarouba*) studbook, 11 are members of AAZPA and 41 are private breeders (Lieberman 1990). While hobbyists and collectors are primarily responsible for the demand for rare species, they also represent an untapped reserve for conservation efforts (Toft 1990).

Commercial Aviculture

Commercial aviculture of domestic species for the pet trade is not a new phenomenon. Import records dating back to 1901 indicate a steady stream of avian imports. Between 1901 and 1942 an average of 350,000 birds were imported each year, of which 71% were canaries (Nilsson 1981). In the 1960s, Hartz Mountain Corporation created a massive cottage industry in the United States for private aviculturists producing Budgerigars (*Melopsittacus undulatus*). These common, highly domesticated species are still the mainstay of the avicultural industry (Meyers 1989).

With the widespread availability of large psittacine species in the pet trade during the last decade, many people became interested in commercial production of macaws, amazons, or other psittacines. While some aviculturists have been successful, many have found the venture unprofitable, with expenses often outweighing sales. Due to the relative difficulty of breeding rare species, commercial aviculturists typically concentrate on common species which are adaptable, marketable, and profitable. Commercial aviculturists are most likely to provide birds in large numbers to meet the demands of the pet industry, but they are less likely to participate in coordinated captive breeding efforts and tend to resent any outside interference in their breeding programs.

Zoos

Zoos have made tremendous strides with many species, primarily mammals, but psittacines are poorly represented in zoo exhibits and breeding programs. This may be due to their destructive nature, which makes them difficult to display attractively. For example, of all psittacine species reported to the International Species Inventory System (ISIS), Blue-and-Yellow Macaws (*Ara ararauna*) are the most numerous. Of 343 participating institutions, 116 hold 415 Blue-and-Yellow Macaws, an average of 3.5 individuals per institution. In 1989 these institutions reported only 43 chicks surviving past 30 days. Of 85 Neotropical psittacine species reported in ISIS, only 22 species are represented by 50 or more individual birds (ISIS 1989). If species survival were to depend on current zoological collections, only a handful of psittacine species would be present in viable numbers.

The zoological community, including the AAZPA, has discouraged private ownership of exotic animals. At the same time it is apparent that zoos have neither the space nor financial resources to sustain genetically viable captive populations of very many species. It is also evident that governmental support will only be available for a limited number of highly endangered species. If psittacine species can be adequately maintained by the private sector, perhaps zoos should encourage such an effort and use their resources to protect species which cannot be maintained privately. Such encouragement and cooperation between zoos and the private sector could result in valuable exchanges of information as well as breeding stock. But the question of who "owns" rare species, or controls their management must be resolved.

Private or Public Foundations, Trusts, or Institutions

Private individuals with proper direction and an identifiable goal can make a significant contribution to conservation, as exemplified by the Peregrine Fund. The Peregrine Fund was started in 1970 by a group of dedicated falconers. They were alarmed by the extirpation of the Peregrine Falcon (*Falco peregrinus*) from the eastern United States, and the dramatic decline of the species on a global basis due to the effects of DDT and dieldrin. Despite tremendous legal and biological difficulties, this group has managed to breed in captivity and release over 3000 Peregrine Falcons. The reintroduction program has been successful and the species is now considered stable in the eastern United States (although reintroductions continue in the western United States). To achieve their successes, the Peregrine Fund pioneered many advances in captive breeding. While now a non-profit organization, the roots of the Peregrine Fund came from private aviculture of Falconiformes (Cade et al. 1988).

Private falconers have also responded to conservation goals. The U.S. Fish and Wildlife Service reports that of the 566 raptors bred in captivity by private breeders in the United States in 1988, 25% were used for conservation (reintroduction), 50% for falconry, and 25% for captive propagation (White 1989). Unfortunately such successes have not yet occurred in aviculture of psittacines.

AVICULTURE MUST BE OPEN TO NEW ATTITUDES

The attitudes of many private aviculturists have been a point of great consternation in the conservation and zoological communities. The most harmful of these attitudes is fear which leads to paranoia and secrecy.

Aviculturists fear regulation on the national, state, or local level, which will limit their right to possess or sell their birds. Confusion about the application of federal law to captive wildlife, and an ever-changing barrage of state laws and local ordinances fuel this fear. For example, in Florida an aviculturist must register in order to sell or exhibit birds in the state. Under the Sunshine Law, a freedom-of-information-styled law, these records are accessible to the public. Aviculturists fear that this makes their birds vulnerable to theft. Certainly the fear of theft or confiscation is a driving force in the development of paranoia among aviculturists, fed by the value of many species and the difficulty of tracing them once stolen.

Private aviculturists are also fiercely independent and resent being told what they can or cannot do with their birds. The prospect of being told where, or to whom, their birds will be transferred will limit the participation by private aviculturists in Species Survival Plans (SSPs) or other cooperative but relatively dictatorial programs. Most of the SSPs are under the direction of zoo personnel. Private aviculturists often feel zoos are unqualified to dictate policy concerning psittacines.

NEOTROPICAL PSITTACINES IN AVICULTURE

Bird sales in the U.S. in 1989 were estimated at approximately 3 to 4 million individuals (Meyers 1989). Approximately 500,000 were wild-caught, imported birds. Most birds sold are budgerigars, canaries, and cockatiels. Of 36,699 birds imported into Connecticut for resale in 1984, 85% were species bred primarily in captivity and 15% were species which were primarily wild-caught (Simon 1984). Captive-bred Neotropical psittacines (including macaws, amazons, pionus, and conures) have been available in larger numbers in recent years and prices on the retail market have been dropping.

According to Low (1989a,b), 13 of the 26 genera of Neotropical psittacines are well represented in aviculture (Table 1). For example, the genus *Aratinga* is highly productive in captivity. Sun Conures (*Aratinga solstitialis*) and Jenday Conures (*A. jendaya*) were the "bread and butter" of many avicultural collections for years, as many aviculturists waited patiently for their macaws and amazons to become productive. Sun conures have been known to breed within a few months of importation. Some other *Aratinga*s, such as Blue-crowned Conures (*A. acuticaudata*) have not been so prolific. *Pyrrhura* species have also adapted well to captivity, but these birds are not as popular as pets. In addition many species of *Pyrrhura* are either rare or unknown in aviculture as well as in the wild.

Macaws of the genus *Ara* are adaptable and hardy for the most part. Some pairs are very prolific and breed almost year-round. Their size and coloration has made macaws popular for exhibition in zoos. One privately owned zoo

Table 1. Status of the genera of Neotropical parrots in aviculture in the United States based on the personal experience of the author and Low (1989a).

Genus	Relative numbers	Ease of breeding	Demand for pets	Pet quality
Amazona	abundant	difficult	high	good
Anodorhynchus	moderate	difficult	high	good
Ara	abundant	prolific	high	good
Aratinga	abundant	prolific	high	good
Bolborhynchus	rare	difficult	low	unknown
Brotogeris	common	difficult	fair	good
Cyanoliseus	common	moderate	low	good
Cyanopsitta	absent			
Deroptyus	rare	difficult	low	poor
Enicognathus	uncommon	moderate	low	good
Forpus	uncommon	moderate	low	fair
Gradydidascalus	absent			
Gypopsitta	absent			
Hapalopsittaca	absent			
Leptosittaca	absent			
Myiopsitta	abundant	prolific	fair	fair
Nandayus	abundant	prolific	fair	good
Nannopsittaca	absent			
Ognorhynchus	absent			
Pionites	uncommon	difficult	high	good
Pionopsitta	rare	difficult	low	poor
Pionus	common	prolific	high	good
Pyrrhura	abundant	moderate	fair	good
Rhynchopsitta	uncommon	difficult	low	poor
Touit	absent			
Triclaria	absent			

in Miami, Florida, has been breeding Scarlet Macaws (*Ara macao*) since 1945 and has bred them to the fifth generation. Hyacinth Macaws (*Anodorhynchus hyacinthinus*) are highly prized by aviculturists, but unlike *Ara* spp. their reproductive rate in captivity has been low, as it is reported to be in the wild (Munn et al. 1989). High demand and low production keeps prices for a captive-bred juvenile of this species extremely high ($7,000 to $12,000). This creates strong incentive for smuggling in spite of international protection efforts (Thomsen 1989).

Amazon parrots (*Amazona* sp.) are favorites of the pet bird industry and typify parrots to many people. Captive breeding of amazons is challenging and often unrewarding (Table 1). They have a short breeding season in captivity, often fail to recycle if eggs are removed or are infertile, and appear to take longer to adapt to captivity and become productive. Thus, it is doubtful that the tremendous demand for amazon parrots can be met by aviculture in the near future. Unfortunately smuggling of Mexican and Central American amazons is pervasive and may fill the void if legal imports are restricted (Clinton-Eitniear 1989). Consumers are typically unaware of the protected status of species. Most aviculturists, on the other hand, will not knowingly buy smuggled birds.

In general, tropical lowland psittacine species (e.g., *Pionus* sp.) are well established in aviculture, whereas mountain species have been more difficult avicultural subjects. *Brotogeris, Pionites, Cyanoliseus,* and *Forpus* have been imported in large numbers but are not commonly bred. *Enicognathus* have been bred quite successfully despite being traded in relatively low numbers.

Approximately 11 genera of Neotropical psittacines are rare or not present in aviculture (Table 1). Some such as Hawk-headed Parrots (*Deroptyus accipitrinus*) have been imported in low numbers but are difficult to breed in captivity. The genus *Pionopsitta* has been regarded as too delicate by importers and has rarely been made available to aviculturists. Others such as *Ognorhynchus* or *Leptosittaca* are rare or poorly known in the wild and have not been imported (Low 1989a).

ECONOMIC ASPECTS OF PRIVATE AVICULTURE

A subjective overview of the pet bird market in recent years indicates a dramatic change in supply and demand. Production has improved as birds are in captivity for longer periods of time. Years ago a captive-bred bird was a novelty commanding a high price. In an attempt to capitalize on this demand, many people began to breed parrots commercially. Many of these farms became productive, prices dropped, and the demand for some species has been exceeded by supply. Now captive-bred birds are common and consumers shop for price. Improved incubation and handrearing techniques have allowed aviculturists to increase production and produce tame pet birds. Many aviculturists directly market their birds by advertising and selling them retail, rather than using pet shops or wholesale outlets for distribution which lowers the retail price.

Some common and popular psittacine species are being bred in large numbers. This produces a glut on the market and has resulted in price reductions. For example, in the early 1980s, juvenile imported Blue-and-Yellow Macaws were sold wholesale for approximately $1,000 and captive-bred birds sold for approximately $1,800. This species has adapted well to captivity and has proven to be quite prolific. Today captive-bred birds are being sold for as little as $650 to $900.

Wild-caught Blue-and-Yellow Macaws imported from Guyana are less expensive than captive-bred birds, selling for $600 to $700, and the majority are being sold to aviculturists (W. Lawson pers. comm.). More than 20,000 Blue-and-Yellow Macaws were imported from 1982 to 1988 (J. B. Thomsen pers. comm.). This species is very hardy and it is not unreasonable to estimate that half of these birds are still alive. If half of the surviving birds were set up for breeding, we would have approximately 2,500 pairs in the United States. If half of those pairs were productive and averaged 4 chicks per year, approximately 5,000 chicks could be produced annually. In this case we could theorize that importation of additional wild-caught birds is unnecessary to meet the demand for this species.

If captive-bred birds are to replace wild-caught birds for the pet trade, price is a vital factor. If import restrictions are legislated, prices for wild-caught birds may increase and discourage sale of those birds as pets. Aviculturists who want to obtain adult birds for breeding may be willing to pay a higher price for sexually mature birds rather than wait years for captive-bred birds to mature. For example, in 1989 the cost of maintaining Neotropical psittacines at two commercial breeding facilities averaged $0.80 to $1.50 per bird per day, including feed, labor, insurance, advertising, veterinary care, etc. (T. Ireland pers. comm.). If we conservatively estimate $350 per year to keep a macaw in captivity, $800 to buy a captive-bred Blue-and-Yellow Macaw cheaply, and four years until a successful reproduction, a sexually mature captive-bred individual would cost roughly $2,200. For this reason, many aviculturists prefer to gamble with imported, wild-caught adult birds even though they may take just as long to adapt to captivity and become productive.

If private aviculturists in the United States cannot meet the demand of the pet market, foreign aviculturists may. Breeding birds in third-world countries may be less expensive and more profitable than raising the same birds in the United States. Costs of shipping and quarantine may be offset by low labor and land costs. For example, prior to the embargo on trade with South Africa, thousands of captive-bred psittacines, primarily cockatiels, were imported into the United States each month. At that time a cockatiel could be purchased in South Africa for $6, while an aviculturist in the United States would need to sell the same bird for approximately $25 to $30 to cover expenses and make some profit. (The cost of feeding a cockatiel for a year in the United States is roughly $25.) It is also likely that other species could be raised in third-world countries, and imported into the United States at prices that are competitive with birds bred by aviculturists in the United States.

DISEASE POSES PROBLEMS FOR PRIVATE AVICULTURE

The growth of private aviculture has been paralleled by the growth of the Association of Avian Veterinarians, a group of veterinarians with a special interest in medicine of companion and aviary birds. A corresponding explosion in the knowledge and application of avian medicine, such as the widespread availability of rapid, accurate sex determination techniques, has made possible a great expansion of aviculture. This proliferation of information would not have been possible without pet owners and aviculturists providing economic support for veterinarians.

Infectious diseases have a profound effect on the aviculture of psittacines. Many diseases, especially viral diseases, can quickly turn successful aviculture into disaster. The incidence and severity of these diseases is compounded by the mixing of species from many regions in captivity, and the mobility of birds between collections. Private aviculturists are extremely concerned about the effects of disease on their collections, and actively seek solutions to disease problems. Some of these diseases, like Pacheco's parrot disease, can now be controlled by vaccination. Other diseases, such as polyomavirus (papovavirus) infections, are a threat to neonatal psittacines, especially in a nursery environment.

Improved husbandry techniques and preventive medicine can minimize the effects of disease. However, the etiology of many recognized syndromes, such as proventricular dilatation syndrome, has not yet been established. The origin of these diseases certainly lies in wild Neotropical bird populations. Their effects on native wild bird populations if carried by escaped birds is unknown, but potentially serious.

A COALITION BETWEEN AVICULTURE AND CONSERVATION

The most important and most achievable conservation goal for private aviculture is to increase captive production of certain psittacine species to fill the demand for pets and take trade pressures off wild populations. However, while this may be an achievable goal for some species, for others it may not be.

The development of avicultural techniques, disease control mechanisms, and diets for common species can contribute to conservation efforts for rare species. To achieve this goal, aviculturists will have to share and disseminate information. Some aviculturists are very open and are willing to share their experiences for the benefit of others. But others closely guard information on numbers and species of birds held in captivity, and their breeding success. More open exchange of information is desperately needed.

Avicultural associations such as the American Federation of Aviculture (AFA), specialty groups, and local bird clubs abound in the United States. Avicultural magazines such as American Cage Bird Magazine, Bird Talk Magazine, the AFA Watchbird, and Bird World have a combined circulation of over 200,000 households. These associations and publications provide an excellent medium for the dissemination of information among aviculturists. If the leaders of private aviculture are convinced of the proper course of action, the means for dissemination of the message is in place.

Sharing of information by participation in studbooks or registries is also vitally needed. Although some studbooks have been established, rates of participation have been low, probably due to the fear of disclosure. Effective population management will require coordinated efforts to manage a significant number of individual birds. For maximum participation, registries and stud-books should be managed by aviculturists for aviculture as well as for con-servation. It is conceivable that smaller groups of private aviculturists could cooperatively strive for captive maintenance of selected psittacine species as a safeguard against future loss of wild populations.

Unfortunately, maintenance in captivity is the only hope for species that have been extirpated in the wild, such as Spix's Macaw. Maintaining and breeding declining species for present or future reintroduction programs is appealing to many aviculturists. But many obstacles will need to be overcome before private aviculturists can make a significant contribution to reintroduction projects. Fear of disclosing avicultural holdings and the unwillingness to relinquish possession of birds will have to be put aside for the common goal of conservation. For these species it is essential that aviculturists cooperate in studbooks, and be willing to trade or transfer birds in order to maximize genetic diversity and minimize artificial selection for adaptation to captivity.

The costs of participation in such projects by aviculturists will be high and the rewards may be limited. Aviculturists must be willing to give up their birds, usually without financial compensation, and risk the return of these birds to the wild. This may be the most difficult undertaking because aviculturists often consider the risks of mortality during reintroduction as unacceptable. Reintro-duced birds are often viewed as being "sacrificed." Extreme caution will also be needed to minimize the introduction of disease into wild populations from avicultural collections.

Future advances in population management and better cooperation with conservation goals could make private aviculture a viable conservation tool. Time is of the essence. The first step can be as simple as breaking down communication barriers and should be followed by the establishment of prac-tical, economically viable management programs. Mistrust must be replaced with mutual respect and a common purpose.

Aviculturists must be made aware of recent advances in population man-agement, recovery plans, and species survival plans. If they wish to participate, they must re-examine entrenched attitudes of fear and independence which discourage participation. While many of the species that they possess are now common, the status of these species in the wild could change with alterations of habitat. The time to develop genetically viable populations is now while most of the breeding stock is of wild origin. Finally, conservationists must also be willing to compromise and assist in the establishment of economically feasible management programs that can be managed by aviculturists to meet the needs of both aviculture and conservation.

LITERATURE CITED

Cade, T. J., J. H. Enderson, C. G. Thelander, & C. M. White (Eds.). 1988. Peregrine Falcon populations, their management and recovery. Boise, Idaho, The Peregrine Fund.

Clinton-Eitniear, J. 1989. Captive status of the Green-cheeked Amazon Parrot, (*Amazona viridigenalis*). AFA Watchbird 16(5):16–18.

Collar, N. J., & A. T. Juniper. 1991. Dimensions and causes of the parrot conservation crisis. This volume.

Desborough, L. 1989. The conservation role of the small breeder in aviculture. AFA Watchbird 16(5):11.

ISIS. 1989. Species distribution report—Birds, as of 31 December. Apple Valley, Minnesota, International Species Inventory System.

Lieberman, A. 1990. International studbook, Golden Conure (*Aratinga guaroba*). San Diego, California, San Diego Zoo.

Low, R. 1989a. Captive breeding of Neotropical parrots. AFA Watchbird 16(5):31–35.

Low, R. 1989b. The American breeders role in conservation. Proceedings of the seminar on breeding psittacines in captivity. Alamo, California, Avian Research Fund.

Marshall, T. 1989. AFA: an organization dedicated to avian captive breeding and conservation. AFA Watchbird 16(5):5.

Meyers, M. 1989. Pet industry profile (fact sheet). Pet Industry Joint Advisory Council.

Munn, C. A., J. B. Thomsen, & C. Yamashita. 1989. The Hyacinth Macaw. Pages 409–419 *in* Audubon Wildlife Report 1989/1990 (W. J. Chandler, Ed.). San Diego, California, Academic Press.

Nilsson, G. 1981. The bird business, a study of the commercial cage bird trade. Washington, District of Colombia, Animal Welfare Institute.

Simon, L. 1984. A study of the Connecticut wild bird trade, 1984. Connecticut General Assembly Environmental Committee. Sharon, Connecticut, Connecticut Audubon Society.

Thomsen, J. B. 1989. When prohibition isn't enough. AFA Watchbird 16(6): 28–31.

Toft, C. A. 1990. Aviculture and the conservation of bird species: the role of captive propagation. Bird World 13(1):49–53.

White, B. 1989. Report on raptor propagators in the United States, 1988. Washington, District of Colombia, U.S. Fish and Wildlife Service.

Resumen.—Los potenciales de la avicultura privada para contribuir a la conservación son muchos pero han sido poco utilizados. Las vías principales por la cual la avicultura puede ayudar con la conservación son: supliendo al comercio de aves mascotas con cantidades significativas de especies comunes a precios competitivos, desarrollando técnicas de avicultura que pueden ser usadas con loros en peligro de extinción, avanzando el estado de conocimiento sobre la medicina avícola, manteniendo reservas genéticas viables en cautiverio de algunas especies, y reproduciendo aves para programas de reintroducción. Desafortunadamente, la desconfianza mutua y temor entre los conservacionistas y avicultores, y entre los avicultores mismos, ha inhibido el progreso positivo para lograr muchas de estas metas. Planes de conservación de especies, organizadas, requieren un nivel de cumplimiento y cooperación que muchos avicultores han sido renuentes de ofrecer. Los zoológicos generalmente han demostrado niveles más altos de cooperación interinstitucional pero en general han demostrado poco interés en reproducir psitácidos. Tal vez las contribuciones futuras más significativas de la avicultura pueden encontrarsen en fundaciones privadas siguiendo el patrón del "Peregrine Fund." Resolviendo conflictos sobre la pertenencia y control de aves, superando actitudes tradicionales de independencia y sigilo, y logrando un buen control sobre la amenaza de enfermedades son entre los retos más importantes para ser superados al integrar la avicultura privada con los esfuerzos de la conservación.

6. Potentials and Limits of Captive Breeding in Parrot Conservation

Scott R. Derrickson and Noel F. R. Snyder

Conservation and Research Center, National Zoological Park, Front Royal, Virginia 22630; and Wildlife Preservation Trust International, P.O. Box 426, Portal, Arizona 85632

Abstract.—The progressive declines in many wild psittacine populations have resulted in widespread calls for the establishment of captive breeding programs. Captive breeding is only one of many possible conservation strategies, however, and its potential contribution to the preservation of endangered parrots is limited by a variety of significant difficulties. Of special concern are problems in: (1) obtaining consistent reproduction in some species; (2) controlling diseases in confinement; (3) avoiding detrimental genetic and behavioral changes; (4) meeting long-term financial and logistical requirements; and (5) securing administrative continuity and commitment. Ideally, captive breeding's direct role in species preservation should be limited to short-term situations where alternative management options have proven ineffective, or can be significantly enhanced. Where practical alternatives exist, they are generally far preferable to captive breeding. The identification of limiting factors and practical management alternatives should be a priority for research, and should be accomplished before populations decline below minimum viable size.

The preservation of species is clearly best served by conservation methods associated with habitat, community, and ecosystem preservation. However, because the rapid decline and fragmentation of wild populations have often outpaced our ability to ensure their survival, there has been a corresponding increase in the application of interventionist techniques, such as captive breeding, reintroduction, embryo transfer, and cryopreservation (Wemmer and Derrickson 1987, Conway 1988, Foose and Ballou 1988, Seal 1988). New technologies clearly need to be developed and applied to species conservation, but should not displace older, more conventional methods in circumstances where the latter are appropriate and can be applied effectively (Cade 1986, 1988). The proliferation of captive breeding and reintroduction programs for endangered and threatened species, in particular, has generated both debate among conservationists (cf. Cade 1988, Ousted 1988, Imboden 1989), and the adoption of specific policy statements by some conservation organizations (e.g., IUCN 1987).

In his book on endangered parrots, Tony Silva (1989) calls for the captive breeding of 31 of 51 species and subspecies of psittacines listed in the International Council for Bird Preservation (ICBP) Red Data Book (King 1977–1979) and Appendix I of the Convention on International Trade in Endangered Species (CITES). Captive breeding efforts of various sorts are already underway for a number of these species, and for some of them, such as Spix's Macaw (*Cyanopsitta spixii*) and the Mauritius Parakeet (*Psittacula echo*), these programs may be crucial for survival. While the preservation of other psittacines will undoubtedly depend upon programs aimed at either long-term captive maintenance or the interactive management of wild and captive populations (Snyder et al. 1987, Foose and Ballou 1988), there are critical questions as to the degree to which captive breeding should be emphasized relative to other conservation approaches. Overall resources for conservation are not infinite, and captive breeding programs are normally quite expensive and labor-intensive if they are to be done comprehensively and for the number of years that may be necessary to achieve success (Cade 1986, 1988; Conway 1988). Furthermore, there are enough other serious constraints that affect captive breeding programs that it is well to be cautious in implementing this approach as a conservation panacea.

The purpose of this chapter is to consider some of the general advantages and disadvantages of captive breeding as they apply to the conservation of psittacines. We also suggest some general principles by which decisions can be made as to when captive breeding should be implemented. The scale of impending extinctions among parrots is large (Collar and Juniper 1991), as are the stakes in selecting optimal conservation strategies to prevent these extinctions.

Although there are a number of significant potential benefits of using captive breeding in conservation, some of the problems inherent in this approach have not received the attention from conservationists that we believe is warranted. Some of these problems are not obvious to those unfamiliar with the field. Some are susceptible to partial control with strenuous efforts. Still others are close to inevitable, and severely limit the long-term value of the technique.

The overall view we will develop is that captive breeding is a valuable and necessary technique for parrot conservation in specific circumstances, but that its values have often been exaggerated, sometimes to the detriment of other potentially promising techniques. Captive breeding is a preferred conservation method only under very specific conditions, and only in a short-term sense. When reliance is placed on this technique in a recovery program, we believe that it should always be coupled with efforts to either supplement or reestablish wild populations as soon as possible.

THE PROBLEMS WITH CAPTIVE BREEDING APPROACHES TO CONSERVATION

Difficulties in Breeding Endangered Parrots

Of the 51 endangered parrots considered by Silva (1989), 36 have been bred at least once in captivity. Of the remaining 15 species, most have not been subjected to comprehensive breeding efforts and undoubtedly some would respond positively under such treatment. Nevertheless, for many of the species that have been bred successfully thus far, breeding successes have been few and scattered, and have involved only a small minority of the individuals held captive. Certainly, infrequent incidents of successful breeding cannot be equated with establishing and maintaining viable, self-sustaining populations.

Captive breeding performance has been especially poor for a number of endangered amazons and macaws (Bennett 1989). For example, although much attention has been given to the propagation of the large Lesser Antillean *Amazona*, the St. Vincent Parrot (*Amazona guildingii*) and the St. Lucia Parrot (*A. versicolor*), success to date has not been substantial enough to allow confidence that self-sustaining captive populations can be achieved. Meanwhile, increased habitat and legal protection, technical assistance, and educational efforts to promote national pride in these species show every sign of being successful in promoting recovery of extant wild populations (Jeggo 1986, Butler 1991). Similar efforts on the island of Dominica will hopefully improve the status of the Red-necked Parrot (*A. arausiaca*) and the Imperial Parrot (*A. imperialis*), neither of which has been bred as yet in captivity. Although efforts to breed members of these species that are already in captivity should be encouraged, the capture of additional wild birds and the allocation of additional resources to captive breeding seem unwarranted at this time.

Intensive efforts to establish a captive population for the Puerto Rican Parrot (*A. vittata*) were not begun until the early 1970s, when the wild population was almost completely lost and hopes for its recovery were at a low ebb (Snyder et al. 1987). Although breeding was first obtained in the captive flock in 1979, annual production has rarely exceeded six fledglings, and breeding has occurred in only a small proportion of the captive pairs. The captive flock, which presently numbers over 50 birds, has been maintained largely through the infusion of additional wild birds, and clearly cannot be considered self-sustaining despite the implementation of a variety of captive husbandry techniques that have been used successfully with other species. The fact that the closely related, non-endangered Hispaniolan Parrot (*A. ventralis*) has bred well in the same aviary suggests that the Puerto Rican Parrot may have an intrinsically low potential for captive breeding. With the continued poor performance of this species in captivity, and the progressive, albeit slow, increase of the wild population under intensive management, the future role of captive breeding in the recovery program for this species remains uncertain.

Many endangered birds have proven to be much more difficult to propagate in captivity than their closely related, non-endangered surrogates. For example, while the captive propagation of the endangered Norfolk Island Red-crowned Parakeet (*Cyanoramphus novaezelandiae cookii*) has posed some difficult hurdles (Hicks and Greenwood 1989), the captive breeding of other *Cyanoramphus* subspecies has progressed relatively easily (Taylor 1985). Similarly, Whooping Cranes (*Grus americana*) and Mississippi Sandhill Cranes (*G. canadensis pulla*) have proven to be much more difficult to maintain, breed, and rear in captivity than either of their non-endangered surrogates, Greater (*G. c. tabida*) and Florida (*G. c. pratensis*) Sandhill Cranes (Kepler 1978, Derrickson and Carpenter 1981). The Aplomado Falcon (*Falco femoralis*) has also proven to be more difficult to breed in captivity than other falcons such as the American (*F. sparvarius*) and Eurasian (*F. tinnunculus*) kestrels, a difference which may prove generally common among many tropical raptors (T. J. Cade pers. comm.).

Because captive stocks of endangered species are normally derived from small wild populations, failures to breed well in confinement may stem in part from a pre-existing loss of genetic variation due to drift or inbreeding (Allendorf and Leary 1986, Danielle and Murray 1986, Ralls and Ballou 1983, Ralls et al. 1986). Alternatively, breeding problems may result from psychological, physiological, or environmental requirements that are lacking in the captive setting (cf. Eisenberg and Kleiman 1977, Millam et al. 1988). We suspect that many of the difficulties in obtaining good reproductive performance from endangered parrots may be related to behavioral problems arising from several widely used captive management practices: hand-rearing and forced-pairing. In Cockatiels (*Nymphicus hollandicus*), hand-rearing produces a number of gender-specific reproductive effects. Whereas hand-reared males show a reduction in fertility, hand-reared females show several changes, including increases in the probability of laying, overall egg production, and the selection of inappropriate oviposition sites (Myers et al. 1988). Although the effects of forced-pairing vary greatly among avian species, the spontaneous choice of mates seems to be crucial for successful pair formation and reproduction in many birds (cf. Kepler 1978, Burley and Moran 1979, Klint and Enquist 1980, Bluhm 1985, and Derrickson and Carpenter 1987), including Cockatiels (Yamamoto et al. 1989). Many psittacines are highly individualistic in their willingness to form pairbonds, and it seems highly probable that social familiarity and sexual compatibility are important determinants of the pairing process. In small captive populations, the absence of reproduction in certain individuals may well trace to the fact that behaviorally compatible mates are simply unavailable.

All of these factors have important implications for the design of psittacine breeding programs. Specific propagation plans (Foose et al. 1986) must address all aspects of captive maintenance as well as genetic and demographic considerations. Unless procedures insuring regular and sustained breeding in endangered parrots can be developed, efforts to establish viable, self-sustaining captive populations and to produce adequate numbers of quality offspring for reintroduction will fail.

Problems in Controlling Avian Diseases

There is a growing body of evidence suggesting that endangered species are relatively susceptible to disease due to reduced genetic diversity that results from small population size (O'Brien et al. 1985, Dein et al. 1986, Jones and Owadally 1988, O'Brien and Evermann 1988, Thorne and Williams 1988). Parrots are susceptible to a wide variety of diseases. Some of these diseases appear limited to the group, some can exist in a carrier state for many months without detection, and some are incurable by presently available methods. Among the most serious diseases threatening captive collections are pox, chlamydiosis (psittacosis), psittacine proventricular dilation syndrome (parrot wasting disease), parrot herpes virus infection (Pacheco's disease), psittacine beak and feather disease, and sarcocystis (Graham and Platt 1978; Clubb 1983; Gerlach 1983; Woerpel et al. 1984; Phalen 1986; Clubb et al. 1987; Gaskin 1989; Ritchie et al. 1989, 1990). Some of these diseases were unknown in this country in past decades, but have now achieved a nearly world-wide distribution, presumably resulting largely from the greatly expanded trade in caged birds in recent times. Various collections of parrots have suffered severe losses from disease outbreaks (e.g., Clubb et al. 1987, Gough 1989), and disease control is especially problematic for institutions and facilities which continually acquire birds from a variety of sources. Normal quarantine procedures (30 days at most institutions) cannot guarantee safety from some of these diseases because of their long potential latencies in asymptomatic carrier individuals.

The potential susceptibility of parrots to disease argues for extreme caution in establishing captive breeding programs for endangered parrots. As a rule, the following principles seem to be sensible: (1) captive breeding facilities should, whenever possible, be located in the species' natural range to reduce the chances of contact with exotic diseases and pathogens to which it may have no resistance. Other potential benefits of siting captive breeding facilities within the species' natural range include natural habitat and climate (Berger 1977, Kear 1977), public education and conservation training (Mallinson 1988), integrated field and captive studies, and reduced logistic costs; (2) the species should be housed in 2–3 geographically isolated, single-species facilities that are distant from other captive breeding facilities, and are essentially "closed"; (3) the facilities should be staffed by individuals who are not simultaneously caring for other captive birds, especially taxonomically similar species; (4) as much as possible, facilities should be sited in areas free from arthropod vectors and feral populations of exotic birds, and should be designed to prevent exposure to such potential disease carriers; and (5) established husbandry protocols should emphasize disease prevention by such policies as exclusion of human visitors and scrubdowns of staff entering facilities, and should incorporate regular health examinations.

Unfortunately, the degree of adherence to the above precautions varies greatly among ongoing breeding programs for endangered parrots. In most instances, birds are being held in multi-species facilities where exposure to insect vectors and feral birds is poorly controlled. It is unusual to find an institution with staff dedicated exclusively to the care of single species, and in many instances staff responsible for endangered parrots possess personal avian pets and have regular contact with many other psittacines. In large part, the failure of many institutions and private aviculturists to implement and maintain rigorous preventive measures for disease stems from the trouble and considerable expense that such efforts demand.

However, without preventive measures, experience shows that the proper question is not whether disease problems will eventually develop, but rather how soon. In recent years, captive breeding programs for a number of endangered birds have suffered losses and sometimes severe setbacks due to disease. Specific examples include eastern equine encephalitis in Whooping Cranes at the Patuxent Wildlife Research Center (Dein et al. 1986), inclusion body disease in Red-crowned (*Grus japonensis*) and Hooded Cranes (*G. monacha*) at the International Crane Foundation (Docherty and Henning 1980, Docherty and Romaine 1983), a herpes virus in Mauritius Pink Pigeons (*Columba mayeri*) at the Rio Grande Zoo (Snyder et al. 1985), parrot wasting disease in several large private collections (D. L. Graham pers. comm.), a sporozoan infection in Tahitian Lories (*Vini peruviana*) at the San Diego Zoo (W. D. Toone pers. comm.), sarcocystis in Thick-billed Parrots (*Rhynchopsitta pachyrhyncha*) at the Gladys Porter Zoo (D. Thompson pers. comm.), an unidentified agent in Puerto Rican Plain Pigeons (*Columba inornata wetmorei*) at Humacao (R. Perez-Rivera pers. comm.), avian tuberculosis in White-winged Wood Ducks (*Cairina moschata*) at Slimbridge (Kear 1986, Cromie et al. 1989), and avian pox (Landolf and Kocan 1976) and atoxoplasmosis (Partington et al. 1989) in Bali Mynahs (*Leucopsar rothschildi*) at the National Zoo. In the last case, retrospective analyses of preserved tissues have revealed the presence of this parasite in the collection dates back to at least 1978, and the sudden outbreak of mortalities was apparently related to the resumption of breeding and the increased susceptibility of young birds.

Most propagation plans for endangered species call for the subdivision of captive populations for genetic, epidemiological, and logistical considerations (Foose et al. 1986, Lacy 1987). But although the risks of disease are theoretically reduced by subdividing populations among a number of facilities, this holds true only if the subpopulations are managed independently and exchanges between subpopulations are infrequent. In most cooperative breeding programs, birds are distributed among facilities as pairs or small groups. While this practice solves the problems of limited off-exhibit space and institutional requirements to maintain diverse collections, it also necessitates the frequent interchange of individuals between facilities to address genetic, demographic, or behavioral problems. We believe that the application of a strategy of extensive subdivision for endangered parrots is a formula for the spread of cryptic diseases, in view of the number of diseases with long latencies affecting this group. Extensive subdivision also severely reduces options for behavioral management and controlled research needed for securing sustained reproduction.

Wild populations of endangered parrots are also vulnerable to disease, particularly when their habitats are greatly modified or are invaded by exotic species. Unfortunately, the potentially important role of disease in the extinction of wild psittacine populations has received essentially no attention, probably because such situations are relatively difficult to document in the absence of intensive study (Warner 1968, Van Riper et al. 1986, May 1988, Scott 1988). The close proximity in which captive parrots are normally housed provides nearly ideal conditions for the spread of disease. In the absence of strict controls, it is likely that captive populations will generally exhibit greater vulnerability to disease than wild populations, where individuals are dispersed. Nevertheless, the comparatively social nature of most psittacines suggests a relatively high vulnerability to disease in both wild and captive populations. Any effort to bolster wild populations through the translocation of wild birds or the release of captive-bred birds should obviously include rigorous disease screening procedures to prevent the unwitting spread of disease organisms. Many reintroduced populations of Wild Turkeys (*Meleagris gallopavo*) in the midwestern United States are infected with a hematozoan parasite (*Plasmodium kempi*), apparently stemming from the translocation of infected birds (Castle and Christensen 1990). Similarly, present difficulties with an upper respiratory disease in wild Desert Tortoises (*Xerobates agassizii*) are believed to be traceable to the releases of infected individuals (Anon. 1989, Jacobson and Gaskin 1990).

Expense and Logistical Difficulties Involved in Long-term Captive Breeding

The long-term costs of maintaining captive populations of vertebrates in the absence of economic payoffs have been estimated by Conway (1986), and the numbers of species that could be housed in existing zoological institutions in minimum viable populations (MVP) (Shaffer 1981) have been calculated by Soulé et al. (1986) at about 925 species, and perhaps more realistically by Conway (1986) at only about 500 species. The costs are far from negligible, running from about $10,000 to $500,000 per year per MVP for various species ranging from Caribbean Flamingos (*Phoenicopterus ruber*) to Siberian tigers (*Panthera tigris altaica*) (Conway 1986). Where endangered parrots would fit in general in this array is hard to specify, although the captive breeding program for the Puerto Rican Parrot has been running at about $250,000 per year, exclusive of cage construction and facility maintenance costs (M. A. Wilson pers. comm.). By comparison, costs associated with the California Condor (*Gymnogyps californianus*) program at the San Diego and Los Angeles Zoos have been running about $500,000 per year (W. D. Toone pers. comm.). Because the captive populations of both of these species have not yet reached minimum viable size, annual costs will presumably be much higher if and when MVP sizes are attained.

One-quarter to one-half million dollars per year for a species summed over the 200-year maintenance period considered reasonable by Soulé et al. (1986) in their "millenium ark" proposal would total 50–100 million dollars per species. Sums of this magnitude would be more than adequate to purchase and endow for perpetual management and control, blocks of habitat that would suffice for the survival of many species of psittacines in the wild, and presumably would also preserve habitat essential for thousands of other plant and animal species sharing their ranges. For example, the 1300-km² Gray Ranch recently purchased by The Nature Conservancy in New Mexico may ultimately provide substantial amounts of habitat not only for Thick-billed Parrots, but also for Aplomado Falcons, California Condors, and a variety of other endangered mammals and reptiles. The total habitat cost will probably come to about $25 million (G. Bonnivíer pers. comm.). Where such opportunities exist to preserve endangered parrots through habitat purchase, it is well to question the logic of pursuing long-term captive breeding.

To the argument that habitat is already gone for many endangered parrot species, we would note that a surprisingly large number of these species are not threatened by habitat destruction nearly as much as by other direct human impacts, such as harvesting for food or for the pet trade (Forshaw 1989, James 1990, Collar and Juniper 1991). Many endangered psittacines are not, in fact, crucially dependent upon virgin habitats. Moreover, where habitat destruction has been an important factor, often there is no reason why habitats cannot be restored and restocked. All too often there seems to be a willingness to advocate captive breeding, without considering alternative courses of action that would be more cost-effective and could benefit many more species.

During the past decade, over 238 organized breeding programs have been established by zoological institutions in North America, the British Isles, Europe, Japan, and Australia and New Zealand for long-term species survival, public education, and exhibition (Baker and George 1988, Bennett 1990, T. J. Foose pers. comm.). Of these programs, approximately 70% have been developed for mammals, 27% for birds, and 3% for reptiles and amphibians. Because existing zoological institutions can only accommodate MVPs of an estimated 500–925 species (Conway 1986, Soulé et al. 1986), it is reasonable to conclude that the majority of space on the "ark" will continue to be devoted to mammals. Parrots will presumably comprise only a small proportion of programs established for birds, and presently endangered parrots an even smaller proportion of those. It is often suggested that space for captive breeding, especially for parrots, can be substantially increased by extending organized breeding programs to include private aviculture. Although this strategy has already been adopted to a very limited extent in programs for cranes, Bali Mynahs, St. Vincent Parrots, and Palm Cockatoos (*Probosciger aterrimus*), we question its broad application to psittacincs because of many considerations, including costs, disease control, and conflicts of interest over ownership and centralized management.

The move toward organized, cooperative breeding programs is a relatively new phenomenon in zoos and involves a major change in programmatic emphasis from the public exhibition of animal diversity to the intensive management of small populations. While major strides have been made in cooperative research, coordinated records-keeping systems, and centralized administration, the extended captive management of MVPs for literally hundreds of species will be a logistically difficult and expensive undertaking involving unprecedented levels of commitment and inter-institutional and international collaboration. Because these logistical and financial constraints may be as formidable as all of the biological problems combined (Conway 1986, Foose et al. 1986), great care should be exercised in establishing captive programs. We strongly support the view expressed by many (cf. Lande 1988, Cade 1988) that captive programs should not be implemented whenever simpler, more cost-effective preservation and restoration methods can be effectively applied.

Genetic and Behavioral Change in Captivity

The establishment of a captive population has a number of genetic consequences. Because such a population will normally be derived from a limited number of founders, its gene pool will differ from that of the source population as rare alleles are lost during the founding event due to sampling (Denniston 1978). Furthermore, if the effective population size (N_e) (Wright 1969) remains small, or fluctuates widely in succeeding generations, genetic variation will be rapidly eroded as a result of inbreeding and random genetic drift (Frankel and Soulé 1981, Allendorf and Leary 1986, Foose et al. 1986, Lacy 1987, Lande 1988, Ralls et al. 1988). Such reductions in heterozygosity and allelic variation will usually result in a lowering of both the average fitness of individuals and the long-term evolutionary potential of the population (Lande 1988, Simberloff 1988, Lacy 1989).

To preserve extant genetic variation, conservation-oriented breeding programs must attempt to minimize the effects of inbreeding, genetic drift, and adaptation to captivity through the deliberate control of reproduction, population size, and population demography (Foose and Ballou 1988, Lacy 1989). This is a difficult task, however, considering the practical limitations of controlling reproduction, the dynamic nature of evolutionary forces in small populations, the types of genetic variation to be maintained, and the uncertain nature of selection in the captive environment (cf. Lande 1988, Simberloff 1988). Because genetic changes resulting from general adaptation to captivity and inadvertent selection for tameness are essentially inevitable, progressive domestication represents a significant problem, especially for long-term programs (Spurway 1955, Franklin 1980, Frankham et al. 1986, Flesness and Cronquist-Jones 1987, Lyles and May 1987, Lande 1988). Although very little is known about the genetic changes which occur during domestication, selection in multilocus (polygenic) developmental, physiological, and behavioral traits appears to be very sensitive to founder effects (Templeton 1980), and many of the traits that accompany domestication have high heritability and can be selected for relatively easily (Franklin 1980).

While domestication may increase relative success in captive breeding over time, it also results inexorably in a captive population that is less and less adapted to the wild. In this regard, it is interesting to note that the one parrot species that has probably been under domestication longer than any other—the Budgerigar (*Melopsittacus undulatus*)—is a species for which feral populations are virtually unknown (Forshaw 1989). Despite frequent escapes of this species from captivity around the world, the only known region where feral populations have become established is in urban areas of southern Florida, where they are favored by low predation and a prevalence of bird feeders and nest sites (Wenner and Hirth 1984). Similarly, the one other psittacine widespread in the bird trade from primarily captive-bred stock, the Cockatiel, has not established feral populations anywhere. Whether the general failures of these species to become established in the wild is due to domestication or other factors has not received careful study, but they appear consistent with domestication effects.

How serious a problem is domestication? How quickly does it proceed? Is it reversible? There is not much information on this subject for parrots specifically, but one can look at other avian species to gain some insights. Domestic Canaries (*Serius canarius*) and species of gallinaceous birds, such as Turkeys and Chickens (*Gallus gallus*), have been under domestication for some time, yet feral populations originating from domesticated forms of these birds are unknown except on predator-free islands. The inability of Wild Turkeys to form feral populations in formerly occupied habitat after only a few generations in captivity has been examined thoroughly (Leopold 1944, Knoder 1959 and unpubl. data), as there have been many attempts to reestablish populations from captivity. In this species, domestication effects are apparent in certain features of the endocrine and nervous system. Size of the adrenals, for example, rapidly declines in captive flocks and seems closely tied to the loss of physiological and behavioral traits essential for survival in the wild (Knoder 1959).

Many phenotypically plastic traits can show considerable non-genetic (environmental) modification in captivity. Complex behavioral traits are especially prone to loss or rapid alteration unless the captive environment is deliberately structured to provide the appropriate physical and social experience during critical developmental periods (Campbell 1980, Kleiman 1980, Lyles and May 1987, Beck et al. in press). Such changes in behavior can adversely affect both reproduction in captivity and later survival in the wild. For example, it has long been known that hand-raised birds are particularly vulnerable to predators following their release to the wild. Recent experiments by Thaler (1986) with Hazel Grouse (*Bonasa bonasa*), Rock Ptarmigan (*Lagopus mutus helveticus*), and Rock Partridge (*Alectoris graeca*) demonstrated that normal antipredator behavior disappears in chicks by about 3 weeks of age unless this behavior is reinforced by the parent. Similarly, even brief exposure to humans early in life can significantly alter the escape reactions of Red-legged Partridge (*A. rufa*) (Csermaly et al. 1983), and Andean Condors (*Vultur gryphus*) (M. P. Wallace pers. comm.). Antipredator behavior in Peregrine Falcons (*Falco peregrinus*) also seems to be learned, as young raised by captive parents that are not fearful of man tend to be tame, while those raised by fearful parents also become fearful of humans (Cade et al. 1989).

Recent attempts to reintroduce captive-bred birds and mammals to the wild have revealed a variety of behavioral deficiencies in addition to those relating to predator recognition and avoidance. These deficiencies have included problems in locating and processing food, interacting and competing with conspecifics, selecting suitable habitat and nest sites, and moving and navigating in complex habitats. As a result, many reintroduction programs have attempted to improve survivorship by incorporating specialized rearing methods, and/or pre-release and post-release conditioning procedures to correct these behavioral deficiencies and ease the transition from captivity to the wild (Ellis et al. 1978, Temple 1978, Cade 1986, Stanley-Price 1986, Derrickson and Carpenter 1987, Wallace and Temple 1987, Horwich 1989, Kleiman 1989, Wiley et al. 1991).

There is abundant evidence that birds and mammals raised under abnormal social conditions are prone to a variety of behavioral problems which later can affect reproduction (Goldfoot 1977, Kleiman 1980). Hand-reared birds can form inappropriate sexual and social bonds with their human foster parents, or in the case of cross-fostering, with their foster parent species (Harris 1970, Immelmann 1972, Cade 1986, Rowley and Chapman 1986). Parrots seem especially vulnerable to mal-imprinting. Yet the hand-rearing of parrots remains a common practice in aviculture, despite its negative effects on future reproductive performance (Myers et al. 1988). Behavioral differences between parent-reared and hand-reared birds are often subtle, but quite important. For example, Snyder (pers. obs.) has observed that parent-raised Thick-billed Parrots are much quicker to learn how to open pine cones than are hand-raised conspecifics. Subtle differences such as this can become especially apparent when captive animals are moved from the benign captive environment to the wild. Not surprisingly, reintroductions involving captive-bred animals have been less successful than those involving wild-born animals (Griffith et al. 1989).

In considering the aforementioned behavioral effects caused by confinement, the Puerto Rican Parrot serves as an important example. The last wild population has endured in a relatively high-predation environment, the Luquillo Mountains of Puerto Rico. Detailed studies of the behavior of these birds have revealed that compared to other wild *Amazona* species, they are especially wary and secretive in nesting behavior, yet at the same time are highly aggressive toward one another in protecting nesting sites, which are in short supply (Snyder et al. 1987). Only a small proportion of the captive population has bred successfully, a problem that some have quickly concluded must be due to failures in husbandry techniques. Yet these same techniques have worked well with the Hispaniolan Parrot and are basically the same techniques used by other *Amazona* breeders. We doubt very much whether the failure of the Puerto Rican Parrot to breed readily in captivity can be attributed primarily to failures in techniques. Very possibly it results from the secretive, wary nature of the birds in the source population in the wild.

It is possible that captive breeding success may increase with the Puerto Rican Parrot over time, but it is well to consider the possibility that this may only occur if the captive population becomes progressively "tamer" and less releasable to the wild. The very features of behavior that do not appear to adapt it well for captive production may be essential for survival in the last wild habitat. Increasing success in captive breeding may eventually result in birds that can exist only in extremely permissive, predator-free environments, if there.

To date, captive-produced Puerto Rican Parrots have been released to the wild primarily by fostering to wild nests and they have survived as well as wild birds. The long-term prospects, however, are not so sanguine. Should the wild population of this species be lost, it would be unwise to wait very long in attempting to reestablish wild populations, as one can predict that there will be increased difficulties with this process over time.

The implications of progressive genetic and behavioral change may well be considerably more serious than are commonly recognized in conservation biology. Proposals such as the now famous "millenium ark" (Soulé et al. 1986) for long-term preservation of species in captivity may, in fact, fail due to this problem. For many species, long-term preservation in captivity, despite all efforts to slow changes by such processes as minimizing inbreeding and equalizing founder representation, may still result in domestic animals that will never be wild animals again. Equal breeding of potential founder individuals cannot be even closely approached in many species, especially many psittacines.

It is sometimes argued that even if domestication cannot be avoided, domestic forms are still a worthwhile goal. But we submit that one is not truly preserving either species or ecosystems by such an approach. Philosophically, it is well to question the value of such efforts and whether much more emphasis should instead be put into saving wild populations, crucial habitats, and ecosystems while they still exist. Moving into a massive "ark" mentality may distract us from implementing more difficult, but, ultimately, much more successful conservation approaches.

In general, the emphasis in theoretical conservation biology has been placed on the undeniably important questions of avoiding inbreeding, preserving genetic diversity in small populations, and determining minimum viable population sizes. Issues relating to selection and the conservation of species' typical behavior in captivity have not as yet received the attention which they deserve. Presumably, some species in long-term captive breeding programs will be more affected than others, and hopefully some will be reestablishable in the wild after many generations. For many others, long-term captive breeding may well prove to be a dead end after only a modest number of generations.

Long-term Administrative Continuity and Commitment

Despite the gravity of the problems considered so far, we fear that the most serious impediment to success in long-term captive breeding efforts will lie in failures in administrative continuity and commitment. These are problems inherent in human programs and institutions, and cut across all cultures and political systems (Wemmer and Derrickson 1987). While some of these problems can hopefully be resolved through increased cooperation, and creative organization and management (cf. Clark and Westrum 1989, Grumbine 1990), the individual and institutional commitments proposed in establishing the "millenium ark" are difficult to assess, since they extend beyond the immediate economic and social sphere. One can foresee sustained commitments being made for certain charismatic species favored for zoo exhibition, but it seems highly unlikely that such commitments will be made for the many other species that will need long-term captive support but lack considerable economic payoffs. Although nothing less than a massive, dedicated, long-range commitment can suffice, this is not likely to be forthcoming considering the inevitability of future periods of human economic stress.

In our own limited experience in the past two decades with species conservation programs, we have come face to face with serious, periodic deteriorations in the quality and commitment to programs for several endangered birds. Personnel involved in these programs have necessarily changed over time, and funding has waxed and waned without regard to programmatic requirements. We know of no reliable mechanism to ensure the continuity of efforts. This same problem, of course, afflicts all human endeavors and institutions, but the penalties for mistakes with endangered species programs are especially severe. The difficulties in guaranteeing long-term, quality efforts for endangered species strongly argue for all possible speed in achieving recovery of wild populations.

ADVANTAGES OF CAPTIVE BREEDING FOR CONSERVING SPECIES IN THE WILD

There are a number of important advantages of captive breeding when it is properly integrated with conservation efforts. First and foremost, captive populations can serve as an important safety net for species whose wild populations are small and fragmented, with a high probability of extinction. With species that do breed readily in captivity, it is sometimes possible to greatly increase the rate of reproduction, through techniques such as multiple-clutching, and thereby speed the recovery of the wild population through the release of captive-bred birds. Theoretically, such releases into the wild can serve a number of purposes such as increasing extant populations, correcting sex-ratio imbalances, infusing genetic variation, infusing new traditions, reestablishing extirpated populations, and/or establishing new populations in natural or altered habitats. Finally, captive birds can provide an important resource for fundamental biological research which cannot be accomplished on wild individuals.

Captive populations also have an important role to play in species preservation when pressures on wild populations are truly overwhelming in the short term and there is no way to sustain wild populations. However, this situation is probably less common than is generally believed, and some "hopeless" cases turn out to be rather more hopeful when imaginative research and conservation efforts are mounted. Nevertheless, truly hopeless situations, such as those faced recently by the California Condor and the Guam Rail (*Rallus owstoni*) do occur. Captive breeding can provide a short-term reprieve for such species, buying time for preparation of reintroduction sites that may permit reestablishment of wild populations. The critical objective of such efforts should always be reestablishment in the wild as soon as possible to avoid domestication and behavioral deficits associated with prolonged captivity. When captive breeding programs are conducted within a species' native range, they can act as an important focal point for establishing subsidiary programs aimed at habitat preservation and restoration, public education, and research training (Durrell and Mallinson 1987, Mallinson 1988, Kleiman 1989, Butler 1991). Because of the widespread interest in psittacines, it is likely that many species could be effectively used as "flagship" species in the development of extensive conservation and education programs.

Still another potential value of captive breeding to endangered parrot conservation comes through providing an alternative source of birds to supply the pet trade and thus indirectly reducing demands on wild populations of species endangered by this trade. This position has been recently espoused by the Cooperative Working Group on the Bird Trade (1990).

However, the argument that commercial captive breeding can relieve pressures on wild populations is basically an economic one, and in the last analysis depends on the costs of captive production relative to the costs of wild harvest and transport. Recent large-scale efforts (e.g., the recently deceased Aviculture Institute in Los Angeles) to breed favored species, such as macaws and amazons, for the commercial market have not managed to achieve profitability. It is questionable if the costs of captive production can ever undercut the few dollars that a compesino may get for harvesting a macaw or amazon nestling in the wild (Thomsen and Brautigam 1991). So long as such small financial rewards are sufficient to motivate harvest, the harvest is likely to continue, and in fact may serve to make the captive breeding of such species an economically inviable endeavor until wild populations are completely extirpated. Although captive breeding of certain prolific species, such as Budgerigars and Cockatiels, currently meets the demands of the marketplace, we remain skeptical that it could ever do so for most amazon parrots and macaws, where reproductive rates are much lower and production costs are much higher. Even for Budgerigars and Cockatiels, captive breeding would probably not be economically viable without the total and effective ban on exports of psittacines from Australia. Bans on the export of macaws and amazons from many countries in the New World have yet to demonstrate much effectiveness.

WHEN IS CAPTIVE BREEDING APPROPRIATE?

Perhaps no other subjects arouse more emotional debate among conservationists than the questions of whether and when to employ captive breeding on behalf of endangered species. On the one hand, it is unwise to wait too long in starting captive breeding efforts, because the chances of success are greatly diminished when the wild population has already lost significant genetic variation as a result of drift and inbreeding. On the other hand, starting too soon can represent unnecessary expense and can focus resources in unproductive directions, preempting other approaches that may have more promise of success. In practice, the major disagreements tend to occur when there is a lack of enough knowledge about an endangered population to allow confident judgements about its potential viability and its prospects for recovery and reestablishment. Very often, only guesses are available as to causes of decline until careful studies are performed, and very often studies are not initiated until a species is already in its final hour.

These issues can only be resolved through intensive biological investigations in the field. These investigations should be initiated before captive breeding or other conservation measures are implemented, and should be aimed at documenting life history characteristics, demographic parameters, and the causes of population decline. Because synergistic models which incorporate genetic, demographic, and environmental uncertainties are presently unavailable, estimates of population viability should be developed primarily on the basis of demographic rather than genetic factors (Lande 1988, Reed et al. 1988, Simberloff 1988, Grumbine 1990). In many cases, remedial actions can be prescribed which are much less expensive and more likely to succeed than captive breeding. For example, thorough studies of the Bahama Parrot (*Amazona leucocephala bahamensis*) have shown clearly that there is no near-term need for captive breeding of this species, and that its conservation can best be served by such measures as education, preserve creation, selective predator control, and translocations to establish new populations (Gnam 1990). Nevertheless, it may be apparent in other cases that alternative conservation measures are unavailable, and that captive breeding may be a necessity for the near-term survival of a species.

Unfortunately, studies often are not begun until a species is all but lost, and there simply is not enough time to reach definitive judgments as to the reversibility of the causes of decline before the species will likely be gone. In such cases there may be no prudent course of action but to start efforts to establish a captive population simultaneous with intensive research of the remnant population, accelerating or decelerating the efforts to establish a captive population in a flexible manner, depending on information gathered. To the extent that a captive population can be established initially through the taking of eggs or young, demographic impacts on the wild population can be minimized, leaving open the option for massive efforts to bolster the wild population if research indicates that this has a good chance of leading to recovery. This was the approach followed in the Puerto Rican Parrot Recovery Program, where the primary function of a captive population has generally been conceded to be a supportive one for the wild population (Snyder et al. 1987). A similar approach is being followed with the Mauritius Parakeet (Jones and Owadally 1988).

In contrast, intensive research into causes of the California Condor's decline eventually revealed that there was no reasonable way to achieve recovery of the remnant wild population. In this case, initial efforts to establish a captive population by taking of eggs and nestlings were followed by efforts to trap all the last wild birds to prevent further losses of genetic diversity (Snyder and Snyder 1989).

By the time that the introduced Brown Tree Snake (*Boiga irregularis*) was identified as the cause of the decline of Guam's native avifauna (Savidge 1987), several species were already biologically extinct and only represented by a few males in the wild. Captive populations of both the Guam Rail and Micronesian Kingfisher (*Halcyon cinnamomina cinnamomina*) were established on an emergency basis by capturing wild adults and, in the case of the rail, the collection of eggs. From the outset of these programs, the principal objective has been the reestablishment of wild populations. Although introduction efforts for the Guam Rail are now underway on the nearby, snake-free island of Rota, reintroduction of the Kingfisher to the wild will have to be delayed until effective snake control measures can be developed, as alternative locations for reintroduction are inhabited by other endemic Kingfishers (Shelton 1987, Derrickson 1987a).

The decision to establish a captive population of Whooping Cranes was only reached after the lone surviving wild population failed to increase substantially despite several decades of protection. The captive population was established by removing single eggs from wild pairs, a practice that has not affected population productivity or growth. The principal goal of the captive effort from its beginning has been to use captive birds to establish additional, disjunct populations in North America to minimize the species' risk of extinction. This objective remains unchanged some 23 years later. Although efforts to establish a self-sustaining population in western North America by cross-fostering Whooping Cranes to Greater Sandhill Cranes appear to have failed, it is still hoped that additional populations can be established elsewhere from captive stock (Drewien and Bizeau 1978, Derrickson 1987b, R. C. Drewien pers. comm.).

In all of the above cases, high priority has been given to the reestablishment of viable wild populations in the near term, simultaneous with increasing the size of captive populations, a strategy in which we heartily concur. In none of these cases is there any necessity to conclude at this point that permanent self-sustaining captive populations will prove to be advisable. If reestablishment efforts are sufficiently successful, the expense of maintaining captive populations can ultimately be foregone. However, if reestablishment efforts are not successful, options still remain open for long-term captive breeding.

Our emphasis on speed of reestablishing wild populations is based both on avoiding behavioral and genetic deterioration in the captive environment and on considerations of habitat preservation in the wild. As a generality, captive breeding should be viewed only as a stopgap emergency measure that will eventually be phased out once wild populations are well on the way to recovery. We do not believe that long-term captive breeding represents a viable approach for conservation either from a biological or human management perspective.

ACKNOWLEDGMENTS

We thank B. B. Beck, J. D. Ballou, G. Bonnivíer, T. J. Cade, R. C. Drewien, T. J. Foose, J. M. Forshaw, D. L. Graham, C. E. Knoder, B. J. Miller, R. Perez-Rivera, D. Thompson, W. D. Toone, M. P. Wallace, and C. Wemmer for providing information and valuable discussions on captive propagation, and S. R. Beissinger and C. E. Knoder for their thorough comments and suggestions on early drafts of this paper.

LITERATURE CITED

Allendorf, F. W., & R. F. Leary. 1986. Heterozygosity and fitness in natural populations of animals. Pages 57–76 *in* Conservation biology: the science of scarcity and diversity (M. E. Soulé, Ed.). Sunderland, Massachusetts, Sinauer.

Anonymous. 1989. Emergency action taken to protect the desert tortoise. End. Sp. Tech. Bull. 14:1,5–6.

Baker, R. M., & G. G. George. 1988. Species management programmes in Australia and New Zealand. Int. Zoo Yb. 27:19–26.

Beck, B. B., D. G. Kleiman, I. Castro, B. Retteburg-Beck, & C. Carvalho. In press. Preparation of the Golden Lion Tamarin for release in the wild. *In* A case study in conservation biology: the Golden Lion Tamarin (D. G. Kleiman & A. Rosenberger, Eds.). Washington, District of Columbia, Smithsonian Institution Press.

Bennett, P. M. 1989. Parrot conservation: the potential of captive breeding. Zoo Fed. News 53:2–6.

Bennett, P. M. 1990. Establishing breeding programs for threatened species between zoos. J. Zool., Lond. 220:513–515.

Berger, A. J. 1977. Fitness of offspring from captive populations. Pages 315–339 *in* Endangered birds: management techniques for preserving threatened species (S. A. Temple, Ed.). Madison, Wisconsin, University of Wisconsin Press.

Bluhm, C. K. 1985. Mate preferences and mating patterns of Canvasbacks (*Aythya valisineria*). Ornithol. Monogr. 37:45–56.

Burley, N., & N. Moran. 1979. The significance of age and reproductive experience in the mate preferences of feral Pigeons, *Columba livia*. Anim. Behav. 27:686–698.

Butler, P. J. 1991. Parrots, pressures, people, and pride. This volume.

Cade, T. J. 1986. Reintroduction as a method of conservation. Raptor Res. Rpts. No. 5:72–84.

Cade, T. J. 1988. Using science and technology to reestablish species lost in nature. Pages 279–288 *in* Biodiversity (E. O. Wilson, Ed.). Washington, District of Columbia, National Academy Press.

Cade, T. J., P. T. Redig, & H. B. Tordoff. 1989. Peregrine Falcon restoration: expectation vs. reality. The Loon 61:160–162.

Campbell, S. 1980. Is reintroduction a realistic goal? Pages 263–269 *in* Conservation biology—an evolutionary perspective (M. E. Soulé & B. A. Wilcox, Eds.). Sunderland, Massachusetts, Sinauer.

Castle, M. D., & B. M. Christensen. 1990. Hematozoa of Wild Turkeys from the midwestern United States: translocations of Wild Turkeys and its potential role in the introduction of *Plasmodium kempi*. Wildl. Dis. 26:180–185.

Clark, T. W., & R. Westrum. 1989. High-performance teams in wildlife conservation: a species reintroduction and recovery example. Environ. Manage. 13:663–670.

Clubb, S. L. 1983. Recent trends in the diseases of imported birds. Pages 63–72 *in* Proceedings of the Jean Delacour/IFCB symposium on breeding birds in captivity (A. C. Risser, Jr., & F. S. Todd, Eds.). North Hollywood, California, International Foundation for the Conservation of Birds.

Clubb, S. L., J. K. Frenkel, C. H. Gardiner, & D. L. Graham. 1987. An acute fatal illness in old world psittacine birds associated with *Sarcocystis falcatula* of opossums. Pages 69–80 *in* Proceedings of the Jean Delacour/IFCB symposium on breeding birds in captivity (A. C. Risser, Jr., Ed.). North Hollywood, California, International Foundation for the Conservation of Birds.

Collar, N. J., & A. T. Juniper. 1991. Dimensions and causes of the parrot conservation crisis. This volume.

Conway, W. G. 1986. The practical difficulties and financial implications of endangered species breeding programmes. Int. Zoo Yb. 24/25:210–219.

Conway, W. G. 1988. Can technology aid species preservation? Pages 263–268 *in* Biodiversity (E. O. Wilson, Ed.). Washington, District of Columbia, National Academy Press.

Cooperative Working Group on Bird Trade. 1990. Findings and recommendations regarding the United States trade in exotic avian species. Washington, District of Columbia, World Wildlife Fund.

Cromie, R. L., J. L. Stanford, M. J. Brown, & D. J. Price. 1989. A progress report of the project to develop a vaccine against avian tuberculosis. Wildfowl 40:146–148.

Csermaly, D., D. Mainardi, & S. Spano. 1983. Escape reaction of captive young Red-legged Partridges (*Alectoris rufa*) reared with or without visual contact with man. Appl. Anim. Ethol. 11:177–182.

Danielle, A., & N. D. Murray. 1986. Effects of inbreeding in the Budgerigar (*Melopsittacus undulatus*) (Aves: Psittacidae). Zoo Biol. 5:233–238.

Dein, F. J., J. W. Carpenter, G. G. Clark, R. J. Montali, C. L. Crabbs, T. F. Tsai, & D. E. Docherty. 1986. Mortality of captive Whooping Cranes caused by eastern equine encephalitis virus. J. Am. Vet. Med. Assoc. 189:1006–1010.

Denniston, C. 1978. Small population size and genetic diversity: implications for endangered species. Pages 281–289 *in* Endangered birds: management techniques for preserving threatened species (S. A. Temple, Ed.). Madison, Wisconsin, University of Wisconsin Press.

Derrickson, S. R. 1987a. Current status and captive propagation of the endangered Guam Rail. Pages 187–195 *in* Proceedings of the Jean Delacour/ IFCB symposium on breeding birds in captivity (A. C. Risser, Jr., Ed.). North Hollywood, California, International Foundation for the Conservation of Birds.

Derrickson, S. R. 1987b. Captive propagation of Whooping Cranes. Pages 377– 386 *in* Proceedings of the 1985 crane workshop (J. C. Lewis, Ed.). Grand Island, Nebraska, Platte River Whooping Crane Maintenance Trust.

Derrickson, S. R., & J. W. Carpenter. 1981. Whooping Crane production at the Patuxent Wildlife Research Center, 1967–1981. Pages 190–198 *in* Proceedings of the 1981 crane workshop (J. C. Lewis, Ed.). Tavernier, Florida, National Audubon Society.

Derrickson, S. R., & J. W. Carpenter. 1987. Behavioral management of captive cranes—factors influencing propagation and reintroduction. Pages 493–514 *in* Proceedings of the 1983 international crane workshop (G. W. Archibald & R. F. Pasquier, Eds). Baraboo, Wisconsin, International Crane Foundation.

Docherty, D. E., & D. J. Henning. 1980. The isolation of a herpesvirus from cranes with an inclusion body disease. Avian Dis. 24:278–283.

Docherty, D. E., & R. I. Romaine. 1983. Inclusion body disease of cranes: a serological follow-up to the 1978 die-off. Avian Dis. 27:830–835.

Drewien, R. C., & E. G. Bizeau. 1978. Cross-fostering Whooping Cranes to Sandhill Crane foster parents. Pages 201–222 *in* Endangered birds: management techniques for preserving threatened species (S. A. Temple, Ed.). Madison, Wisconsin, University of Wisconsin Press.

Durrell, L., & J. Mallinson. 1987. Reintroduction as a political and educational tool for conservation. Dodo, J. Jersey Wildl. Preserv. Trust 24:6–19.

Eisenberg, J. F., & D. G. Kleiman. 1977. The usefulness of behavior studies in developing captive breeding programs. Int. Zoo Yb. 17:81–89.

Ellis, D. H., S. J. Dobrott, & J. G. Goodwin, Jr. 1978. Reintroduction techniques for Masked Bobwhites. Pages 345–354 *in* Endangered birds: management techniques for preserving threatened species (S. A. Temple, Ed.). Madison, Wisconsin, University of Wisconsin Press.

Flesness, N. R., & K. G. Cronquist-Jones. 1987. Possible selection in captive *Panthera tigris altaica*. Pages 363–370 *in* Tigers of the world: the biology, biopolitics, management, and conservation of an endangered species (R. L. Tilson & U. S. Seal, Eds.). Park Ridge, New Jersey, Noyes Publications.

Foose, T. J., & J. D. Ballou. 1988. Management of small populations. Int. Zoo Yb. 27:26–41.

Foose, T. J., R. Lande, N. R. Flesness, G. Rabb, & B. Read. 1986. Propagation plans. Zoo Biol. 5:139–146.

Forshaw, J. M. 1989. Parrots of the world, 3rd revised edition. Willoughby, Australia, Lansdowne Editions.

Frankel, O. H., & M. E. Soulé. 1981. Conservation and evolution. New York, Cambridge University Press.

Frankham, R., H. Hemmer, O. A. Ryder, E. G. Cothran, M. E. Soulé, N. D. Murray, & M. Snyder. 1986. Selection in small populations. Conserv. Biol. 5:127–138.

Franklin, I. R. 1980. Evolutionary change in small populations. Pages 135–150 *in* Conservation biology: an evolutionary-ecological perspective (M. E. Soulé & B. A. Wilcox, Eds.). Sunderland, Massachusetts, Sinauer.

Gaskin, J. M. 1989. Psittacine viral diseases: a perspective. J. Zoo Wildl. Med. 20:249–264.

Gerlach, H. 1983. Virus diseases that can interfere with efforts for conservation in birds. Pages 399–410 *in* Proceedings of the Jean Delacour/IFCB symposium on breeding birds in captivity (A. C. Risser, Jr., & F. S. Todd, Eds.). North Hollywood, California, International Foundation for Conservation of Birds.

Gnam, R. S. 1990. Conservation of the Bahama Parrot. Am. Birds 44:32–36.

Goldfoot, D. A. 1977. Rearing conditions which support or inhibit later sexual potential of laboratory monkeys: hypothesis and diagnostic behaviors. Lab. Anim. Sci. 27:548–556.

Gough, J. F. 1989. Outbreak of Budgerigar fledgling disease (BFD) in three aviaries in Ontario. Can. Vet. J. 30:672–674.

Graham, D. L., & K. B. Platt. 1978. Herpes virus infections in captive birds. Pages 526–530 *in* Proceedings of the first international birds in captivity symposium (A. C. Risser, Jr., L. F. Baptista, S. R. Wylie, & N. B. Gale, Eds.). North Hollywood, California, International Foundation for the Conservation of Birds.

Griffith, B., J. M. Scott, J. W. Carpenter, & C. Reed. 1989. Translocation as a species conservation tool: status and strategy. Science 245:477–480.

Grumbine, R. E. 1990. Viable populations, reserve size, and federal lands management: a critique. Conserv. Biol. 4:127–134.

Harris, M. P. 1970. Abnormal migration and hybridization of *Larus argentatus* and *L. fuscus* after interspecies fostering experiments. Ibis 12:488–498.

Hicks, J., & D. Greenwood. 1989. Rescuing Norfolk Island's parrot. Birds International 1:34–47.

Horwich, R. H. 1989. Use of surrogate parental models and age periods in a successful release of hand-reared sandhill cranes. Zoo Biol. 8:379–390.

Imboden, C. 1989. Parrots, trade, and captive breeding. World Birdwatch 11:2.

Immelmann, K. 1972. Sexual and other long-term aspects of imprinting in birds and other species. Adv. Study Behav. 4:147–176.

International Union for Conservation of Nature and Natural Resources (IUCN). 1987. The IUCN policy statement on captive breeding. Gland, Switzerland, International Union for Conservation of Nature and Natural Resources.

Jacobson, E. R., & J. M. Gaskin. 1990. Clinicopathologic investigations on an upper respiratory disease of free-ranging desert tortoises, *Xerobates agassizii*. U.S. Department of the Interior, Bureau of Land Management. Riverside, California, Contract Rep., 37 p.

James, F. 1990. The selling of wild birds: out of control? Living Bird 7:8–15.

Jeggo, D. 1986. The St. Lucia Parrot *Amazona versicolor* 1975–1986: turning the tide for a vanishing species. Dodo, J. Jersey Wildl. Preserv. Trust 23:59–68.

Jones, C. G., & A. W. Owadally. 1988. The life histories and conservation of the Mauritius Kestrel *Falco punctatus* (Temminck 1823), Pink Pigeon *Columba mayeri* (Prévost 1843), and Echo Parakeet *Psittacula eques* (Boddaert 1783). Proc. Royal Soc. of Arts & Sci. of Mauritius 5(1):80–130.

Kear, J. 1977. The problems of breeding endangered species in captivity. Int. Zoo Yb. 17:5–14.

Kear, J. 1986. Captive breeding programmes for waterfowl and flamingoes. Int. Zoo Yb. 24/25:21–25.

Kepler, C. B. 1978. Captive propagation of Whooping Cranes: a behavioral approach. Pages 231–241 *in* Endangered birds: management techniques for preserving threatened species (S. A. Temple, Ed.). Madison, Wisconsin, University of Wisconsin Press.

King, W. B. 1977–1979. Red data book, 2 Aves. Morges, Switzerland, International Union for the Conservation of Nature and Natural Resources.

Kleiman, D. G. 1980. The sociobiology of captive propagation. Pages 243–261 *in* Conservation biology—an evolutionary-ecological perspective (M. E. Soulé & B. A. Wilcox, Eds.). Sunderland, Massachusetts, Sinauer.

Kleiman, D. G. 1989. Reintroduction of captive mammals for conservation. Bioscience 39:152–160.

Klint, T., & M. Enquist. 1980. Pair formation and reproductive output in domestic Pigeons. Behav. Processes 6:67–62.

Knoder, E. 1959. Morphological indicators of heritable wildness in the Turkey (*Meleagris gallopavo*) and their relation to survival. Pages 116–134 *in* Proceedings of the first national wild turkey symposium. Memphis, Tennessee, Southeast Section of The Wildlife Society.

Lacy, R. C. 1987. Loss of genetic diversity from managed populations: interacting effects of drift, mutation, immigration, selection, and population subdivision. Conserv. Biol. 1:143–158.

Lacy, R. C. 1989. Analysis of founder representation in pedigrees: founder equivalents and founder genome equivalents. Zoo Biol. 8:111–123.

Lande, R. 1988. Genetics and demography in biological conservation. Science 241:1455–1460.

Landolf, M., & R. M. Kocan. 1976. Transmission of avian pox from Starlings to Rothschild's Mynahs. J. Wildl. Dis. 12:353–356.

Leopold, A. S. 1944. The nature of heritable wildness in Turkeys. Condor 46:133–197.

Lyles, A. M., & R. M. May. 1987. Problems in leaving the ark. Nature 326:245–246.

Mallinson, J. C. 1988. Collaboration for conservation between the Jersey Wildlife Preservation Trust and countries where species are endangered. Int. Zoo Yb. 27:176–191.

May, R. M. 1988. Conservation and disease. Conserv. Biol. 2:28–30.

Millam, J. R., T. E. Roudybush, & C. R. Grau. 1988. Influence of environmental manipulation and nest-box availability on reproductive success of captive Cockatiels (*Nymphicus hollandicus*). Zoo Biol. 7:25–34.

Myers, S. A., J. R. Millam, T. E. Roudybush, & C. R. Grau. 1988. Reproductive success of hand-reared vs. parent-reared Cockatiels. Auk 105:536–542.

O'Brien, S. J., & J. F. Evermann. 1988. Interactive influences of infectious disease and genetic diversity in natural populations. TREE 3:254–259.

O'Brien, S. J., M. E. Roelke, L. Marker, A. Newman, C. A. Winkler, D. Meltzner, L. Colly, J. F. Evermann, H. Bush, & D. E. Wildt. 1985. Genetic basis for species vulnerability in the Cheetah. Science 227:1428–1434.

Ousted, M. L. 1988. Attempts by The Wildfowl Trust to establish the White-winged Wood Duck and the White-headed Duck, *Cairina scutulata* and *Oxyura leucocephala*. Int. Zoo Yb. 27:216–222.

Partington, C. J., C. H. Gardiner, D. Fritz, L. G. Phillips, Jr., & R. J. Montali. 1989. Atoxoplasmosis in Bali Mynahs (*Leucopser rothschildi*). J. Zoo Wildl. Med. 20:328–335.

Phalen, D. N. 1986. An outbreak of psittacine proventricular dilation syndrome (PPDS) in a private collection of birds and an atypical form of PPDS in a Nanday Conure. Proc. Am. Assoc. Zoo Vet. 1986:27–34.

Ralls, K., & J. Ballou. 1983. Extinctions: lessons from zoos. Pages 164–184 *in* Genetics and conservation (C. M. Schoenwald-Cox, S. M. Chambers, B. Mac-Bride, & L. Thomas, Eds.). Menlo Park, California, Benjamin/Cummings.

Ralls, K., J. D. Ballou, & A. Templeton. 1988. Estimates of lethal equivalents and the cost of inbreeding in mammals. Conserv. Biol. 2:185–193.

Ralls, K., P. H. Harvey, & A. M. Lyles. 1986. Inbreeding in natural populations of birds and mammals. Pages 35–56 *in* Conservation biology (M. E. Soulé, Ed). Sunderland, Massachusetts, Sinauer.

Reed, J. M., P. D. Doerr, & J. R. Walters. 1988. Minimum viable population size of the Red-cockaded Woodpecker. J. Wildl. Manage. 52:385–391.

Ritchie, B. W., F. D. Niagro, K. S. Latimer, P. D. Lukert, W. L. Steffens III, P. M. Rakich, & N. Pritchard. 1990. Ultrastructural, protein composition, and antigenic comparison of psittacine beak and feather disease virus purified from four genera of psittacine birds. J. Wildl. Dis. 26:196–203.

Ritchie, B. W., F. D. Niagro, P. D. Lukert, W. L. Steffens, & K. S. Latimer. 1989. A review of psittacine beak and feather disease and characteristics of the PBFD virus. J. Assoc. Avian Vet. 3:143–148.

Rowley, I., & G. Chapman. 1986. Cross-fostering, imprinting and learning in two sympatric species of Cockatoos. Behav. 96:1–16.

Savidge, J. A. 1987. Extinction of an island forest avifauna by an introduced snake. Ecology 68:660–668.

Scott, M. E. 1988. The impact of infection and disease on animal populations: implications for conservation biology. Conserv. Biol. 2:40–56.

Seal, U. S. 1988. Intensive technology in the care of *ex situ* populations of vanishing species. Pages 289–295 *in* Biodiversity (E. O. Wilson, Ed.). Washington, District of Columbia, National Academy Press.

Shaffer, M. L. 1981. Minimum population sizes for species conservation. BioScience 31: 131–134.

Shelton, L. C. 1987. Captive propagation to the rescue of Guam's birds. Pages 53–61 *in* Proceedings of the Jean Delacour/IFCB symposium on breeding birds in captivity (A. C. Risser, Jr., Ed.). North Hollywood, California, International Foundation for the Conservation of Birds.

Silva, T. 1989. A monograph of endangered parrots. Pickering, Ontario, Canada, Silvio Mattachione.

Simberloff, D. 1988. The contribution of population and community biology to conservation science. Annu. Rev. Ecol. Syst. 19:473–511.

Snyder, B., J. Thilsted, B. Burgess, & M. Richard. 1985. Pigeon herpesvirus mortalities in foster reared Mauritius Pink Pigeons. Proc. Am. Assoc. Zoo Vet. 1985:69–70.

Snyder, N. F. R., & H. A. Snyder. 1989. Biology and conservation of the California Condor. Current Ornithology 6:175–263.

Snyder, N. F. R., J. W. Wiley, & C. B. Kepler. 1987. The parrots of Luquillo: natural history and conservation of the Puerto Rican Parrot. Los Angeles, California, Western Foundation of Vertebrate Zoology.

Soulé, M., M. Gilpin, W. Conway, & T. Foose. 1986. The millenium ark: how long a voyage, how many staterooms, how many passengers? Zoo Biol. 5:101–114.

Spurway, H. 1955. The causes of domestication: an attempt to integrate some ideas of Konrad Lorenz with evolution theory. J. Genetics 53:325–362.

Stanley-Price, M. R. 1986. The reintroduction of the Arabian Oryx (*Oryx leucoryx*) into Oman. Int. Zoo Yb. 24/25:179–188.

Taylor, R. H. 1985. Status, habits and conservation of *Cyanoramphus* parakeets in the New Zealand region. Pages 195–211 *in* Conservation of island birds (P. J. Moors, Ed.). Cambridge, International Council for Bird Preservation Tech. Publ. No. 3.

Temple, S. A. (Ed.) 1978. Endangered birds: management techniques for preserving threatened species. Madison, Wisconsin, University of Wisconsin Press.

Templeton, A. R. 1980. The theory of speciation via the founder principle. Genetics 92: 1265–1282.

Thaler, E. 1986. Studies of the behaviour of some Phasianidae chicks at the Alpenzoo—Innsbruck. Int. Conf. World Pheasant Assoc. 3:82–89.

Thomsen, J. B., & A. Brautigam. 1991. Sustainable use of Neotropical parrots. Pages 359–379 *in* Neotropical wildlife use and conservation (J. G. Robinson & K. H. Redford, Eds.). Chicago, University of Chicago Press.

Thorne, E. T., & E. S. Williams. 1988. Disease and endangered species: the Black-footed Ferret as an example. Conserv. Biol. 2:66–74.

Van Riper III, C., S. G. Van Riper, M. L. Goff, & M. Laird. 1986. The epizoology and ecological significance of malaria in Hawaiian land birds. Ecol. Monogr. 56:327–344.

Wallace, M. P., & S. A. Temple. 1987. Releasing captive-reared Andean Condors to the wild. J. Wildl. Manage. 51:541–550.

Warner, R. E. 1968. The role of introduced diseases in the extinction of the endemic Hawaiian avifauna. Condor 70:101–120.

Wemmer, C., & S. R. Derrickson. 1987. Reintroduction: the zoobiologists dream. Am. Assoc. Zool. Parks & Aquariums Ann. Proc. 1987:48–65.

Wenner, A. S., & D. H. Hirth. 1984. Status of the feral Budgerigar in Florida. J. Field Ornithol. 55:214–219.

Wiley, J. W., N. F. R. Snyder, & R. S. Gnam. 1991. Reintroduction as a conservation strategy for parrots. This volume.

Woerpel, R. W., W. J. Rosskopf, Jr., & E. Hughes. 1984. Proventricular dilation and wasting syndrome: myenteria ganglioneuritis and encephomyalitis of psittacines: an update. Proc. Am. Assoc. Zoo Vet. 1984:25–28.

Wright, S. 1969. Evolution and the genetics of populations. Vol. 2. The theory of gene frequencies. Chicago, University of Chicago Press.

Yamamoto, J. T., K. M. Shields, J. R. Millam, T. E. Roudybush, & C. R. Grau. 1989. Reproductive activity of force-paired Cockatiels (*Nymphicus hollandicus*). Auk 106:86–93.

Resumen.—Las reducciones progresivas en muchas de las poblaciones silvestres de los psitácidos ha resultado en un llamado general para el establecimiento de programas de reproducción en cautiverio. Sin embargo, la reproducción en cautiverio es solamente una de muchas posibles estrategias de conservación y su contribución potencial para la preservación de loros en peligro de extinción es limitado por una variedad de dificultades significativas. De preocupación particular son problemas con: (1) obtener la reproducción segura en algunas especies; (2) controlar las enfermedades en cautiverio; (3) evitar cambios genéticos y de comportamiento detrimentales; (4) llenar los requisitos financieros y logísticos a largo plazo; y (5) asegurar continuidad y apoyo administrativo. Idealmente, la función directa de la reproducción en cautiverio para la preservación de especies debiera ser limitada a situaciones de corto plazo donde otras alternativas de manejo no han sido efectivas, o pueden ser mejoradas en forma significativa. Donde existen alternativas prácticas, generalmente son mucho más preferibles que la reproducción en cautiverio. La identificación de factores limitantes y alternativas de manejo prácticas debieran ser una prioridad para la investigación, y se debe lograr antes de que las poblaciones se reduscen por debajo del nivel mínimo viable.

7. Reintroduction as a Conservation Strategy for Parrots

James W. Wiley, Noel F. R. Snyder, and Rosemarie S. Gnam

U.S. Fish and Wildlife Service, Ventura, California 93003; Wildlife Preservation Trust International, P.O. Box 426, Portal, Arizona 85632; and Bird Department, American Museum of Natural History, Central Park West at 79th St., New York, New York 10024

Abstract.—Deliberate reintroduction as a conservation tool has been little tested with psittacines. Nevertheless, large feral populations of exotic parrots in many urban areas around the world suggest that translocated parrots can form viable wild populations with some facility in permissive environments. Experiments with Hispaniolan and Thick-billed Parrot releases suggest that translocated wild-caught birds are superior to captive-reared birds in establishment potential and that parent-reared birds are superior to hand-reared birds. Behavioral and genetic deterioration under captive conditions argues for attempting reintroductions with stocks taken as recently from the wild as possible. In general, reintroductions are advisable only under circumstances where the original factors causing extirpations have been corrected. However, many parrots do not appear to be extreme habitat specialists and can be expected to survive even in modified habitats, if stress factors such as shooting and harvest for the pet trade can be controlled. The many advantages of wild populations over captive populations argue for expanded utilization of this technique.

The term *reintroduction*, if used rigorously, would be limited to situations where organisms are being introduced into an area not for the first time, but as a repeated process. The term is rarely used in this limited sense, and is generally employed in a much looser way to cover a variety of situations in which organisms are established in the wild from other populations, either captive or wild (Cade 1986, Conway 1988). In common usage, the term is not limited to attempts to establish wild populations in areas where a species is known to have occurred in the past, but also includes translocations to non-native regions. Our purpose here is not to redefine or limit terms, but to indicate at the outset something of the breadth of situations we will be considering in our discussion of parrot reintroductions.

The techniques of reintroduction have long been used by fish and wildlife managers in the limited sense of "put-and-take" manipulations—e.g., restocking streams with hatchery-produced trout or releasing non-native pheasants from game farms for harvest by sportsmen (Everhart 1979, Harmon 1979). These reintroductions or restockings normally consist of large numbers of animals set free with little or no subsidization. Naive to hazards in the wild environment, the released animals usually suffer heavy losses, not only from harvesting by sportsmen, but also from natural predation, starvation, and exposure to weather. Self-sustaining wild populations have not usually been the primary goal, and repeated releases on a continuing basis have normally been necessary to maintain the presence of the species in the wild.

Reintroduction has not been as widely used in conservation efforts for non-game species. But recently, with expanding concerns for declining populations of animals worldwide, wildlife conservationists have been turning increasingly to reintroduction efforts to reestablish self-sustaining wild populations of threatened species, either in localities from which they have been extirpated or in totally new sites where the animals may have better chances for survival. Sometimes these efforts have involved simple translocations of animals from one region to another. The most complex efforts have involved the intermediate steps of establishing captive populations, producing releasable progeny, and then freeing offspring at suitable sites.

Reintroductions have been particularly prominent in the recovery programs for several high-profile species—e.g., the Peregrine Falcon (*Falco peregrinus*) (Cade et al. 1988), the California Condor (*Gymnogyps californianus*) (Snyder and Snyder 1989), and the Whooping Crane (*Grus americana*) (Erickson and Derrickson 1981). The success of many of these efforts is still to be determined, but certainly reintroductions do offer hope for saving some species from local or global extinction, and may ultimately play an important overall conservation role in recovery of failing populations.

Reintroduction techniques have been little tested and utilized in conservation programs for parrots. Parrots have been severely persecuted in their interactions with people, and populations of many species are declining in numbers and range (Collar and Andrew 1988, Forshaw 1989, Collar and Juniper 1991). The causes of these declines are typically a complex of problems resulting from man-caused alterations of the natural environment. In this chapter, we will discuss the utility of reintroduction as part of a strategy for conservation of parrots and will present a review of some attempts to create new wild parrot populations through reintroduction efforts. We will also present information on the limitations of the reintroduction technique and suggest some factors to be considered in developing programs of reintroductions.

A SURVEY OF PARROT INTRODUCTIONS

Prehistoric Introductions

There is a strong possibility that some parrots were introduced in non-native lands by aboriginal man. Parrots have long been kept as pets (Amadon 1942), and aboriginal peoples sometimes took their feathered companions with them as they made distant voyages among islands, as in the West Indies (Snyder et al. 1987) and Polynesia. Perhaps in addition to their roles as companions, the parrots served as emergency food reserves for the travelers when other foods were not obtainable. Some of these captives may have escaped or have been deliberately released in non-native lands. While many undoubtedly succumbed in exotic environments, others probably survived and, where suitable mates were also available, bred and prospered. The extent to which aboriginal peoples contributed to the historical distribution of parrots through the introductions of birds into new regions is largely undocumented, but may have been substantial.

The St. Croix Macaw (*Ara autocthones*), known only from skeletal remains, may have been named from a species carried to that small island from other parts of the Caribbean by Carib Indians in their conquest of more northern tribes (Snyder et al. 1987). When Thomas Street explored Washington Island, in the Line Group, in 1874, he met a party of natives who had come from islands to the south to harvest coconuts. They carried with them several Kuhl's Lories (*Vini kuhlii*) as pets. Thus, the species' presence on both Washington (now Teraina) and Fanning (now Tabueran) islands may have resulted from introductions by such wandering gatherers (Forshaw 1989). On both islands the lory is common, especially around coconut plantations, and often is encountered in or near settlements (Pratt et al. 1987). Similarly, the Tahitian Lory (*Vini peruviana*) was apparently introduced by aboriginal Polynesians to Aitutaki, Cook Islands (Forshaw 1989).

Historic Establishment of Feral Populations

Many species of parrots have proven to be excellent colonizers under proper conditions (Hardy 1973, Owre 1973, Arrowood 1981, Long 1981). Feral exotic parrot populations have become established in urban areas around the world, probably mainly resulting from random frustration releases (as owners became tired of their birds' screeches and demands) or following accidental escapes. Probably in most cases, the releases have been as single birds, although some releases may have involved large numbers, as is rumored in the case of Hispaniolan Parrots (*Amazona ventralis*) turned loose off western Puerto Rico (Snyder et al. 1987, Forshaw 1989). For most feral populations, little or nothing is known of the source of the original release(s) or of the size of the initial inoculum.

Introductions of some parrots, like the Brown-throated Parakeet (*Aratinga pertinax*) which was probably established before 1860 on St. Thomas, U.S. Virgin Islands, occurred before the modern era of massive importations of pet birds (Knox 1852, Sclater 1859, Wiley unpubl. MS). With the increasingly cosmopolitan nature of the modern world and the routine traffic of cage birds through modern transportation networks, the numbers of introductions have increased dramatically. Some introductions have been quite local, whereas in other cases, species have been established in numerous populations in widely separated areas. The Monk Parakeet (*Myiopsitta monachus*) occurs in feral populations in the United States, Puerto Rico, and in some major cities in Europe. The locations of these populations, often in proximity to cities, zoos, seaports, or airports, suggest that birds were turned loose, escaped from their owners, or were inadvertently liberated through handling mishaps (Bump 1971, Forshaw 1989).

Introduced populations of the Canary-winged Parakeet (*Brotogeris versicolorus*) are found in Puerto Rico, the Miami district of Florida, and localities in California (Bond 1971a, Arrowood 1981, Forshaw 1989, Raffaele and Kepler in press). Also, a small population originating from escaped cage birds is now established in the Lima district of Peru (Koepcke 1970). Another species with a wide distribution of feral populations is the Red-crowned Parrot (*Amazona viridigenalis*), which is found on Puerto Rico and in suburban areas of such cities as Miami, Brownsville, and Los Angeles (Hardy 1973, Owre 1973, Froke 1981, Raffaele and Kepler in press).

Many other examples of feral parrot populations exist. The following represent only a sampling: Fischer's Lovebird (*Agapornis fischeri*), introduced to the Tanga and Dar es Salaam districts, coastal Tanzania, to Mombasa, coastal Kenya, and to the Nairobi, Athi River, Vaivasha and Isiolo districts, inland Kenya (Forshaw 1989); Nyasa Lovebird (*Agapornis lilianae*), introduced to the Lundazi district, eastern Zambia, and southern Namibia (aviary escapees; Benson et al. 1971, Clancey 1965); Rose-ringed Parakeet (*Psittacula krameri*), established in southern Britain, Spain, Germany, the United States, and many other locations (Long 1981, Forshaw 1989); Moustached Parakeet (*Psittacula alexandri*), probably introduced to southern Borneo (Smythies 1968); Gang-gang Cockatoo (*Callocephalon fimbriatum*), introduced to Kangaroo Island, South Australia (Forshaw 1989); Lesser Sulphur-crested Cockatoo (*Cacatua sulphurea*), introduced to Singapore and Hong Kong (Long 1981, Forshaw 1989); Sulphur-crested Cockatoo (*Cacatua galerita*), established in New Zealand, Palau Islands, western Australia, and in Ceramlaut and Goramlaut, Indonesia (Long 1981, Forshaw 1989); Salmon-crested Cockatoo (*Cacatua moluccensis*), introduced to Amboina in the southern Moluccas (Forshaw 1989); Goffin's Cockatoo (*Cacatua goffini*), probably introduced to Tual in the Kai Islands, Indonesia (Forshaw 1989); Eclectus Parrot (*Eclectus roratus*), introduced to Goram Islands, Indonesia and to Palau Archipelago in the Pacific (Forshaw 1989); Pale-headed Rosella (*Platycercus adscitus*), introduced to Hawaii in 1877, but not recorded since 1928 (Munro 1960); Palm Cockatoo (*Probosciger aterrimus*), introduced to Kai Kecil Island, in the Kai Islands,

Indonesia, but the population may not be viable (White and Bruce 1986, Forshaw 1989); and a feral breeding population of the Nanday Conure (*Nandayus nenday*) that originated from escaped cage birds in California (Forshaw 1989). A much more thorough, though still incomplete account of feral parrot establishments worldwide is given by Long (1981).

Some alien species have apparently benefited from the destruction of native forests in their new homes. Introduced populations of the Eastern Rosella (*Platycercus eximius*) in New Zealand are increasing in numbers and range, as they thrive in areas managed as pasturelands and for the cultivation of cereal crops (Rostron 1969, Forshaw 1989). Similarly, Monk Parakeets apparently find second-growth habitats to be congenial in many areas of introduction. Many other species have been able to colonize human-made second-growth habitats, for example the Rainbow Lory (*Trichoglossus haematodus*) and the Dusky Lory (*Pseudeos fuscata*), whereas other closely related species, for example the Black-capped Lory (*Lorius lory*), have not been able to take advantage of these areas and remain confined to shrinking virgin forests (Forshaw 1989).

Some species may do well in some regions, but may not become established in others, for reasons that are not entirely clear. Despite numerous accidental releases of pet Budgerigars (*Melopsittacus undulatus*) in many areas of the world, feral populations have become established only in suburban areas of southern Florida (Wenner and Hirth 1984, Forshaw 1989). The Green-rumped Parrotlet (*Forpus passerinus*) has been introduced to Curaçao, Jamaica, Barbados, Tobago, and possibly to Martinique in the West Indies (ffrench and ffrench 1966, Bond 1971b, Forshaw 1989). Since its introduction to Jamaica in about 1918, this species has steadily increased its range and is now widespread in lowland open country on the southern side of the island (Bond 1971b). However, it has not been as successful on the other islands (Bond 1952, 1971b; ffrench and ffrench 1966; Forshaw 1989).

Factors Allowing Establishment of Feral Populations

It may appear that many feral populations of parrots have become established without subsidization. But it is important to recognize that many feral populations have presumably been derived from birds that were originally wild-caught and many have colonized very favorable, artificially protective environments. Many of the suburban areas where feral populations have become established have complex mosaics of vegetation that offer a vast array of foods. Some of the exotic plants in suburban backyards are indeed native to the alien parrots' homelands. In addition, feral parrots often learn to take foods in backyard bird feeders and, in fact, people often encourage these colorful and exotic birds to use their feeders (Neidermyer and Hickey 1977, Forshaw 1989).

Protective roosting, feeding, and nesting habitat is often available in such settings, sometimes in sizeable tracts, as large parks or as patches of neighborhood backyards or as windbreaks around agricultural areas. Some parrot species have taken enthusiastically to roosting and even nesting on or in such artificial structures as building facades or in bird houses. Many of the other avian inhabitants of these environments are also aliens, fitting into empty niches with little or no competition from native species.

Certainly, the security of birds within urban and suburban areas is often superior to that in natural areas. There are serious penalties in most urban areas for discharge of firearms, for example, whereas just outside city limits shooting can be much more of a threat. In addition, people in economically advanced countries are not generally dependent on wildlife as a source of food and, in fact, often work actively to prevent molestation of urban birds. Regulations exist for the protection of most exotic bird species in many urban areas, and such regulations even extend in some areas to penalties for harvesting of chicks for pets.

Many predator populations are also lower in urban areas than in natural areas. Although some kinds of exotic predators, like domestic cats, may occur in large numbers within cities, raptors are often relatively scarce (Emlen 1974, Beissinger and Osborne 1982).

With all these advantages, it is no surprise that many alien parrots have been able to establish sizeable populations in urban environments. In fact, the diverse artificial ecosystems that have developed in some metropolitan areas, like Miami and Ft. Lauderdale, have led us to speculate that such habitats may represent adequate locations for reestablishing wild populations of some endangered parrot species.

Organized Releases as Part of Conservation Programs

Although deliberate translocations and releases have not been a commonly used strategy in the conservation of parrots, several attempts have been made. These attempts have met with varying success. Twelve Antipodes Island Parakeets (*Cyanoramphus unicolor*) were transferred to Kapiti Island off the west coast of the North Island of New Zealand in 1907 (Waite 1909). Several of these survived there until at least 1923. None have been released on other islands. In another effort, six Kuhl's Lories (*Vini kuhlii*) were introduced to Christmas (now Kiritimati) Island in December 1957. Although some observers have reported that this introduction effort eventually failed (Backus 1967, Pratt et al. 1987), C. B. Kepler (pers. comm.) reports that a small population has persisted there.

Translocation is now being attempted by the New Zealand government to save the critically endangered Kakapo (*Strigops habroptilus*) from extinction (King 1977–1979, Merton and Empson 1989, Triggs et al. 1989). The Kakapo is threatened within its native range by several environmental problems that have proved impractical to control, but especially by predation by introduced cats, rats, and stoats. The New Zealand Wildlife Service has embarked on a desperate program to transfer birds from remnant predator-stressed populations to predator- and competitor-free islands. Initial releases have resulted in good survival but as yet no reproduction. The Service has had outstanding success with translocations of other endangered species, for example the Black Robin (*Petroica traversi*) and the Saddleback (*Creadion carunculatus*), to offshore islands (Merton 1975a, Mills and Williams 1979), but whether success will also be achieved with the Kakapo is as yet uncertain.

The first translocations of Kakapos actually occurred in the 1890s when the government transferred several hundred birds from Dusky Sound to Resolution Island, one of New Zealand's first bird sanctuaries. Unfortunately, within a few years exotic stoats (*Mustela putorius*) managed to reach the sanctuary and wiped out the Kakapos.

In the modern program, three Kakapos were trapped from an all-male remnant population in the Milford Sound area of South Island and transferred to predator-free Maud Island in the Marlborough Sounds in 1974 and 1975 (Merton 1975b, D. Merton *in* King 1977–1979). Then, in 1977, a remnant population including both males and females was discovered on Stewart Island off South Island. Unfortunately, it quickly became obvious that this population was rapidly declining from predation by feral cats, and another six birds, including three females from Stewart Island, were transferred to Maud Island. Five of the nine birds on Maud Island still survived in July of 1981, but a stoat somehow got to the island in 1982, and the four surviving Kakapos were soon transferred to Little Barrier Island off North Island, from which cats had just been removed. In the same year (1982) 18 more Kakapos (11 males and 7 females) were also transferred to Little Barrier Island from Stewart Island. Breeding has not yet been confirmed on Little Barrier Island, though lekking activities have been documented and the birds appear to be adapting well there. Finally, in late 1987, five females and 11 males were transferred from Stewart Island to nearby Codfish Island, which had recently been cleared of all predatory mammals except the Polynesian rat (*Rattus exulans*). Only about 20 individuals now persist on Stewart Island, and efforts will continue to move these birds to Codfish and Little Barrier Islands.

Conservation of the Kakapo has enormous importance because of this species' unique biological characteristics. As yet, this extraordinary flightless, lekking parrot has been extremely difficult to keep alive, let alone to breed, in captivity, so the emphasis on translocations has been reasonable. However, there are serious concerns as to whether the food resources on Little Barrier and Codfish Islands are adequate to support reproduction in the species, and attention is now focused on improving food availability in these locations.

Other parrot translocation efforts in New Zealand have been more clearly successful. For example, the nominate race of the Red-crowned Parakeet (*Cyanoramphus novaezelandiae*) has been successfully established from captive stock on Tiritiri Matanga and Cuvier Islands in the Hauraki Gulf (Dawe 1979, Taylor 1985).

In 1986 a program was begun by the Arizona Game and Fish Department and several cooperating agencies to investigate the feasibility of reestablishing Thick-billed Parrots (*Rhynchopsitta pachyrhyncha*) in Arizona (Snyder et al. 1989). This species occurred naturally in the southern part of the state until the 1930s and was apparently extirpated largely by unregulated shooting. A small-scale release effort, utilizing Mexican thick-bills confiscated from the illegal bird trade in the United States, has demonstrated the willingness of some thick-bills to remain and breed in Arizona. Numbers are presently too low to constitute a viable population, however, and efforts are being made to establish a quantitatively significant source of birds for release. The remaining Mexican population of this species has been under increasing pressure from habitat destruction and harvest for the pet trade, so establishment of a United States population could have significant conservation benefits. Because the heavy shooting pressures that characterized Arizona in the early part of the century are no longer in existence, there are good reasons to believe that a viable population can be reestablished.

The Ultramarine Lory (*Vini ultramarina*) was, until recently, restricted to two of the Marquesas Islands, but was introduced to Uahuka after World War II through releases of birds from Huapu (Forshaw 1989). On Uahuka (78 km²), the species appears to be restricted to two or three valleys (Holyoak 1975, Thibault 1973) and numbers 225 ± 25 pairs (Thibault undated). Another apparently successful psittacine introduction is that of Blue-throated Conures (*Pyrrhura cruentata*) to Tijuca National Park in Guanabara, Brazil (Silva 1989).

Other efforts to transplant parrots have failed or have shown only very limited success. Although Polynesians apparently introduced the Tahitian Lory (*Vini peruviana*) to Aitutaki centuries ago, it is not now plentiful (Amadon 1942, King 1977–1979). By 1904, Wilson (1907) suspected the species no longer nested on Tahiti, and it presumably became extinct there shortly thereafter. About 1940, attempts were made to reintroduce it there, but apparently these were not successful (Yealland 1940).

Efforts to transplant the Uvea Horned Parakeet (*Eunymphicus cornutus uvaeensis*) from Uvea, Loyalty Islands, to other islands with better habitat have thus far failed. There have been two attempts to transplant the parakeet to Lifou, the next largest island of the chain: 100 birds in 1925 and 14 in 1963. However, neither attempt was successful, possibly because the transplanted birds were able to fly the 60 km back to Uvea (Delacour 1966, H. Bregulla *in* King 1977–1979). Bregulla (*in* King 1977–1979) proposed attempting further transplants, preferably aviary-raised birds, to other islands with suitable habitat.

The Vasa Parrot (*Coracopsis vasa*) was introduced to Réunion, Mascarene Islands. There are no reports of its continued presence there, so the introduction was presumably unsuccessful (Forshaw 1989).

The Grey-headed Lovebird (*Agapornis cana*) was introduced to Rodriguez,

Mauritius, the Comoro Islands, the Seychelles, and Zanzibar and Mafia Islands, but populations on Mauritius, Zanzibar, and Mafia Island have not endured to the present (Gill 1967, Penny 1974, Long 1981). Possibly an unsuccessful attempt was made to introduce this species to Natal in the late 1890s (Clancey 1964).

SITUATIONS WHERE REINTRODUCTION AND RELEASES ARE APPROPRIATE

Reintroduction can be a valuable tool for conservation in a number of circumstances. Where populations have been extirpated locally, but the limiting factors causing extirpation have been partially or wholly corrected, it may be feasible to reestablish populations from other sources. This can greatly increase a species' security by increasing the number and geographic distribution of its populations (Soulé 1987).

Where species have been lost completely from the wild, successful reintroductions can represent a far preferable alternative, economically and biologically, to long-term captive breeding. But determining rigorously whether environmental conditions are permissive for reintroduction generally necessitates a comprehensive understanding of the causes of extirpation. In many cases, wild populations have been lost without being studied, and causes of extirpation are highly speculative. This should not rule out attempts at reintroductions necessarily, but such attempts should at least be based on corrections of what appear to be the most reasonable potential causes of extirpation. *Reintroductions in former range in the absence of any actions to modify limiting factors are difficult to justify.*

In this age of rapid habitat loss and alteration, many species have become subdivided into fragmented small populations with decreasing contact with one another over time. Populations sufficiently isolated from one another lose the capacity for genetic exchange, and may ultimately fall below critical demographic levels where they lose the capacity for self-maintenance or become vulnerable to catastrophic loss (Gilpin and Soulé 1986, Gilpin 1987, Lande and Barrowclough 1987). Reintroduction efforts can potentially counter such trends by providing the security against catastrophic loss that is inherent in additional populations, and by increasing genetic diversity in small fragmented populations.

Examples of Potentially Advantageous Reintroductions

For some species in the West Indies, opportunities exist for repopulating islands with parrots under conditions more favorable than existed at the time of loss of original populations. For example, Vieques Island off Puerto Rico once sustained a population of the Puerto Rican Parrot (*Amazona vittata*) that apparently was wiped out largely by subsistence hunting. The island now has large areas of protected habitat that could potentially support a Puerto Rican Parrot population, and reestablishing the species there could greatly increase its overall security.

The Bahama Parrot (*Amazona leucocephala bahamensis*) survives only on Abaco and Inagua islands, although historically the species was much more widely distributed among the Bahama Islands (Snyder et al. 1982, Gnam 1990). The parrot population on Inagua apparently is not in critical danger (other than from hurricane catastrophe). But the Abaco population is moderately threatened by habitat alteration, predation by feral cats, and harvesting of chicks by the pet and avicultural trade (Gnam 1990). Thus, there would seem to be merit in following a course of establishing additional populations of this parrot on suitable islands through a program of releases. Habitat destruction has abated on several other unpopulated islands, and shooting and harvesting of parrots could potentially be controlled with the proper sorts of educational and legal preparations (Butler 1991). The Forestry Section (Department of Lands and Surveys) has recommended that Andros, the largest island in the Bahamas, be considered as a release site for parrots from Abaco. Additional populations would surely increase the security of the Bahama Parrot against extinctions caused by catastrophes.

Translocations may be an especially useful technique among some of the smaller islands in the Pacific. Populations of some Pacific species (e.g., *Cyanoramphus*) show a high degree of subspeciation, have very limited distributions on isolated islands, and are highly vulnerable to extinction. Forshaw (1989) recommended that consideration be given to translocating some Norfolk Island Red-crowned Parakeets (*Cyanoramphus novaezelandiae cookii*) from their threatened habitat on Norfolk Island to neighboring Lord Howe Island, where a rat-control program is in place and there are no known avian competitors. The species was last reported on Lord Howe Island in 1869 and presumably some of the habitat formerly occupied by the species is still available. However, introduced rats (*Rattus rattus*) are the major known stress for the population on Norfolk Island, and still exist on Lord Howe Island. An alternative reintroduction site already free of rats, Philip Island, has recently been suggested by Hicks and Greenwood (1989). The primary drawback of Philip Island is its relatively small size (190 ha).

Virtually nothing is known of the habits of Spix's Macaw (*Cyanopsitta spixii*) in the wild (King 1977–1979). The last few wild individuals of this Brazilian species were under intense pressure of harvest for aviculture and the pet trade in the 1980s (Thomsen and Munn 1988). This macaw is certainly one of the world's most endangered species of birds. Only a single individual is known to remain in the wild, and perhaps 20 to 40 exist in captivity. The only chance for saving this species from extinction in the near term has been generally acknowledged to lie in a cooperative captive breeding program, but many hurdles lie in the way of success here, as the captive individuals are scattered all over the world in diverse hands. Reestablishment of this bird in the wild might well succeed if human depredations could be controlled, but as yet all attention has been focused on attempting to achieve a self-sustaining captive population. Unfortunately, little has been accomplished in the way of captive production with this species, and there are no guarantees that a self-sustaining captive population can be achieved. It is conceivable that a comprehensive near-term reintroduction program with the remaining captives, were that politically possible, might have as much or more chance of success.

Translocations to Non-native Habitat

Some parrots may be lost forever from their native lands if habitat destruction, shooting, and exploitation continue unchecked. In such cases, a species may have to be translocated to a non-native region to save it from extinction. Such translocations must be performed with careful consideration of the consequences of introducing alien animals and the risks to natural ecosystems. However, especially on islands and in disturbed mainland regions, enough ecological space may exist to allow such translocations without significant detrimental effects on native species. The relatively small island of Puerto Rico (11,489 km²) has no fewer than six and perhaps as many as 10 established species of alien parrots, some with populations numbering several hundred individuals (Raffaele and Kepler in press). Yet these populations have become established exclusively in lowland urban and second-growth forests, and no direct competition between aliens and native species in original habitat has been reported. In contrast, introduced Crimson Rosellas (*Platycercus elegans*) have proved to be an important nest-site competitor for the endangered Red-crowned Parakeet on Norfolk Island (Hicks and Greenwood 1989). Caution in introducing parrots into new areas is especially relevant where other threatened hole-nesting species exist.

An example of a parrot population that could potentially benefit by a reintroduction program to non-native lands is the critically endangered Cayman Brac race of the Cuban Parrot (*Amazona leucocephala hesterna*). The wild population of this race is only in the low hundreds and is restricted to Cayman Brac, a 38-km² island where human-caused habitat alterations even further limit its distribution (Bradley 1986, Wiley pers. obs.). The population is thus at considerable risk from hurricanes or other natural disasters. Establishing a disjunct population through translocations of wild birds or releases of captive-produced fledglings on Little Cayman and on other distant islands (e.g., a suitable Bahama Island where reintroductions of native Bahama Parrots are not planned) might give this race a substantially improved chance of survival (Wiley in press).

Bolstering Existing Wild Populations and other Special Management Applications

Release programs can also play a positive role in maintaining a species in the wild through a period of population stress while environmental rehabilitation takes place. Such releases have aided the recovery of certain populations of the Peregrine Falcon (*Falco peregrinus*) in the western United States during the period of subsiding levels of organochlorine contaminants, which were largely responsible for the species' decline (Cade et al. 1988). The fostering of captive-produced eggs and chicks into wild nests of Puerto Rican Parrots and releases of free-flying birds have been important in the survival and bolstering of the wild population in Luquillo Forest (Snyder et al. 1987).

In other cases, a population may be doomed to extinction by threats that cannot be corrected in the foreseeable future. Birds removed from the wild may be held in captivity and their progeny released back to the wild in a different, safer environment. This technique may be used to rid a population of some of the behavioral traditions that led to decline. All California Condors were removed from the wild by 1987 to avoid inevitable extinction resulting from intractable environmental problems (Snyder and Snyder 1989). None of the wild-trapped birds will be released, as they presumably retain behavioral traditions, especially traditional use of certain dangerous habitats, that led them into trouble originally. If released, they could potentially transmit such maladaptive traditions to other released birds. Plans call for the eventual releases of naive captive-produced progeny, which do not carry these traditions. Released birds will be conditioned to feed in safe areas on clean food provided through the recovery period.

Reintroduction as Ecosytem Re-creation

We emphasize that we greatly favor the concept of not just reintroducing individual species but of reconstructing entire ecosystems, where opportunities for doing this exist (Wingate 1985). An example of such a reconstruction proposal is the avifauna of the Río Abajo Forest of northwestern Puerto Rico. Río Abajo was once occupied by the extirpated Puerto Rican Parrot, Puerto Rican Plain Pigeon (*Columba inornata wetmorei*), White-necked Crow (*Corvus leucognaphalus*), and Limpkin (*Aramus guarauna*). All of these species survive elsewhere and, through a program of planned reintroductions, could eventually be returned to the forest (Wiley 1985).

Another such opportunity exists with the Gray Ranch of southwestern New Mexico. This 1,295-km² region, recently acquired by The Nature Conservancy, apparently once hosted Thick-billed Parrots, Aplomado Falcons (*Falco femoralis*), and California Condors, plus several species of large mammals that now exist only in captivity or in threatened populations elsewhere (Snyder and Snyder 1989). Reintroductions of many of these creatures in such a setting could result in significant savings in expenditures in overall conservation efforts, compared with a piecemeal species-by-species approach, and would have considerable biological and aesthetic advantages.

CONDITIONS REQUIRED FOR SUCCESSFUL REINTRODUCTION

Clearly, before any program of reintroduction is instituted, the original factors causing the decline or extirpation of a species should be identified and an adequate plan for removing these threats should be developed. Identifying the sources of a population's problems is often no easy task. Obvious problems, like complete habitat loss, are readily determined. But environmental problems that have created population declines are seldom as simple as they first appear. Rather, the most obvious problems are often underlain by an array of more subtle and complex factors. Ferreting out the complex interrelationships between a population and its biotic and abiotic limiting factors takes time and intensive study, and needs to be accomplished while the species still exists in the wild. Unfortunately, studies are often made difficult by the reduced numbers of individuals available for study. With only a few individuals in existence, experimental approaches to determining the importance of various limiting factors are often inadvisable. Also, determining the normal wild behavior and ecology of some species may be extraordinarily difficult when populations survive only in greatly degraded environments.

To some extent, insights may be gained by study of closely related species inhabiting similar environments. However, generalizing from one species to another is an approach with many pitfalls.

Habitat Protection

Habitat is shrinking throughout the range of most species of parrots. An aggressive effort to protect, maintain, and create suitable habitat is essential for any reintroduction program. In many cases this includes setting aside sizeable tracts of forested lands wherein management practices must be compatible with the goals of wildlife conservation. Habitat management must ensure that resources vital to the parrots' survival are available. This generally implies an emphasis on natural forests, rather than monocultures of a few economically valuable species. If timber management programs are to be included in the area of reintroduction, the program should provide for leaving substantial tracts in undisturbed condition so that adequate numbers of nest and roost sites, and adequate diversity of foods may be available. Cavity availability is normally crucially dependent on the maturity of forest stands. Unless one is dealing with a species that is willing to use nest boxes (Fig. 6 in Beissinger and Bucher 1991), reintroductions are likely to fail in areas where all forested stands are subject to frequent cutting.

Control of Other Limiting Factors

Even where suitable habitat has been secured, other limiting factors are often sufficiently important that success cannot be achieved unless they are controlled. The threats of hunting, chick harvesting, human disturbance (e.g., recreation), competitors, disease, and predators must all be evaluated and handled in a reintroduction plan. The parrots, as well as their habitat, must be assured protection through legislation and effective enforcement of regulations. Also essential to any program of protection are aggressive education efforts, like those developed for the Lesser Antillean parrots by Gabriel Charles and Paul Butler (Butler 1991). Such efforts should be aimed at creating a public conservation awareness and concern for the species in question. A reintroduction program may also need to develop biologically sound means for controlling competitors and predators of the released birds, particularly during the early period of releases. However, once the population shows good indication of recovery, such efforts, like some education efforts, may be scaled back with little effect on recovery. For example, control of raptor predation may play a vital role in a species' recovery during early phases when released birds are still low in numbers and naive to the wild environment. Later on, with larger numbers, larger flock sizes, and greater sophistication of birds, such efforts may be unnecessary.

Although it is questionable in this vastly changed world whether many reestablished parrot populations can become totally self-sufficient, the hope is that some may and others may require only minimal continuing conservation efforts. Regardless of the initial estimates of the time needed to achieve success, reintroduction programs should be prepared for a long-term commitment. If intensive management is to be incorporated into a program, plans should include a careful evaluation of alternative reintroduction sites and methods, and choices should be based among other things on the level of management needed in various sites.

Use of Wild vs. Captive-produced Parrots as Release Candidates

Where wild-caught parrots are available as release candidates they offer a number of important advantages over captive-reared birds. Wild-caught birds are already sophisticated in matters of foraging, food handling, roosting, and predator avoidance. In general, they can also be expected to be in fit physical condition if taken recently from the wild and to survive relatively well in unfamiliar areas. No training of wild-caught birds may be necessary, outside of familiarizing them with the specific foods available in the release area and socializing them with one another prior to release. Birds need not be held at the release site longer than the time it takes to achieve these straightforward goals, and after release they may need little or no subsidization if resources such as food and water are readily available in the release area.

Releases involving only the trapping of birds from one area and the relatively quick release in another are comparatively inexpensive, and are often the most likely to succeed. However, they have the drawback that the released birds may be inclined to long-distance homing behavior and may not remain in the release area. Such tendencies, if they prove to be a problem, can potentially be combated by holding birds in the release area for relatively long periods before release and perhaps by retaining some birds in field aviaries to serve as an attractant for released birds. If such strategies as these do not prevent movements of birds from the release region, there may be no alternative but to use captive-bred birds in releases. Arizona releases of wild-caught Thick-billed Parrots from Mexico have shown that at least many individuals will not home to their lands of origin if held for some months in captivity prior to release (Snyder et al. 1989), although such tendencies may well vary from species to species and with varying details of release procedures.

Once some birds are established in the wild, subsequent releases of wild-caught birds can often be accomplished by direct introduction of birds into the wild flock, relying on the gregarious nature of most species to encourage quick integration into the social hierarchy. In such releases with Thick-billed Parrots, we have found that the fastest integration seems to be achieved when one introduces birds as singletons into a wild flock. Birds in larger release groups appear to be less motivated to join the wild flock, probably because they have other members of the released group available for socialization. Where direct integrations into a wild flock are possible, released birds can quickly learn important information regarding location of food, water, and roosting sites from experienced birds and quickly become as sophisticated as the experienced birds in interacting with their new environment.

Captive-reared birds, in contrast, are at best disadvantaged in a great variety of ways on release. Experimental releases of Hispaniolan Parrots (*Amazona ventralis*) have shown that subsidy is generally crucial to their survival in the period after release (Wiley 1983, Snyder et al. 1987). This is apparently especially true if they are released where there are no wild members of the species. Totally ignorant of many aspects of survival outside of their cages, and often in less than hardened physical condition, captive-reared birds are best managed in a gradual transition to wild existence (Fig. 1). Failures to find food and water in the wild, for example, can be compensated by subsidy at the release cages. Such subsidy can be terminated once a capacity to find such resources in the wild is achieved by trial and error. Such transitions can be speeded by prior training in the cage environment, especially with foods available in the release area. The transition to the wild can also be greatly aided by the presence of wild birds of the same species in the release area which the released birds can join.

Hand-reared birds are characteristically the most unsuitable for release because of their almost total lack of fear of humans, and their reluctance to socialize with wild-caught or parent-reared members of their own species (Fig. 2). In releases of hand-reared Thick-billed Parrots, we have observed grave deficiencies in flocking tendencies, abilities to find food in the wild environment, vigilance against raptors, and interest in joining wild flocks, despite intensive training to counter such problems in the cage environment (Snyder et al. 1989).

Captive-bred birds also represent a relatively enormous expense in the full sense of the husbandry investments necessary for their production. Gearing up production to supply the numbers necessary for release programs often takes many years and many dollars both in labor and in capital investments for maintenance and health-care necessities. Furthermore, over a period of generations, captive birds can be expected to deteriorate in their potential for successful release because of behavioral and genetic selection for the captive environment (Derrickson and Snyder 1991). Captive-bred birds for release should be as close to wild stocks in time and generations as possible.

Fig. 1. *A*. "Hard release" of captive-raised Hispaniolan Parrots (*Amazona ventralis*) during experiments in the Dominican Republic in 1982. Birds were released in an area of good habitat, with wild populations of parrots, but were given no further food subsidization or shelter after their release. *B*. Captive-reared Hispaniolan Parrots released experimentally in the Dominican Republic without conditioning to local foods showed maladaptive foraging behavior, like searching for food on the ground.

Captive-bred birds can also pose risks of disease transmission to wild flocks, especially where captives are not held in isolation from other avian species and/ or are obtained from sources with unknown exposure to avian diseases. Some severe avian diseases (e.g., parrot wasting disease and Pacheco's disease) can be carried asymptomatically for periods of years (Graham 1978, Flammer 1978, Clubb 1983, Gaskin 1989). They can potentially be transmitted to wild flocks in reintroduction efforts, without any overt indications that a problem exists. Such developments could be disastrous.

Nevertheless, where good disease control can be achieved, and where the proper circumstances exist, captive breeding can represent a valuable component of release efforts. Perhaps the most important advantage is that captive flocks can help take pressures off wild flocks if established in a comprehensive manner. Captive stock harvested as wild eggs or chicks can have relatively low impacts on wild populations if the species in question readily recycles after harvest of progeny. Under some circumstances it is possible to greatly increase overall reproduction of an endangered species by such manipulations, and ultimately to significantly bolster wild populations with released captives (Snyder et al. 1987).

When Should Captive Breeding Be Used?

While reintroductions are generally best done using wild-caught birds as a source, in some cases this option is not available or advisable, and there is no reasonable alternative to an intermediate step of captive breeding. In some instances, though a wild source population may be available for releases, it may be so depleted itself that taking birds from it would jeopardize its own survival. In more than a few instances, the decision as to whether to pursue reintroduction with wild-caught birds or captive-reared birds, or some combination of the two, is a very difficult one. It often involves the weighing of risks that are largely unknown in severity and that are very difficult to compare with one another.

A current example of such difficulties can be seen in strategy debates for the Puerto Rican Parrot recovery program. Over the past 15 years the last remnant population of this species, averaging about 30 birds, has been slowly recovering under intensive management. During this same period a captive flock of about 50 birds has been established, but it has never shown a very encouraging level of reproduction, despite implementation of a variety of techniques successful with other species. Most observers agree that it would be valuable to establish at least one new wild population and one new captive population to provide security from catastrophes, but this can only be done at the expense of the existing wild and captive populations. The extent to which current captive production should be dedicated to bolstering the existing wild population or to the establishment of a new captive population has been the subject of vigorous controversy. Similarly, there is no consensus as to whether establishment of a new wild population should be attempted at the expense of bolstering the existing wild population, and whether it should be done with captive-bred birds or translocated wild birds. Experience from other release programs suggests that the existing wild population, since it has been recovering, represents an extremely valuable resource and can greatly facilitate the introduction of captive-bred birds into the wild. Establishing a new wild population strictly from captives poses prospects of very low survival in released birds. Splitting up the captive flock into several parts reduces the opportunities for re-pairing birds to achieve good pairs laying fertile eggs, and can increase the chances of disease transmission if movements of birds are made between various captive populations to reduce this problem.

Our own favored strategy for the Puerto Rican Parrot is (1) a single split of the captive flock into two parts in the near term, (2) a basically even split of captive production between bolstering of the existing wild population and increasing the numbers of birds in captivity, and (3) a delay in starting a second wild population until the existing wild population is large enough (possibly 60–70 birds) to offer a few birds to serve as core birds for a combined release of wild-caught and captive-reared birds in a new area. This judgment depends heavily on a weighing of "apples and oranges" risks and benefits that cannot be quantified in any rigorous way. But it is based on what appear to be inherent problems in the captive breeding of this species and severe problems in introducing captive-bred birds into an environment lacking wild members of the species.

The advisability of a role for captive breeding in reintroduction efforts has to be evaluated on a species-by-species basis, and it is very difficult to generalize from one species to another. Where good alternatives exist, they are generally

Fig. 2. Captive-raised Hispaniolan Parrots liberated as part of the experimental "hard release" in the Dominican Republic showed poor survival. Losses to predators, including man, were recorded. Radio transmitters carried by released birds were tracked to the shelter of a Haitian family, who had captured and eaten the naive birds.

much less expensive than captive breeding, and for many species (e.g., the Kakapo and the Puerto Rican Parrot) the difficulties in achieving successful captive reproduction are sufficiently great as to greatly limit its potentials. In many cases (e.g., the Bahama Parrot) captive breeding may be an unnecessary intermediate phase to creating new populations, and this objective can be met through simple translocations from still reasonably healthy wild populations. The Abaco population of the Bahama Parrot has averaged about 1,000 individuals in recent years (Gnam and Burchsted 1991) and is clearly large enough and vigorous enough to safely donate the few dozen individuals that should be required for a translocation effort. The Inagua population of this parrot, though not yet accurately censused, may well be even larger and even better able to serve as a donor. Attempting to establish new populations of this species through releases of captive-reared birds would be far more expensive and less likely to succeed, and offers no clear advantages over simple translocations.

Unfortunately, the vigor of wild populations and the potentials for captive breeding to succeed with a species are often little known at the outset. Waiting too long in starting captive breeding can in itself greatly reduce its chances of success through genetic deterioration and through delays in developing proper husbandry techniques. On the other hand, effective conservation can often be achieved without captive breeding. Implementing this technique too soon can rob resources and attention from needed efforts to sustain wild populations and allow administrators to avoid commitments to preserve crucial tracts of habitat. Achieving a proper balance between captive breeding and other conservation efforts has been, and promises to continue to be, a battleground in endangered species recovery efforts.

PROCEDURES FOR RELEASING BIRDS

Pre-conditioning Captive-reared Birds for Release

As summarized above, captive-reared birds are at a considerable survival disadvantage compared to wild-caught parrots when released. Their deficiencies must be addressed for successful release. Probably, the best strategy for reintroducing captive-reared parrots into the wild is to foster the birds as eggs or chicks into wild nests, where they are raised by wild parents and potentially fledge without any behavioral or physical deficits. Fostering is also inexpensive compared to releases of free-flying birds. However, this technique has severe limitations in that it can only be used in situations where (1) wild pairs are breeding, (2) some of these pairs have subnormal brood sizes, and (3) captive production is synchronized with that in the wild. These constraints considerably limit the number of birds that can be released into the wild by fostering.

Releases of free-flying captives are limited only by the numbers of birds available for releases, but certain training and care protocols must be met above usual husbandry procedures to achieve adequate levels of success. Primary among these protocols is an avoidance of associations of pre-release birds with humans. Birds accustomed to humans may continue to center their activities around areas used by humans and even come to people to beg for food. These activities, of course, place the parrots at risk from human molestation and capture, and may interfere with the development of normal "wild" behavior. A program of allowing chicks destined for release to be raised by their parents or by foster parents is far preferable to one utilizing hand-raised birds. In many cases, it may be advisable to shield the releasable young parrots from the sounds and view of their human keepers, especially from the sight of humans associated with food.

Also of critical concern is the development of appropriate predator-avoidance behavior in captive-reared birds. Where birds are held in company with wild-caught birds in large field aviaries, there are opportunities for the birds to see predators such as raptors and learn adaptive responses from the responses of their cage mates. Parent-reared Thick-billed Parrots in our Arizona release program witness wild Northern Goshawks (*Accipiter gentilis*) hitting their cages with some frequency and soon learn to respond as a flock to the thick-bill alarm call. Additional training in raptor avoidance can potentially be achieved with use of trained hawks (Ellis et al. 1978).

Physical conditioning is also a fundamental component of preparing young captive-produced birds for release. Although most aviaries do not have adequate room to allow birds to make long flights, some techniques may encourage the birds to be more active within their limited spaces. Creative arrangements of the perches within an aviary can encourage exercise (e.g., food can be placed on a pedestal in the middle of the cage, separated from other perches). In general, the larger the pre-release cage, the better.

Parrots destined for release are generally best placed in communal cages, where social relationships and rudimentary flocking behavior can develop among individuals. Before release, parrots should be gradually weaned from prepared aviary foods to natural items present in the release area. This allows the birds to develop an appropriate search image for typical foods they will find after release. Foods should be presented as much as possible in the form that they take in the wild (e.g., clusters of fruits still attached to stems or branches). It often requires many weeks of practice for birds to become proficient in handling natural foods. For example, it takes young Thick-billed Parrots months to become expert in pine-cone husking, whether they are fledged in

Fig. 3. The primary food of wild Thick-billed Parrots (*Rhynchopsitta pachyrhyncha*) is seeds of pine cones. The development of skills to handle cones properly takes many months of learning, and captive-reared thick-bills destined for release must become expert in this process prior to release.

captivity or in the wild (Fig. 3). Skills in searching for, recognizing, and manipulating natural food items are all absolutely essential for survival in the wild.

Release Procedures

Several factors must be addressed when considering the actual release of parrots to the wild, including the timing of releases and numbers and genetic composition of birds. Season of release is important in assuring a high probability of survival and good integration into wild flocks, particularly if captive-produced birds are used. Integration into a resident flock is particularly helpful for the survival of released juveniles. If the birds are to be released into an existing wild population, the releases should preferably coincide with seasons when the wild birds are stationary and flocking. For many species, the breeding season may not be the best time to conduct releases because the resident population has dispersed into breeding pairs, each defending a discrete territory. Raptor predation threats also tend to be relatively high during the breeding season. The post-breeding period may often be more favorable, as birds often tend to clump at this season and are presumably most receptive to new birds entering the population at this time. Care should be taken with nomadic or migratory species that releases are not done at a time when the wild populations are likely to leave the area abruptly. Care should also be taken to conduct releases at a time of favorable food availability.

Another important consideration is the numbers of animals to be used in releases. In general, if birds are being released into an area lacking a wild population, relatively large numbers, perhaps 50 to 100 birds with relatively even sex ratio, are more likely to succeed than smaller numbers (Griffith et al. 1989). With the inevitable losses of some individuals in making an initial transition to wild existence, it is important that enough birds survive to constitute a viable social group, particularly with respect to vigilance against predators (Westcott and Cockburn 1988). Depending on survival of individuals in initial release attempts, it may be essential to follow up with subsequent releases over a period of several years until birds begin to breed in the wild and achieve significant capacities for intrinsic growth in numbers. However, as discussed earlier with the Thick-billed Parrot, once a wild flock is established, there may actually be advantages to releasing additional birds in a one-by-one fashion to encourage rapid integration into the flock and discourage tendencies for birds to split up into several flocks.

Release candidates should be of diverse genetic stocks to avoid problems with inbreeding within the released population. Such considerations of genetic management should be a part of any captive-production program directed at reintroduction of parrots. Genetic considerations are more difficult to incorporate into a program of translocating wild parrots under current technology. However, with improvements in genetic analysis techniques such considerations could also become a part of translocation efforts.

Monitoring

A long-term monitoring program is an important component of any reintroduction program. Factors that decrease the chances for reestablishment, whether
they be mortality or reproductive factors, must be identified and corrected on
a continuing basis to achieve success. Without comprehensive monitoring and
a capacity for flexible responses to unpredictable developments, the chances
of failure are greatly increased.

Several elements are critical. A periodic determination of population size is
one of the most essential. Also of great importance is a determination of the
frequency and extent of movements. Interactions with other species, especially
predators, are often of crucial importance, but cannot be evaluated without close
study. Similarly, initiation of reproduction cannot be studied effectively without
detailed tracking of released birds.

For many species of parrots, movements are sufficiently long range that there
is no alternative to radiotelemetry as an aid to monitoring the progress of
releases. Nevertheless, radiotelemetry involves some difficulties and risks as
well as some moderate expense. Wildlife telemetry technology, although quite
improved in recent years, is still a field of compromises, primarily finding the
best balance between range and lifetime of transmitters. In practical terms,
transmitters are now available that give lifetimes over a year and ranges of 4–
10 km, and such units have proved extremely useful in following releases of
medium-sized parrots (Snyder et al. 1987, 1989).

Because of the flocking tendencies of most parrot species, it may not be
necessary to radio all birds released. But because of inevitable losses of birds
in early stages and the values of recovering lost birds to determine causes of
mortality, a substantial fraction of released birds should generally be radioed
in early releases. In later stages, when movements of released birds stabilize
and become more predictable, and when much more is known about causes
of mortality, the needs for large numbers of radioed birds will decline. No radio
package should be considered entirely innocuous (Gessaman and Nagy 1988),
and harmful effects may range from enhanced susceptibility to predation to
decreases in foraging efficiency (Wanless et al. 1988, Brigham 1989). Optimally, radio units should be designed to fall off birds after batteries have been
exhausted.

THE LIMITATIONS OF REINTRODUCTION AS A CONSERVATION TOOL

Despite the economic, aesthetic, and biological advantages of successful reintroductions in overall conservation of parrots, especially versus a strict captive-breeding approach, experience to date suggests that only a fraction of reintroduction efforts will prove successful. In part, this will stem from insufficient control of limiting factors causing the original extirpation; in part it will trace to insufficient numbers of birds available to constitute a viable release population; in part it will trace to basically insurmountable genetic limitations; and in part it will trace to technical failures in properly conditioning birds or in other release procedures. Techniques of getting birds into the wild successfully are improving rapidly, but these comprise only part of the necessary conditions for success. The need for sustained and flexible efforts is paramount, and such efforts are difficult to achieve for many human institutions.

Perhaps the biggest overall stumbling block will be difficulties in achieving effective control over major limiting factors in the wild environment. In many cases, reintroduction efforts will be attempted in the absence of critical information on causes of decline, simply because no studies have been conducted during the declines. And even if causes may be understood, there may be no guarantee that the causes can be sufficiently lessened in severity to allow reestablishment of the species in the same regions.

It is important to recognize that even if there is no way to counter some limiting factors in native habitats, it still may be possible to reestablish wild populations in other more permissive environments. If this can be done, it may be a far more economical and successful means for sustaining the existence of species than captive breeding alone. The major risks involved with such efforts are that the released birds may come to represent threats to other species in these permissive environments, either through their direct interactions with other species or by indirect effects such as their carrying undetected diseases which can spread to other members of the community (Scott 1988, Castle and Christensen 1990). Nevertheless, the experience with numerous unintentional establishments of feral parrots in urban environments around the world suggests that such risks may sometimes be acceptable. Careful study of potential risks before reintroductions are attempted can reduce the chances of damage.

Introductions into non-native areas have not generally enjoyed widespread support among wildlife conservationists (see discussions in Owre 1973, Cade 1986). Yet, to completely forego such introductions may mean that many psittacines will be lost from the wild forever. Species retained only as captive populations may eventually be unreleasable to the wild because of unavoidable genetic and behavioral changes due to the captive environment (Derrickson and Snyder 1991).

LITERATURE CITED

Amadon, D. 1942. Birds collected during the Whitney South Sea Expedition: notes on some non-passerine genera. Am. Mus. Novit. No. 1176:1–21.

Arrowood, P. C. 1981. Importation and status of Canary-winged Parakeets (*Brotogeris versicolorus* P.L.S. Muller) in California. Pages 425–429 *in* Conservation of New World parrots (R. F. Pasquier, Ed.). Washington, District of Columbia, Smithsonian Institution Press, International Council for Bird Preservation Tech. Publ. No. 1.

Backus, G. J. 1967. Changes in the avifauna of Fanning Island, central Pacific, between 1924 and 1963. Condor 69:207–209.

Beissinger, S. R., & E. H. Bucher. 1991. Sustainable harvesting of parrots for conservation. This volume.

Beissinger, S. R., & D. R. Osborne. 1982. Effects of urbanization on avian community organization. Condor 84:75–83.

Benson, C. W., R. K. Brooke, R. J. Dowsett, & M. P. S. Irwin. 1971. The birds of Zambia. London, Collins.

Bond, J. 1952. Second supplement to the Check-list of Birds of the West Indies (1950). Philadelphia Acad. Nat. Sci. 1–24.

Bond, J. 1971a. Birds of the West Indies, 2d edition. London, Collins.

Bond, J. 1971b. Seventeenth supplement to the Check-list of Birds of the West Indies (1956). Philadelphia Acad. Nat. Sci. 1–11.

Bradley, P. E. 1986. A report of a census of *Amazona leucocephala caymanensis* and *Amazona leucocephala hesterna* in the Cayman Islands. George Town, Grand Cayman, Cayman Islands Government Tech. Publ. No. 1.

Brigham, R. M. 1989. Effects of radio transmitters on the foraging behavior of Barn Swallows. Wilson Bull. 101:505–506.

Bump, G. 1971. The South American Monk, Quaker, or Grey-headed Parakeet. Wildlife Leaflet No. 496. Washington, District of Columbia, U.S. Dept. Interior, Fish Wildl. Serv.

Butler, P. J. 1991. Parrots, pressures, people, and pride. This volume.

Cade, T. J. 1986. Reintroduction as a method of conservation. Pages 72–84 *in* Raptor conservation in the next 50 years (S. E. Senner, C. M. White, & J. R. Parrish, Eds.). Raptor Research Foundation Report No. 5.

Cade, T. J., J. H. Enderson, C. G. Thelander, & C. M. White (Eds.). 1988. Peregrine Falcon populations, their management and recovery. Boise, Idaho, The Peregrine Fund.

Castle, M. D., & B. M. Christensen. 1990. Hematozoa of Wild Turkeys from the midwestern United States: translocation of Wild Turkeys and its potential role in the introduction of *Plasmodium kempi*. J. Wildl. Dis. 26:180–185.

Clancey, P. A. 1964. The birds of Natal and Zululand. Edinburgh, Oliver and Boyd.

Clancey, P. A. 1965. A catalogue of birds of the South African sub-region, Part II: families Glareolidae-Pittidae. Durban Mus. Novit. 7:305–386.

Clubb, S. L. 1983. Recent trends in the diseases of imported birds. Pages 63–72 *in* Proceedings of the Jean Delacour/IFCB symposium on breeding birds in captivity (A. C. Risser, Jr., & F. S. Todd, Eds.). North Hollywood, California, International Foundation for the Conservation of Birds.

Collar, N. J., & P. Andrew. 1988. Birds to watch, the ICBP world checklist of threatened birds. Washington, District of Columbia, Smithsonian Institution Press, International Council for Bird Preservation Tech. Publ. No. 8.

Collar, N. J., & A. T. Juniper. 1991. Dimensions and causes of the parrot conservation crisis. This volume.

Conway, W. 1988. Editorial. Conserv. Biol. 2:132–134.

Dawe, M. R. 1979. Behaviour and ecology of the Red-crowned Parakeet (*Cyanoramphus novaezelandiae*) in relation to management. University of Auckland, Auckland, New Zealand, M.Sc. Thesis.

Delacour, J. 1966. Guide des Oiseaux de la Nouvelle Caledonie et de ses Dependances. Neuchatel, Switzerland, Delachaux et Niestle.

Derrickson, S. R., & N. F. R. Snyder. 1991. Potentials and limits of captive breeding in parrot conservation. This volume.

Ellis, D. H., S. J. Dobrott, and J. L. Goodwin, Jr. 1978. Reintroduction techniques for Masked Bobwhites. Pages 345–354 *in* Endangered birds: management techniques for preserving threatened species (S. A. Temple, Ed.). Madison, Wisconsin, University of Wisconsin Press.

Emlen, J. T. 1974. An urban community in Tucson, Arizona; derivation, structure, regulation. Condor 76:184–197.

Erickson, R. C., & S. R. Derrickson. 1981. The Whooping Crane. Pages 104–118 *in* Crane research around the world (J. C. Lewis & H. Masatomi, Eds.). Baraboo, Wisconsin, International Crane Foundation.

Everhart, W. H. 1979. Fishery management principles. Pages 234–237 *in* Wildlife conservation: principles and practices (R. D. Teague & E. Decker, Eds.). Washington, District of Columbia, The Wildlife Society.

ffrench, R. P., & M. ffrench. 1966. Recent records of birds in Trinidad and Tobago. Wilson Bull. 78:5–11.

Flammer, K. 1978. Chlamydiosis (Psittacosis) in captive psittacine birds. Pages 81–85 *in* Proceedings of the first international symposium on breeding birds in captivity (A. C. Risser, Jr., L. F. Baptista, S. R. Wylie, & N. B. Gale, Eds.). North Hollywood, California, International Foundation for the Conservation of Birds.

Forshaw, J. 1989. Parrots of the world, 3rd revised edition. Willoughby, Australia, Lansdowne Editions.

Froke, J. B. 1981. Populations, movements, foraging and nesting of feral *Amazona* parrots in southern California. Humboldt, California, California State University, M.S. Thesis.

Gaskin, J. M. 1989. Psittacine viral diseases: a perspective. J. Zoo Wildl. Med. 20:249–264.

Gessaman, J. A., & K. A. Nagy. 1988. Transmitter loads affect the flight speed and metabolism of homing pigeons. Condor 90:662–668.

Gill, F. B. 1967. Birds of Rodriguez Island (Indian Ocean). Ibis 109:383–390.

Gilpin, M. E. 1987. Spatial structure and population vulnerability. Pages 125–139 *in* Viable populations for conservation (M. E. Soulé, Ed.). Cambridge, Cambridge University Press.

Gilpin, M. E., & M. E. Soulé. 1986. Minimum viable populations: processes of species extinction. Pages 19–34 *in* Conservation biology: the science of scarcity and diversity (M. E. Soulé, Ed.). Sunderland, Massachusetts, Sinauer.

Gnam, R. S. 1990. Conservation of the Bahama Parrot. Am. Birds 44:32–36.

Gnam, R., & A. Burchsted. 1991. Population estimates for the Bahama Parrot on Abaco Island, Bahamas. J. Field Ornithol. 62:139–146.

Graham, D. L. 1978. Herpes virus infections in captive birds. Pages 526–530 *in* Proceedings of the first international symposium on breeding birds in captivity (A. C. Risser, Jr., L. F. Baptista, S. R. Wylie, & N. B. Gale, Eds.). North Hollywood, California, International Foundation for Conservation of Birds.

Griffith, B., J. M. Scott, J. W. Carpenter, & C. Reed. 1989. Translocation as a species conservation tool: status and strategy. Science 245:477–480.

Hardy, J. W. 1973. Feral exotic birds in southern California. Wilson Bull. 85:506–512.

Harmon, K. W. 1979. Private land wildlife—a new program is needed. Pages 146–155 *in* Wildlife conservation: principles and practices (R. D. Teague & E. Decker, Eds.). Washington, District of Columbia, The Wildlife Society.

Hicks, J., & D. Greenwood. 1989. Rescuing Norfolk Island's parrot. Birds International 1(4):34–47.

Holyoak, D. T. 1975. Les oiseaux de iles Marquises. L'Oiseau et R. F. O. 45:207–233.

King, W. B. 1977–1979. Red data book, vol. 2: Aves, part 2. Morges, Switzerland, International Union Conservation Nature and Natural Resources.

Knox, J. P. 1852. A historical account of St. Thomas, W.I. New York, C. Scribner.

Koepcke, M. 1970. The birds of the Department of Lima, Peru, revised edition translated by E. J. Fisk. Newton Square, Pennsylvania, Harrowood Books.

Lande, R., & G. F. Barrowclough. 1987. Effective population size, genetic variation, and their use in population management. Pages 87–123 *in* Viable populations for conservation (M. E. Soulé, Ed.). Cambridge, Cambridge University Press.

Long, J. L. 1981. Introduced birds of the world. London, David and Charles.

Merton, D. V. 1975a. Success in re-establishing a threatened species: The saddleback—its status and conservation. ICBP Bull. 12:150–158.

Merton, D. V. 1975b. Kakapo. Wildlife: a review 6:39–51.

Merton, D., & R. Empson. 1989. But it doesn't look like a parrot. Birds International 1(1):60–72.

Mills, J. A., & G. R. Williams. 1979. The status of endangered New Zealand birds. Pages 147–168 *in* Status of endangered Australian wildlife (M. Tyler, Ed.). Adelaide, South Australia, Proc. Cent. Symp. Roy. Zool. Soc.

Munro, G. C. 1960. Birds of Hawaii, 2d revised edition. Tuttle, Rutland Press.

Neidermyer, W. J., & J. J. Hickey. 1977. The Monk Parakeet in the United States, 1970–75. Am. Birds 31:273–278.

Owre, O. T. 1973. A consideration of the exotic avifauna of southeastern Florida. Wilson Bull. 85:491–500.

Penny, M. 1974. The birds of Seychelles and the outlying islands. London, Collins.

Pratt, H. D., P. L. Bruner, & D. G. Berrett. 1987. A field guide to the birds of Hawaii and the tropical Pacific. Princeton, New Jersey, Princeton University Press.

Raffaele, H. A., & C. B. Kepler. In press. Earliest records of the recently introduced feral exotic avifauna of Puerto Rico. Ornithologia Caribeña.

Rostron, A. 1969. Rosella parrots: New Zealand's most beautiful pests. New Zealand Agric. J. March:40.

Sclater, P. L. 1859. Descriptions of two new species of American parrots. Ann. Mag. Nat. Hist., Ser. 3, 4:224–226.

Scott, M. E. 1988. The impact of infection and disease on animal populations: implications for conservation biology. Conserv. Biol. 2:40–56.

Silva, T. 1989. A monograph of endangered parrots. Pickering, Ontario, Canada, Silvio Mattacchione.

Smythies, B. E. 1968. The birds of Borneo, 2d edition. Edinburgh, Oliver and Boyd.

Snyder, N. F. R., W. B. King, & C. B. Kepler. 1982. Biology and conservation of the Bahama Parrot. Living Bird 19:91–114.

Snyder, N. F. R., & H. A. Snyder. 1989. Biology and conservation of the California Condor. Current Ornithology 6:175–267.

Snyder, N. F. R., H. A. Snyder, & T. B. Johnson. 1989. Parrots return to the Arizona skies. Birds International 1(2):40–52.

Snyder, N. F. R., J. W. Wiley, & C. B. Kepler. 1987. The parrots of Luquillo:

the natural history and conservation of the Puerto Rican Parrot. Los Angeles, California, Western Foundation of Vertebrate Zoology.

Soulé, M. (Ed.). 1987. Viable populations for conservation. Cambridge, Cambridge University Press.

Taylor, R. H. 1985. Status, habits and conservation of *Cyanoramphus* parakeets in the New Zealand region. Pages 195–211 *in* Conservation of island birds (P. J. Moors, Ed.). Cambridge, International Council for Bird Preservation Tech. Publ. No. 3.

Thibault, J. C. 1973. Notes ornithologiques polynesiennes. II. Les Iles Marquises. Alauda 41:301–316.

Thibault, J. C. Undated. Fragilite et protection de l'avifaunne en Polynesie Française. Unpublished report to the International Council for Bird Preservation.

Thomsen, J. B., & C. A. Munn. 1988. *Cyanopsitta spixii*: a non-recovery report. Parrotletter 1:6–7.

Triggs, S. J., R. G. Powlesland, & C. H. Daugherty. 1989. Genetic variation and conservation of Kakapo (*Strigops habroptilus*: Psittaciformes). Conserv. Biol. 3:92–96.

Waite, E. R. 1909. The vertebrata of the subantarctic islands of New Zealand. Pages 542–600 *in* The subantarctic islands of New Zealand. Vol. II. (C. Chilton, Ed.). Christchurch, New Zealand, Philosophical Institute of Canterbury.

Wanless, S., M. P. Harris, & J. A. Morris. 1988. The effect of radio transmitters on the behavior of Common Murres and Razorbills during chick rearing. Condor 90:816–823.

Wenner, A. S., & D. H. Hirth. 1984. Status of the feral Budgerigar in Florida. J. Field Ornithol. 55:214–219.

Westcott, D. A., & A. Cockburn. 1988. Flock size and vigilance in parrots. Aust. J. Zool. 36:335–349.

White, C. M. N., & M. D. Bruce. 1986. The birds of Wallacea. London, British Ornithologists' Union, B. O. U. Check-list No. 7.

Wiley, J. W. 1983. The role of captive propagation in Puerto Rican Parrot conservation. Pages 441–453 *in* Jean Delacour/IFCB symposium on breeding birds in captivity (A. C. Risser, Jr., & F. S. Todd, Eds.). North Hollywood, California, International Foundation for Conservation of Birds.

Wiley, J. W. 1985. Bird conservation in the United States Caribbean. Pages 107–159 *in* Bird conservation 2 (S. A. Temple, Ed.). Madison, Wisconsin, University of Wisconsin Press.

Wiley, J. W. In press. Status and conservation of parrots and parakeets in the Greater Antilles, Bahama Islands, and Cayman Islands. Bird Cons. Int.

Wilson, S. B. 1907. Notes on birds of Tahiti and the Society Group. Ibis, 9th ser., 1:373–379.

Wingate, D. B. 1985. The restoration of Nonsuch Island as a living museum of Bermuda's pre-colonial terrestrial biome. Pages 225–238 *in* Conservation of island birds (P. J. Moors, Ed.). Cambridge, England, International Council for Bird Preservation Tech. Publ. No. 3.

Yealland, J. 1940. The blue lories. Avicult. Mag., 5th ser., 5:308–313.

Resumen.—La reintroducción deliberada como método de conservación ha sido poco probado en los psitácidos. Sin embargo, poblaciones grandes de loros exóticos en muchas áreas urbanas del mundo señalan que los loros originarios de otro lugar pueden formar poblaciones silvestres viables con cierta facilidad en ambientes poco exigentes. Experimentos con la liberación del loro Hispaniola (*Amazona ventralis*) y Piquigrueso (*Rhynchopsitta pachyrhyncha*) señalan que las aves capturadas en su habitat natural son superiores a las aves criadas en cautiverio, en cuanto a su potencial de establecimiento, y que aves criadas por sus parientes son superiores a aves criadas a mano. La deteriorización en el comportamiento y la genética bajo condiciones de cautiverio hacen razonar que se debe intentar reintroducciones con aves tomadas, lo más recién posible, de su habitat natural. En general, las reintroducciones solo se recomiendan bajo circunstancias donde los factores que causaron la extirpación de la población original han sido corregidos. Aún así muchos loros no parecen ser especialistas en su uso de habitat y pueden sobrevivir, hasta en habitat modificados, si factores de presión como la caza y la explotación para el comercio de mascotas pueden ser controladas. Las muchas ventajas de poblaciones silvestres sobre poblaciones en cautiverio indican que se debe ampliar el uso de esta técnica.

8. Neotropical Parrots as Agricultural Pests

Enrique H. Bucher

Centro de Zoología Aplicada, Universidad de Córdoba, Casilla de Correos
122, Córdoba 5000, Argentina

Abstract.—Neotropical parrots that are agricultural pests present peculiar management
and conservation problems. Some species that are considered pests are also valued in
the pet trade and/or are simultaneously endangered as wild populations. Conflicts
between parrots and agriculture have increased as agriculture has expanded into
forested areas. Common agricultural problems caused by parrots include damage to
fruits and grain crops, with a few cases of damage to trees or man-made structures.
Damage by parrots tends to be exaggerated, is irregularly distributed, and is commonly associated with agricultural frontiers and poor agricultural practices. Parrots
have several characteristics that are similar to other avian pest species including
morphological adaptations, dietary and distributional opportunism, and certain
reproductive and behavioral adaptations. However, parrots also possess a variety
of characteristics that limit their abilities to depredate crops. As predominantly
K-strategists, they tend to have low productivity and strict nesting habitat requirements. Proper management of pest parrots requires strategies that combine available
techniques and resources in ways that minimize crop damage without endangering the
survival of the parrot species involved, and with minimal environmental side effects.
Several approaches are discussed. Priority is given to crop substitution and bird
repellency over lethal techniques. Promotion of unrestricted trapping is neither an
efficient nor a justifiable method for reducing agricultural damage, and may lead to
extinction of some species.

Many species of parrots are considered agricultural pests, particularly in Australia and in the Neotropics (Halse 1986, Forshaw 1989). Parrots are hardly unique among birds in this respect, but they present some peculiar problems. Many species considered pests are also valued in the pet trade and/or are simultaneously endangered as wild populations. Adequate management of such species, for example the Blue-fronted Amazon (*Amazona aestiva*), is especially difficult.

In Latin America conflicts between man and parrots began with pre-European cultures, which had problems with parrots attacking their corn plantations (Bibar 1558). Scenes of parrots eating corn or being frightened away from crops are found in the Incas' pottery (Anthropological Museum of Lima, Peru, pers. obs.). Problems with crop depredation by parrots continued after European colonization. When Charles Darwin visited Uruguay in 1833, he was told that Monk Parakeets (*Myiopsitta monachus*) were killed by the thousands along the Uruguay River to prevent crop damage (Darwin 1833).

Conflicts between New World parrots and agriculture have increased as agriculture has continued to expand into forested areas (Bucher and Nores 1988). In addition, a new dimension to human-parrot interactions emerged when a dramatic increase in the demand for parrots as pets began during the 1980s, resulting in a massive increase in trapping. Although this increase in trade has been under considerable scrutiny from international conservation organizations (Thomsen and Mulliken 1991), some countries, particularly Argentina, have allowed unlimited exportation of parrots under the justification of their pest status.

An analysis of the problem of parrots as agricultural pests is long overdue, bearing in mind the important implications that pest status may have in terms of parrot management, trade, and conservation. It is particularly important to consider both conservation and control under the broader scope of management, instead of treating them in isolation. Maintaining a balance between the needs of preserving biodiversity and of increasing food production requires a rational, comprehensive approach, which is precisely what the concept of management implies.

The present review deals with the Neotropical region, and particularly Argentina, where the conflicts between pest considerations and conservation needs are most intense. Still, I believe that the basic patterns and principles discussed here apply to any country or region where similar problems may arise.

AGRICULTURAL CROPS DAMAGED BY PARROT PESTS

Common problems caused by parrots include damage to fruits and grain crops (Table 1). Damage to trees from bud-eating has been reported in only a few cases. In addition, the huge communal nests of the Monk Parakeet sometimes cause damage to structures such as transmission lines (Bucher 1984, Bucher and Martin 1987).

In Argentina, parrots frequently feed on citrus plantations, particularly in the Northwest (Tucumán, Salta, and Jujuy) where citrus groves are located in valleys surrounded by mountains covered with subtropical humid forests. Several species of parrots, including the Blue-fronted Amazon, the endemic Tucuman Amazon (*Amazona tucumana*), and to a lesser extent the Scaly-headed Parrot (*Pionus maximiliani*), fly daily from their roosts in the forests to feed in the groves. Parrot damage, although widespread, is not intense (Bucher et al. unpubl. data). Damage to citrus has also been reported in the Yucatán Peninsula of Mexico (Berlanga et al. 1989) and in the West Indies (Snyder et al. 1987). Grapes and olives are sometimes eaten by the Burrowing Parrot (*Cyanoliseus patagonus*) in the irrigated valleys of western Argentina (provinces of La Rioja, Catamarca, and San Juan). The Burrowing Parrot also feeds on the fruits of the native mesquite tree (*Prosopis alba*), whose pods are harvested for human and domestic animal consumption. In all cases damage is usually light (Bucher and Rinaldi 1986).

Peaches, pears, and other temperate-climate fruits are sometimes damaged in Argentina by the Monk Parakeet, the Blue-crowned Parakeet (*Aratinga acuticaudata*), and the Burrowing Parrot (Bucher 1984). None of these parrots is abundant in the main fruit-growing areas of Argentina (provinces of Neuquén and Mendoza). Most of the reported damage has been to small plantations or house orchards. The overall economic impact has been minor (Bucher 1984).

Corn, sunflower, and to a lesser extent wheat and sorghum, are the most frequently affected grain crops in Argentina (Bucher 1984). Corn and sunflower

Table 1.   Crops affected by parrots in Argentina (1 = sporadic, 2 = frequent, 3 = common).

Crop	Blue-fronted Amazon	Blue-crowned Parakeet	Monk Parakeet	Scaly-headed Parrot	Burrowing Parrot
Fruit					
Citrus, peaches	3		2	1	
Grapes					1
Olives					1
Mesquite					1
Grain					
Corn		2	3	2	
Sunflower		2	3	1	2
Wheat			1		2
Sorghum			1		1
Tree buds			1		

are attacked mainly by the Burrowing Parrot, the Scaly-headed Parrot, the Blue-crowned Parakeet, and the Monk Parakeet (Table 1). In Uruguay the Monk Parakeet is an important pest of corn and sunflower (Fig. 1). Wheat is affected by the Burrowing Parrot in northern Patagonia (Rio Negro Province) and in western Argentina (Catamarca), involving plantations in marginally suitable areas (Bucher and Rinaldi 1986). Sorghum is also eaten occasionally by the Monk Parakeet but damage is usually minimal.

Forest plantations are sometimes affected when parrots eat buds. Damage to poplars by the Burrowing Parrot is frequent in Rio Negro (Bucher and Rinaldi 1986). Occasionally Monk Parakeets damage pine trees in the province of Entre Rios (pers. obs.). In all observed cases damage has been minimal.

Transmission lines are frequently affected by the huge communal nests of the Monk Parakeet. The nests can produce short circuits when built around isolated supports on poles. The problem can be serious enough to require continuous patrolling and nest destruction in some places (Bucher and Martin 1987).

Fig. 1. Typical damage caused by Monk Parakeets to sunflower plants in western Uruguay, where losses may be important in some years (see Bucher 1985).

PARROTS AS PESTS: COMMON PATTERNS AND CHARACTERISTICS

Conflicts between parrots and agriculture show common characteristics throughout the group's range, some of which are similar to those found in other bird groups (Murton and Wright 1968, Bucher 1984).

Parrots are easy to detect: Parrots are usually noisy and sometimes bright-colored, and tend to gather in flocks. Their presence in or near a crop rarely remains unnoticed by farmers. Other causes of crop losses such as pathogenic viruses or fungi are often much less obvious, although generally more serious.

Damage tends to be exaggerated: There is a worldwide tendency to overstate bird damage by farmers (Dyer and Ward 1977). This tendency may be especially great for parrots, given their already mentioned conspicuousness. Damage is commonly overstated in regions where control of vertebrate pests is carried out by government agencies. Thus, the matter sometimes becomes a political issue (Bucher 1984).

Damage is irregularly distributed in space and time: Damage by parrots, like most other bird damage, occurs very unpredictably. Usually a few plots are severely damaged and many are left slightly damaged or untouched (Dyer and Ward 1977; pers. obs.). As a result, damage at the regional level is usually minimal. This generally makes the implementation of large-scale control campaigns uneconomical because costs rapidly become higher than losses (Bucher 1984).

Damage is commonly associated with agricultural frontiers: The expansion of agriculture into previously forested areas is an accelerating process in Latin America and provides an ideal combination of feeding habitat (crop patches) and nesting habitat (forest patches) for many species of parrots. Good examples of this situation can be observed in the previously mentioned citrus groves in the inter-montane valleys of northwestern Argentina, and in the semi-arid Chaco savannas of Argentina, Paraguay, and Bolivia (Bucher and Nores 1988).

Damage is usually related to poor agricultural practices: Plots with considerable open spaces and low plant density, or those that are left unharvested long after ripening are likely to suffer more damage by parrots than those properly managed (Table 2). Plantations located in marginally suitable areas, where the plants tend to be weaker, are also more affected (Bucher 1984). For example, wheat damage by the Burrowing Parrot occurs in northern Rio Negro province in Argentina, an area so clearly unsuitable for the crop that cultivation is discouraged by the local Ministry of Agriculture (Bucher and Rinaldi 1986). Increased damage in citrus groves has also occurred when fruit harvesting was delayed by farmers who were speculating for better prices in northwestern Argentina (C. Saravia Toledo, pers. comm.). Unfortunately, cultivation of marginal lands and poor farming practices are widespread in tropical Latin America, where subsistence agriculture is predominant.

Table 2.   Damage caused by Monk Parakeets to corn plantations in Entre Rios, Argentina, in relation to crop condition (estimated from ear density; data from Bucher 1984).

Crop condition	Ear density[1]	% Damaged ears	Sample size[2]
Good	1.46	14	23
Poor	0.46	98	10

[1]Number of ears per meter in a row.
[2]Number of 20-m transects.

CURRENT CONTROL PRACTICES AND THEIR IMPACTS

Almost invariably, authorities confronted with a new bird-pest situation plunge into lethal control without adequate consideration of alternative approaches (Dyer and Ward 1977). This tendency certainly applies to the case of parrots in Latin America. In all cases that I know, lethal methods have been used as the first (and usually the only) alternative. Common methods of lethal control include shooting, dispersion of poisoned baits, and nest destruction and poisoning (Table 3). Control campaigns have been largely unsuccessful in the long term because of the economic, logistic, and political problems associated with government agencies (Bucher 1984, 1985). However, some of the presently available techniques, such as nest poisoning in Monk Parakeets, have the potential for causing a serious impact if applied with enough intensity and persistence (pers. obs.).

More recently, unrestricted trapping and unlimited exportation quotas have been authorized for nearly all native species of parrots by Argentine authorities under the justification of their pest status (Thomsen and Mulliken 1991). Unfortunately, the decision to label a given species as a pest usually has not been based on reliable damage evaluation. Moreover, in many provinces no clear distinction has been made between parrot species. In some cases the generic

Table 3. Current parrot control methods in Argentina (excluding trapping for the pet trade) (1 = sporadic, 2 = frequent, 3 = common).

Method	Blue-fronted Amazon	Blue-crowned Parakeet	Monk Parakeet	Scaly-headed Parrot	Burrowing Parrot
Poisoned baits					1
Shooting	1	1	2	1	1
Nest destruction			1		1
Nest poisoning			3		

classification "parrot" has been used in the legislation without any further taxonomic specification (Reynoso and Bucher 1989).

As a result, about 900,000 parrots were exported from Argentina between 1982 and 1988 (Thomsen and Mulliken 1991). Given that nestlings are preferred by trappers to adults because of their higher market value, most of the trapping has not been directed toward those individuals that cause damage, but instead has affected whole populations. Furthermore, nestling capture is nearly always associated with massive nesting habitat destruction, because the campesinos usually ruin nests or fell trees to extract nestlings (Bucher and Martella 1988, Bucher et al. unpublished report to the World Wildlife Fund). Unlike traditional control measures, the combination of unlimited trapping and habitat destruction has had a very serious effect on some parrot populations (Beissinger and Bucher 1991).

ECOLOGICAL CONSIDERATIONS OF PARROTS AS PESTS

Parrots exhibit several adaptations and behaviors that are commonly found in other successful granivorous pest species. These include morphological adaptations, dietary and distributional opportunism, and reproductive and behavioral adaptations (Wiens and Johnston 1977). However, parrots also have a variety of characteristics that limit the success with which they can depredate crops, largely related to predominantly K-strategist life history patterns.

Morphological adaptations of parrots that assist them in exploiting agriculture include a strong beak, a flexible foot structure, and in some cases perhaps the ability to produce crop milk to feed their young. A parrot's bill is an extremely versatile tool which allows parrots to open and eat many fruits and seeds, including very hard seeds like palm fruits and protected grains like corn. Their peculiar foot structure allows them to hang in the vegetation, to get at food items, and to handle food items expertly. A crop secretion may be synthesized by a few parrots (Forshaw 1989). Although not as well developed as in pigeons, it may help to make some parrots independent from animal food while feeding their young. In contrast, other granivorous birds require sources of animal protein during breeding (Murton 1972).

Dietary opportunism is shown by some species like the Monk Parakeet and Burrowing Parrot, which can feed on seeds, fruits, buds, pollen, and even insects, both in trees and on the ground (pers. obs.). Other species are much more restricted and specialized in their diet. Amazons, for example, normally feed in trees and not on the ground. Their diet tends to be restricted to fruits and buds (Forshaw 1989).

Distributional opportunism in parrots is normally restricted to the non-breeding season, given their marked nest site fidelity and their general tendency to breed in dispersed small groups (Forshaw 1989). Several species, including the Burrowing Parrot and the Blue-fronted Amazon, are partly nomadic outside the breeding season (pers. obs.). Other species, like the Monk Parakeet (pers. obs.), show limited mobility and year-round feeding territories. A few are colonial breeders, like the Burrowing Parrot (Forshaw 1989).

Reproductive habits exert the strongest limitation on the abilities of parrots to become "efficient" pests. In general parrots have very specific breeding habitat requirements. Many species nest in tree cavities, which are usually associated with mature forests. Cliff-nesting species, like the Burrowing Parrot, require escarpments that satisfy specific height and texture requirements (Bucher and Rinaldi 1986). Only the Monk Parakeet, which builds its own nests, can be somewhat more flexible about breeding sites.

Neotropical parrots also tend to have a well defined and short breeding season. Often they nest only once a year, as in the case of the Puerto Rican Amazon (*Amazona vittata*) (Snyder et al. 1987), the Monk Parakeet (Bucher et al. in press) and the Burrowing Parrot (Bucher et al. 1987). This lack of breeding opportunism is important, given that varying the number of successful broods during a breeding period has a far greater influence on natality potential than varying clutch size. Changing the number of broods produced per breeding season is how birds most often respond to year-to-year changes in environmental conditions (Wiens and Johnston 1977). As in other cavity-nesting birds, the breeding cycle of parrots is relatively long and nestling growth rate is slow (Forshaw 1989, Navarro and Bucher 1990). In addition, delayed breeding is common in parrots, and has been observed in the Puerto Rican Parrot (Snyder et al. 1987) and the Monk Parakeet (Bucher et al. in press). The combination of delayed maturity, a fixed breeding season, and an absence of multiple-brooding make it difficult for these birds to increase rapidly in response to abundant but ephemeral resources such as crops. Neither do these traits favor quick population recovery from lethal control campaigns. Overall, Neotropical parrots show more K-strategist reproductive characteristics than the r-strategist patterns that are typical of many pest bird species (Wiens and Johnston 1977).

Parrots commonly feed and roost in flocks outside the breeding season (Forshaw 1989). Both of these aspects of social organization may facilitate detection and exploitation of abundant but short-lived resources (Ward and Zahavi 1973). However, true colonial breeding is uncommon in parrots, limiting the potential for gathering large numbers of birds in good feeding areas during the breeding season. Perhaps this explains why much of the agricultural damage by parrots in Argentina occurs in early autumn, after the breeding season (pers. obs.).

CONTROL STRATEGIES AND TACTICS

No single magic recipe is available for solving all bird-damage problems. The toxic chemical approach that has become popular in insect or weed control, after the development of potent insecticides and herbicides, cannot be applied to parrots, given the many ecological, logistic, economic, and sociological constraints associated with bird management (Murton 1972).

There is ample scope, however, for the development of management strategies that combine available techniques in ways that maximize damage reduction without endangering the survival of pest species, and with minimal and acceptable environmental side effects. This integrated approach, which has already proven effective in insect control (Pimentel 1978), deserves priority attention when dealing with bird problems.

A strategic approach to parrot control should give preference to techniques that are the least expensive, the least environmentally damaging, and most permanent instead of those that are expensive, repetitive, and damage non-target species. Such a strategy implies four consecutive steps or lines of action: (1) determine that damage is important enough to justify action, (2) substitute less susceptible crops, (3) deter the birds from the crops, and (4) only as a last resort, consider population reduction (Table 4) (Dyer and Ward 1977). Crop substitution, exclusion of birds from crops, changes in agricultural practices, frightening techniques, and compensation for damage should always be considered prior to resorting to population control (see below).

Proper damage evaluation, using sound statistical methodology, is essential for a rational approach to any parrot damage problem. As mentioned previously, damage may be exaggerated by farmers, as well as trappers and dealers involved in the pet trade. Establishing a regional pattern of occurrence and intensity of damage is also important to separate problems that affect a whole regional economy from isolated cases that, even if severe, are not regionally significant. These two categories deserve different management approaches.

Crop substitution may provide a one-step, definitive solution when applicable. It is particularly feasible in those cases where the affected crops are located in marginally suitable areas where productivity is low and costs are high. For example, crop substitution could be a valid alternative for the wheat plantations in northern Rio Negro, Argentina, previously discussed.

Complete exclusion of birds from crops is a very efficient, although expensive technique. It is advisable only in cases of heavy damage to expensive crops in small plots. Netting is useful to protect grapes and other fruit crops, and parent plants used to produce hybrid seeds in cereals. A variation on the netting technique involves the use of fluorescent monofilament fishing line or reflective tape strung approximately 1 m above the canopy in rows parallel to tree rows (Tipton et al. 1989).

Table 4.   Recommended strategy for managing parrot damage.

Alternative	Action	Environmental impact of action
Damage below economic threshold?	No action or compensation	None
Damage sporadic but locally intense, or caused by an endangered species?	Compensation	None
Crop substitution possible?	Crop substitution	Low or none
Change in agronomic practices possible?	Agronomy change	Low
Birds can be frightened from crop?	Frightening away	Low
Crop protection by limited population reduction possible and desirable?	Local population reduction	High
Crop protection by massive population reduction possible and desirable?	Regional population reduction	Very high
No viable or acceptable alternative?	More research	None

Changes in agronomic practices, such as using resistant cultivars, synchronic planting, or providing alternative foods, are probably the easiest and most acceptable approach in terms of minimizing environmental impact (Dyer and Ward 1977). Use of resistant cultivars for repelling birds has considerable potential and has already proved successful in protecting sorghum against doves in Argentina (Bucher 1984). Early harvesting may also avoid damage in cereal crops, although costs are high (Bucher 1984). Anticipating harvest before the arrival of migratory birds may help to avoid damage in appropriate circumstances. Planting of crops that lure or divert the attack of birds may be effective, but requires a careful cost/benefit analysis. To my knowledge, this approach has not been used to control parrots.

Techniques for frightening birds away from crops include visual, sound, and taste repellents. As a rule, birds tend to habituate rapidly to both visual and auditory repellents, rendering them ineffective in a short time (Inglis 1980, Slater 1980). Visual repellents include kites, balloons, and reflecting tapes (Inglis 1980, Shirota et al. 1983, Connover 1984, Tipton et al. 1989). Auditory repellents include pyrotechnics and exploders (Slater 1980, Connover 1984). More recently, electronic synthesizers have been developed that can produce a wide range of noises with variable intensity, frequency, and duration (Murton and Wright 1968). Finally recorded distress and alarm calls have also been used with varied success (Murton and Wright 1968). The last two methods deserve attention in parrots, given their usually rich and complex vocalizations. In the Monk Parakeet (Martella and Bucher 1990) and in the Burrowing Parrot (pers. obs.), agonistic calls tend to attract rather than disperse other birds, whereas alarm calls usually elicit dispersal flights in the Monk Parakeet.

Patrolling is widely used in third world countries to repel parrots from crops. Usually, patrolling is done by children, sometimes on horseback. Although this technique has not been adequately evaluated, it seems one of the more cost-effective approaches in tropical countries.

Taste repellents have been widely used to protect cereal crops (Wright 1980). The best known repellents are methiocarb and carbamates, and also amino-pyridines which produce a stress reaction that results in agonistic displays and calls, which in turn disperse the birds. Cost is one of the main limitations of taste repellents, particularly in the third world (Bucher 1984). The application of these chemicals is economic only in cases of very heavy damage to high-priced crops. Repellents have been used experimentally against Monk Parakeets in Uruguay with mixed results (E. Rodriguez pers. comm.). Research and development of new repellents is now very limited, given a restricted demand and the U.S. Environmental Protection Agency's costly requirements for research on environmental safety.

Compensation programs for damage may be a viable alternative when damage is caused by an endangered species, or is restricted both in geographical range and intensity. Individual farmers should not be expected to bear the full costs of wildlife conservation. However, implementing damage compensation programs may be complicated, requiring substantial investments in damage evaluation. Compensation should not discourage farmers from using acceptable techniques to avoid damage. Compensation for damage has already been implemented in Canada for waterfowl crop damage (Boyd 1980), and could be applied to protect the relic population of the Lear's Macaw (*Anodorhynchus leari*) in Brazil, for example.

Population control options include sterilants and lethal methods, such as trapping, shooting, nest poisoning, and poison baits. Sterilants have been used with limited success, and only in a few cases, because they require the treatment of a large proportion of the population to overcome density-dependent compensatory effects (Murton 1968, 1972). Population control using lethal methods on a regional scale has proven to be generally unsuccessful in species with opportunistic breeding habits, high mobility, and a high reproductive output like the Quelea (*Quelea quelea*) and the Eared Dove (*Zenaida auriculata*) (Dyer and Ward 1977, Bucher 1984). Given that food availability is often a key limiting factor, natural mortality tends to compensate rather than add to mortality from control campaigns, greatly reducing their impact (Murton 1968, Newton 1981).

A regional approach to parrot control is rarely justified, given the relative ecological "weakness" of parrots in terms of their generally low reproductive output. Intensive killing and trapping at a regional scale may overcome compensatory mechanisms and result in a severe population reduction, particularly in some species with very low productivity like amazons. Besides, given the localized dispersion of damage incidents, massive killing will probably affect many individuals that will never attack a crop. Finally, costs of control may rapidly become higher than losses, particularly in areas of low crop density.

Many of the same considerations apply to the legalization of massive trapping and trade as a population control strategy. This practice allows for uncontrollable excesses in exploitation not directly related to damage intensity or distribution, but driven instead by the build-up of vested interests along the trade chain. Such interests are likely to resist any attempt to cancel trapping permits even if a decline in population becomes clear. Any significant delay between the onset of a population decline and the banning of trade, resulting from economic pressures or even bureaucratic delays, may prove to be fatal for any parrot species subject to intensive exploitation. This could well be the future for the Blue-fronted Amazon in Argentina (Bucher and Martella 1988, Beissinger and Bucher 1991). Moreover, as trappers concentrate more on the more marketable nestlings than on adults, massive nesting habitat loss is caused by their widespread habit of felling trees or opening the nest cavity for capturing the nestlings (Bucher and Martella 1988).

Massive exportation of parrots as a control method also poses risks of introducing parrot pest species into other countries. The Monk Parakeet has become successfully established after accidental releases in Puerto Rico and the continental United States (Niedermyer and Hickey 1977), where it is already causing problems to electricity transmission lines in Florida (J. Burnham pers. comm.).

CONCLUSIONS

Neotropical parrots do not fit the typical profile of a successful pest species. They lack the typical combination of high mobility, flock feeding and roosting, opportunistic breeding, and high productivity that characterize successful pest birds. Consequently, Neotropical parrots appear in general to be weakly adapted to exploit ephemeral resources such as crops, and cannot sustain heavy losses such as those resulting from control practices.

Techniques and approaches other than lethal methods are available for controlling damage by parrots. Unfortunately, experience with non-lethal techniques is still extremely limited in Latin America. Such techniques deserve increased attention in the future.

There is no rational justification for promoting unrestricted trapping and trade quotas under the guise of controlling agricultural damage. This policy allows for uncontrollable excesses in exploitation not directly related to damage intensity or distribution, and results in a build-up of vested interests along the trade chain. A significant delay between the onset of a population decline and the banning of trade, due to economic pressures or bureaucratic procedures, may prove to be fatal for any parrot species subject to intensive exploitation. Moreover, this practice also stimulates capture of nestlings over adults and in the case of tree-hole nesting parrots may cause massive destruction of nesting habitat by trappers.

ACKNOWLEDGMENTS

This paper was completed while on sabbatical leave at Colorado State University. I am grateful to John Wiens for his support and to the Colorado State University for hosting me. I thank the World Wildlife Fund (US) and the Consejo Nacional de Investigaciones Científicas y Técnicas of Argentina for financing my sabbatical, and my thanks to TRAFFIC (USA) and the World Wildlife Fund for supporting my research on the Blue-fronted Amazon. I also thank Steven Beissinger and Noel Snyder for their valuable comments on the original manuscript.

LITERATURE CITED

Beissinger, S. R., & E. H. Bucher. 1991. Sustainable harvesting of parrots for conservation. This volume.

Berlanga, M. Gutierrez, & R. Castillo. 1989. Aspectos ecológicos y perspectivas de conservación de los loros yucatecos *Amazona xantholora* y *Amazona albifrons*. Yucatán, México, Pronatura, Capítulo Yucatán.

Bibar, G. 1558. Crónica y relación copiosa de los reynos de Chile hecha pr Gerónimo de Bibar. Transcription from the original made by I. A. Leonard. Fondo Histórico Toribio Medina, Chile, 1966.

Boyd, H. 1980. Waterfowl crop damage prevention and compensation programs in the Canadian Prairie Provinces. Pages 20–27 *in* Bird problems in agriculture (E. N. Wright, I. R. Inglis, & C. J. Feare, Eds.). London, British Crop Protection Agency Publications.

Bucher, E. H. 1984. Las aves como plaga en Argentina. Centro de Zoología Aplicada. Publ. No. 9. Córdoba, Argentina, Universidad de Córdoba.

Bucher, E. H. 1985. Ecología de aves plaga en el Uruguay. Consultant report. Montevideo, Food and Agriculture Organization, United Nations.

Bucher, E. H., & M. B. Martella. 1988. Preliminary report on the current status of *Amazona aestiva* in the western Chaco, Argentina. Parrotletter 1:9–10.

Bucher, E. H., & L. F. Martin. 1987. Los nidos de cotorras (*Myiopsitta monachus*) como causa de problemas en líneas de transmisión eléctrica. Vida Silvestre Neotropical 1:50–51.

Bucher, E. H., L. F. Martin, M. B. Martella, & J. L. Navarro. In press. Social behaviour and population dynamics of the Monk Parakeet. Christchurch, New Zealand, Proceedings of the XX International Ornithological Congress.

Bucher, E. H., & M. Nores. 1988. Present status of birds in steppes and savannas of northern and central Argentina. Pages 71–79 *in* Ecology and conservation of grassland birds (P. D. Goriup, Ed.). Cambridge, International Council for Bird Preservation Tech. Publ. No. 7.

Bucher, E. H., & S. Rinaldi. 1986. Distribución y situación actual del loro barranquero (*Cyanoliseus patagonus*) en la Argentina. Vida Silvestre Neotropical 1:55–61.

Bucher, E. H., A. Santamaria, & M. A. Bertin. 1987. Reproduction and molt in the Burrowing Parrot (*Cyanoliseus patagonus*). Wilson Bull. 99:107–109.

Conover, M. R. 1984. Comparative effectiveness of Avitrol, exploders, and hawk kites in reducing blackbird damage to corn. J. Wildl. Manage. 48:109–116.

Darwin, C. 1833. Charles Darwin's diary of the voyage of H.M.S. Beagle. Edited from the MS by Nora Barlow (1934). Cambridge, Cambridge University Press.

Dyer, M. I., & P. Ward. 1977. Management of pest situations. Pages 267–300 *in* Granivorous birds in ecosystems (J. Pinowsky & S. C. Kendeigh, Eds.). Cambridge, Cambridge University Press.

Forshaw, J. 1989. Parrots of the world, 3d revised edition. Willoughby, Australia, Lansdowne Editions.

Halse, S. A. 1986. Parrot damage in apple orchards in Southwestern Australia. A review. Dept. of Conservation and Land Management, Western Australia. Technical Report No. 8.

Inglis, I. R. 1980. Visual scarers: an ethological approach. Pages 121–143 *in* Bird problems in agriculture (E. N. Wright, I. R. Inglis, & C. J. Feare, Eds.). Croydon, British Crop Protection Agency.

Martella, M. B., & E. H. Bucher. 1990. Vocalizations of the Monk Parakeet. Bird Behaviour 8:101–110.

Murton, R. K. 1968. Some predator-prey relationships in bird damage and population control. Pages 157–180 *in* The problem of birds as pests (R. K. Murton & E. N. Wright, Eds.). New York, Academic Press.

Murton, R. K. 1972. Man and birds. New York, Taplinger Publishing Company.

Murton, R. K., & E. N. Wright (Eds.). 1968. The problem of birds as pests. New York, Academic Press.

Navarro, J. L., & E. H. Bucher. 1990. Growth of nestling Monk Parakeets in a wild population. Wilson Bull. 102:520–525.

Newton, I. 1981. The role of food in limiting bird numbers. Pages 11–30 *in* The integrated study of bird populations (H. Klomp & J. W. Woldendorp, Eds.). Amsterdam, North Holland Publishing Company.

Neidermyer, I. J., & J. J. Hickey. 1977. The Monk Parakeet in the United States, 1970–75. Am. Birds 31:237–278.

Pimentel, D. (Ed.). 1978. Pest control strategies. New York, CRC Press.

Reynoso, H., & E. H. Bucher. 1989. Situación legal de la fauna silvestre en la República Argentina. Ambiente y Recursos Naturales 6:22–28.

Shirota, Y., M. Sanada, & S. Masaki. 1983. Eyespotted balloons as a device to scare gray starlings. Appl. Entomol. Zool. 18:545–549.

Slater, P. J. 1980. Bird behaviour and scaring by sounds. Pages 105–114 *in* Bird problems in agriculture (E. N. Wright, I. R. Inglis, & C. J. Feare, Eds.). Croydon, British Crop Protection Agency.

Snyder, N. F. R., J. W. Wiley, & C. B. Kepler. 1987. The parrots of Luquillo: natural history and conservation of the Puerto Rican Parrot. Los Angeles, California, Western Foundation of Vertebrate Zoology.

Thomsen, J. B., & T. A. Mulliken. 1991. Trade in Neotropical psittacines and its conservation implications. This volume.

Tipton, A. R., J. H. Rappole, A. H. Kane, R. H. Flores, D. B. Johnson, J. Hobbs, P. Schulz, S. L. Beasom, & J. Palacios. 1989. Use of monofilament line, reflective tape, beachballs, and pyrotechnics for controlling grackle damage to citrus. Pages 126–128 *in* Proceedings of the ninth Great Plains wildlife damage control workshop. Fort Collins, Colorado.

Ward, P., & A. Zahavi. 1973. The importance of certain assemblages of birds as "information-centres" for food finding. Ibis 115:517–534.

Wiens, J. A., & R. F. Johnston. 1977. Adaptive correlates of granivory in birds. Pages 301–340 *in* Granivorous birds in ecosystems (J. Pinowsky & S. C. Kendeigh, Eds.). Cambridge, Cambridge University Press.

Wright, E. N. 1980. Chemical repellents—a review. Pages 164–172 *in* Bird problems in agriculture (E. N. Wright, I. R. Inglis, & C. J. Feare, Eds.). Croyden, British Crop Protection Agency.

Resumen.—El manejo y la conservación de los loros neotropicales considerados como plagas agrícolas presenta problemas propios. Algunas especies consideradas como plagas también son valoradas para el comercio de mascotas y simultaneamente sus poblaciones silvestres están en peligro. Conflictos entre loros y la agricultura han aumentado con la expanción de la agricultura a areas boscosas. Problemas agrícolas comunes, causados por loros, incluyen daños a frutales y a siembras de granos con algunos casos de daños a árboles o a estructuras erigidas por el hombre. Los daños hechos por loros se tienden a exagerar, son irregulares en su distribución, y frecuentemente están asociados con fronteras agrícolas o prácticas de agricultura deficientes. Los loros comparten varias características con otras aves que son plagas incluyendo adaptaciones morfológicas, oportunismo en la dieta y la distribución, y ciertas adaptaciones reproductivas y comportamientos. Sin embargo, los loros también demuestran una variedad de características que limitan su capacidad de depredar los cultivos. Con una estrategia de vida predominantemente de selección "K," tienden a tener una productividad baja y requisitos de habitat para anidar estrictos. El manejo adecuado de los loros considerados plagas requieren estrategias que combinen técnicas y recursos existentes de tal manera que reduscan al máximo los daños, sin poner en peligro de extinción a la especie de loro con que se trata, y con mínimos efectos ambientales secundarios. Se discuten varias alternativas. Se da prioridad al uso de cultivos alternos y repelentes avícolas sobre técnicas letales. La promoción de la caza irrestringida no es ni eficiente ni un método justificado para reducir los daños agrícolas y puede causar la extinción de algunas especies.

9. Trade in Neotropical Psittacines and Its Conservation Implications

Jorgen B. Thomsen and Teresa A. Mulliken

TRAFFIC International, World Conservation Monitoring Centre, 219C
Huntingdon Rd., Cambridge CB3 0DL, United Kingdom

Abstract.—Approximately 6% to 10% of the households in the United States keep
exotic pet birds, mostly parakeets and Cockatiels. An estimated 1.8 million Neotropical psittacines were legally exported for trade from 1982 to 1988. The United
States accounted for up to 80% of all Neotropical psittacines traded, followed by
countries in the European Economic Community and Japan. Argentina exported
nearly half of all parrots that were traded from 1982 to 1988. Other countries that
legally exported significant numbers of parrots included Guyana, Surinam, and Peru.
This multi-million dollar trade threatens the existence of some wild parrot populations
and even entire species. Although nearly all exporting and importing countries are
members of CITES, and many exporting countries have trade regulations, the
domestic and international laws which are supposed to ensure that trade does not
result in species declines have been only moderately effective. The role of habitat
destruction appears to have been exaggerated and trade somewhat minimized as the
main causes of the decline of many parrots, although conclusive data are lacking.
Intensive management techniques such as captive breeding and sustained harvesting
(or ranching) may help to meet the demand for pet parrots while reducing pressures
on wild populations. Draft legislation is under development in the United States by
The Cooperative Working Group on Bird Trade that would phase out imports of
wild-caught birds for the pet trade over a five-year period. However, until measures

to control trapping and export are based on species biology and are adequately enforced, international trade is likely to continue to deplete wild Neotropical parrot populations.

Keeping parrots in captivity is a passion and hobby that has appealed to people the world over for centuries. It is also big business. According to Thomsen and Brautigam (1991), the estimated retail value of all Neotropical parrots imported into the United States alone in 1986 was over $300 million. To millions of bird owners, however, the value of exotic birds comes from the pleasure and companionship that they provide, not from their monetary worth.

Although statistics provided by several recent surveys of pet owners vary greatly, they all indicate that avian pets are gaining in popularity in the United States, the world's largest market for wild-caught birds. According to a survey conducted on behalf of the American Pet Products Manufacturers Association, Inc. (APPMA), an estimated 5.2 million residences (6% of all residences) in the United States were home to approximately 13.9 million exotic birds in 1988 (Anon. 1988a). Of these, 43% were "parakeets," 18% were Cockatiels (*Nymphicus hollandicus*), and 14% were other psittacines. Canaries and finches each represented 7% of the total. A survey conducted by Kaytee Products, Inc. (Anon. 1988b), one of the leading pet food and supply manufacturers, estimated that there were over 31 million pet birds in the United States, a figure well over twice that of APPMA. Kaytee's survey indicated that 10% of the households in the United States owned at least one exotic bird. With respect to the relative popularity of different "types" of avian pets, Kaytee's results were similar to those of the APPMA: "parakeets" accounted for 35% of all pet birds, cockatiels for 16%, other psittacines for 10%, and canaries for 6%.

Sixty-three percent of the bird owners polled in the APPMA survey stated that the primary benefits of keeping pet birds were companionship and love. In the Kaytee survey, only 36% of the respondents stated that companionship was their primary reason for purchasing a bird, 24% received a bird as a gift, and 22% purchased a pet as a gift for their children. It is interesting to note that 8% of the bird owners in the Kaytee study stated that they bought a bird for "home decor."

THE MAGNITUDE OF THE COMMERCIAL PARROT TRADE

Home decor or not, their beauty and bright colors, ability to learn to talk, and relative ease of care make Neotropical parrots valued pets and ideal targets for the cage-bird industry. The diversity of Neotropical parrots can accommodate the tastes of almost any keen aviculturist or bird keeper, making these species among the most popular in trade.

Recent studies have documented the use of parrots for food, as sources of feathers for aboriginal plumeary art, and as pets in some South American countries (Thomsen and Brautigam 1991). However, it is the international trade in Neotropical parrots that is the primary source of concern among conservation biologists. More than 1.8 million (43%) of the 4.2 million parrots reported in international trade worldwide between 1982 and 1988 were from the Neotropics (Thomsen and Brautigam 1991, Thomsen unpubl. data). These figures clearly demonstrate the economic importance and popularity of Neotropical parrots as pets.

The estimated volume of international trade in Neotropical parrots cited above probably represents only a fraction of the total number of birds removed from the wild for trade from 1982 to 1988. A number of exporting and importing countries did not report their trade in parrots during some or all of these years. Therefore, it is likely that an additional but unknown number of birds were legally traded during this time. Smuggled birds, having crossed international borders undetected, would further add to the total number of birds in trade. As many as 150,000 parrots may be smuggled across the Mexican border into the United States every year (Thomsen and Hemley 1987). Neotropical birds are smuggled to many other countries as well.

Furthermore, any effort to assess the actual number of birds removed from the wild to support the trade would have to take into account the number of birds dying during the capture and holding process prior to export. If one were to apply the 60% pre-export mortality estimate determined by Ramos and Iñigo (1985) for Mexican parrots to all Neotropical parrot exports, the total harvest from the wild for international trade from 1982 to 1988 would have been almost four million birds.

The monetary value of Neotropical parrots that survive until export is sig-

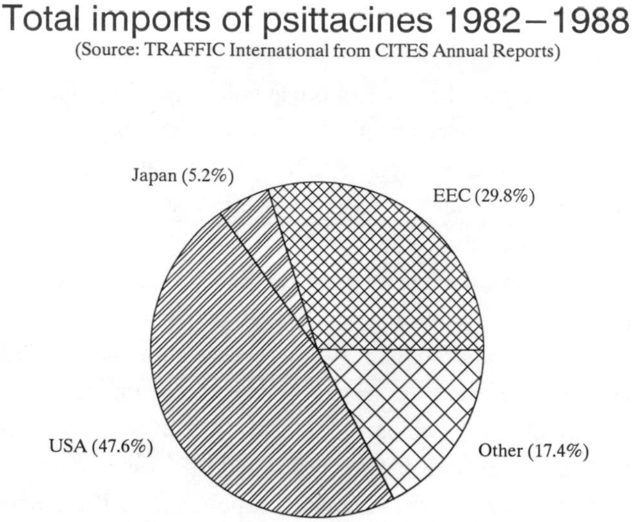

Total imports of psittacines 1982–1988
(Source: TRAFFIC International from CITES Annual Reports)

Fig. 1. Reported volume of psittacines imported by the European Economic Community (EEC), Japan, and the United States from 1982 to 1988.

nificant. The estimated total retail value of the 1.4 million parrots that were legally exported by mainland Neotropical countries from 1982 to 1986 was $1.6 billion (Thomsen and Brautigam 1991).

COUNTRIES INVOLVED IN THE NEOTROPICAL PARROT TRADE

The United States is by far the largest importer of parrots in the world, accounting for nearly half of all psittacines reported in international trade (Fig. 1). The United States consumes an even greater share of the Neotropical psittacines traded internationally. In a given year, up to 80% of the New World parrots reported in trade were exported to the United States. The European Economic Community countries and Japan are also important consumers of Neotropical parrots (Fig. 1). EEC countries consume about 15% to 20% and Japan <3% of the New World parrots traded annually.

The single most important exporter of Neotropical parrots in recent years

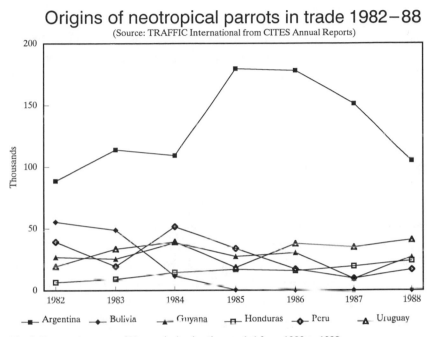

Fig. 2. Reported exports of Neotropical psittacines traded from 1982 to 1988.

has been Argentina (Fig. 2). This country exported more than 920,000 parrots from 1982 to 1988, or 49% of all Neotropical parrots reported in trade during that period. Using retail sales prices from the United States, the total gross retail value of Argentina's parrots was close to one billion dollars (estimate based on Thomsen and Brautigam 1991). Argentina itself received only about one-tenth of this amount.

Major shifts in the Neotropical psittacine trade have taken place since the first United States trade data were published in 1970 (Banks 1970). Both the species composition and the exporting countries involved in the trade have changed dramatically, not so much because of changing tastes of the parrot-buying public but because of changes in the export policies of the countries involved (Fig. 2). In the early 1970s the major exporter nations were Peru, Colombia, Paraguay, and Mexico. Legal exports from the latter three countries virtually ceased following domestic export bans, although illegal trade appears to have continued. Perhaps in response to these bans, other countries, particularly Argentina and Bolivia, assumed larger exporting roles. Bolivia banned wildlife exports in mid-1984 in response to allegations that it had become a trading center for wildlife illegally taken in neighboring countries. Soon after, Argentinean exports increased dramatically, and this country became the single largest exporter of Neotropical parrots.

CURRENT EFFORTS TO CONTROL THE INTERNATIONAL TRADE

Exporting and importing countries have adopted a number of multilateral and domestic measures to control the international trade in Neotropical psittacines and other wildlife. The most widely recognized and implemented international trade control agreement is the Convention on International Trade in Endangered Species of Wild Fauna and Flora (CITES). All of the mainland Neotropical countries are parties to CITES, as are the three key importers of Neotropical psittacines: the United States, the European Economic Community (EEC), and Japan. CITES requires exporting parties to prohibit commercial trade in endangered species listed on CITES Appendix I and to maintain exports of species listed on Appendix II within levels that will not be detrimental to the survival of those species. Exporting parties are required to provide CITES permits for all exports of listed species; these permits are to be inspected upon import to confirm that the wildlife shipments were exported within the framework established by the Convention.

All Neotropical psittacine species are listed on the CITES Appendices: 28 species (see Appendix) are listed on Appendix I, and the remaining species are on Appendix II. International trade in all Neotropical parrots is therefore theoretically controlled in such a manner that no species are endangered by that trade.

Unfortunately, exporting countries generally lack the resources to adequately assess the status or reproductive capacity of their wild parrot populations. As a result, a number of Appendix II species are being trapped for legal export in numbers which appear to threaten local parrot populations and, in some cases, species as a whole. Furthermore, Neotropical countries often lack the enforce-

Table 1. Mainland Neotropical countries prohibiting commercial exports of indigenous wild-caught parrots [compiled from Fuller et al. (1985), Fuller and Gaski (1987), Inskipp et al. (1988), and Anon. (1990)].

Country	Year export ban instituted	Country	Year export ban instituted
Belize	1981	French Guiana*	1986
Bolivia	1984	Guatemala	1986
Brazil	1967	Honduras	1990
Colombia	1973	Mexico	1982
Costa Rica	1970	Paraguay	1975
Ecuador	1981	Venezuela	1970

*French Guiana is a territory of France.

ment personnel necessary to ensure that exports adhere to established CITES control mechanisms. Inadequate inspection, document forgery, and smuggling undermine these countries' efforts to control wildlife exports (Thomsen and Hemley 1987; Gruss and Waller 1988; Anon. 1989a,b; Barzdo et al. 1989). Although Appendix I species such as Hyacinth Macaws (*Anodorhynchus hyacinthinus*) are prohibited from commercial international trade, there is evidence that trapping from the wild for export continues (Munn et al. 1989).

A number of exporting countries have established trade controls which go beyond the minimum requirements of CITES. Thirteen Central and South American countries (Table 1) prohibit commercial exports of indigenous wild-caught birds. All other Neotropical countries have instituted one or more trade-control mechanisms, including licensing requirements for trappers and/or exporters, quota systems, "closed" trapping seasons, and prohibition of trade in certain species (Table 2).

However, the same problems that hinder enforcement of CITES trade controls also reduce the effectiveness of unilateral export control efforts. Countries which prohibit exports, such as Mexico, are often unable to halt illegal trapping and smuggling of their indigenous parrots. Quotas such as those established by the

Table 2. Mainland Neotropical countries allowing commercial export of wild-caught specimens of one or more indigenous parrot species (compiled from references listed in Table 1 and the U.S. Fish and Wildlife Service Computerized Wildlife Trade Data).

Country	Export limited to certain species	Trapper/Exporter licensing required	Quota system	Additional information
Argentina	x	x	x	Quota system established in 1990.
Chile	x			Exports of *Cyanoliseus patagonus* prohibited. Exports to U.S. virtually ended after 1986.
El Salvador				Exports must be authorized by Servicio de Parques Nacionales. Only 6 birds exported to U.S. 1986–1988.
Guyana	x	x	x	Quota system established in 1987.
Nicaragua			x	Quota system established 1991.
Panama	x			Exports of *Ara* spp. and *Amazona ochrocephala* prohibited. Only 42 birds commercially exported to U.S. from 1986 to 1988.
Peru	x	x	x	Quota system established in 1983. Trapping prohibited east of Andes.
Surinam	x	x	x	Quota system established in 1985.
Uruguay	x			Only exports of *Myiopsitta monachus* allowed.

governments of Guyana and Argentina do not appear to be based on a scientific review of parrot populations, and may be in excess of sustainable trade levels.

In Surinam, however, the government has developed a trade control system combining low quotas and exporter licensing which may be maintaining trade within sustainable levels. Surinam established what appears to be conservative export quotas for 21 parrot species based on available population and biological data (Thomsen and Brautigam 1991). Lower quotas were set for larger parrots, such as macaws, than for smaller psittacines. Quotas are reevaluated annually, with initial results indicating that some quotas could be increased in the future without detriment to parrot populations. An export authorization system for parrot exporters, which requires prior membership in an exporters' association, appears to have effectively encouraged compliance with the quotas.

THE IMPACT OF TRADE ON WILD POPULATIONS

The quality of evidence documenting the impacts of trapping for trade on wild populations is often poor. While it is reasonable to assume for species which are both declining and under heavy harvest that the harvest must be at least an important cause contributing to the decline, this is rarely established in a rigorous manner. Nevertheless, if there is any doubt regarding the effects of trade on any psittacine species, many would argue that the easiest and safest option with respect to conserving that species is simply to assume that any and all exploitation has a negative impact on wild populations.

Until quite recently, the only systematic effort to place the international trade of Neotropical parrots in a biological context was provided by Ridgely (1982). He argued that habitat destruction was the greatest threat to the continued survival of Neotropical parrots. Based on extensive surveys throughout Central and South America, Ridgely concluded that the impact of trade on populations of many Neotropical parrot species was not great. Further, he appeared convinced that many of the more numerous species, such as some parakeets, would not decline in the wild even if subject to a considerably greater harvest than that taking place at the time of his study.

Trade has continued largely unabated since the completion of Ridgely's thesis. In fact, trade in many Neotropical parrot species has increased significantly.

A recent study of species traded in "significant" numbers (Inskipp et al. 1988), carried out under the auspices of CITES, concluded that trade represented a threat to many parrot species. In fact, for certain species trade may be the primary factor threatening the survival of wild populations (Collar and Juniper 1991).

The lack of baseline data for wild populations of most parrot species in the trade prevents us from quantitatively assessing the effects of different trade levels on specific populations. However, we do know that the habitats of most species are either changing or being destroyed at great speed (Ridgely 1982). Ironically, this fact is often used to justify the continued large volume of trade. To use the argument of some in the pet industry and aviculture: "if we don't remove the birds from the wild, they'll die anyway due to habitat destruction."

From the perspective of conservation biology, it must be questioned whether for many parrot species the threat caused by habitat alteration has not been somewhat exaggerated. At least 27 species of parrots are free-living and breeding in the United States (Thomsen unpubl. data), indicating that many species can adapt to different food and habitat types. That wild-caught parrots generally do very well in captivity without access to natural food sources also indicates great adaptability. Despite problems presented by the specialized breeding needs of certain species, it seems for a great many species that the prospect of existence in secondary or completely human-made habitats presents less of a threat than the systematic removal from the wild of large components of their populations for the pet trade.

ARE PRESENT TRADE LEVELS SUSTAINABLE?

The problem of determining the sustainability of current or future trade levels is perhaps best illustrated using the example of the United States, the world's largest importer of Neotropical psittacines, and Argentina, the largest exporter of New World parrots. Both countries are party to CITES, but Argentina lacks effective CITES trade control mechanisms (Gruss and Waller 1988). From 1986 to 1988, the United States imported an annual average of 94,000 Neotropical parrots for which international trade presented a "problem" or "possible problem" (Inskipp et al. 1988, Mulliken and Thomsen unpubl. data). Inskipp et al.

(1988) noted that the export of hundreds of thousands of CITES "possible problem" parrots from Argentina accounted for 92% of all Argentinean parrots imported by the United States. "Possible problem" species of the genus *Aratinga* were the most heavily traded, with over 100,000 specimens imported from 1986 to 1988. In addition, over 45,000 Blue-fronted Amazons (*Amazona aestiva*), another CITES "possible problem" species, were imported from Argentina during this time (Mulliken and Thomsen unpubl. data).

Argentina freely allows wildlife to be exported without assessing whether the numbers of animals removed from the wild for international trade are within sustainable limits (Barzdo et al. 1989). Furthermore, little attempt has been made to verify CITES documents accompanying wildlife exports. This suggests that the Argentinean government may not be able to ensure that trade in CITES "problem," "possible problem," or other species is within government-established levels.

It is not a lack of concern but rather a shortage of funds and personnel that prevents Argentinean wildlife authorities from assessing trade impacts and tightening export controls. Recently, Argentina's Dirección Nacional de Fauna Silvestre implemented additional trade control mechanisms, including a quota system for avian exports, which should help that country to more effectively control the utilization of its avian wildlife resources.

Although aware of the trade control problems in Argentina and other South American countries, the United States nevertheless remains the world's single largest importer of CITES "problem" and "possible problem" species. In effect, demand by the United States is driving potentially unsustainable trade in these and perhaps many other avian species. This raises serious questions regarding the willingness of the United States to actively support the sustainable trade goals of CITES and its own domestic legislation.

POTENTIAL FOR SUSTAINABLE EXPLOITATION OF PARROTS

Although 99% of the Neotropical parrots currently in trade are derived from wild sources (Thomsen and Brautigam 1991), it is likely that the parrot trade will go the way of other wildlife trade and increasingly consist of birds originating from intensive management operations. These include captive breeding programs, where parent stock is maintained in a closed environment (Clubb 1991), and sustained harvest or "ranching" operations (Beissinger and Bucher 1991). Ranching involves the collection of eggs and/or young from the wild for rearing in captivity until they reach a size or age when they can be sold commercially. Sustained harvesting may also involve the manipulation of the wild environment to increase the number of birds available for collection by increasing food or nesting opportunities (Beissinger and Bucher 1991).

These intensive management techniques have enjoyed varied economic and conservation success when applied to other animals. The success or failure of captive breeding or ranching operations depends on many factors, including changes in prevailing fashions and therefore demand, other market trends, and rising capital investment and operational costs. Other factors include the reproductive capacity and behavioral adaptability of the species in question, which remain unknown for many species. Even if captive breeding or ranching operations are successful, the changing nature of the trade in a given species may limit their long-term utility. This has been the case with sea turtle ranching, where what otherwise might have been "acceptable" operations have been closed to international markets due to concerns over continued exploitation of wild populations and illegal trade in these globally threatened species.

Although programs such as ranching may have increasing relevance to the potential for sustainable trade, a thorough analysis of whether trade is actually sustainable must be based on the biology of the wild populations in question, and the trade-monitoring and control capacities of exporting and importing countries. Ranching and captive breeding should not be the primary focus of discussion with respect to trade in Neotropical parrots. Instead, the greatest attention should be given to assessing the ability of governments and other responsible institutions to ensure that the removal of birds from the wild, whether for management programs or for domestic or international trade, is either not detrimental to the survival of the species, or is at a level which is sustainable for a species or given population.

It is important to recognize that the ability to develop, let alone implement, any system to ensure that trapping is sustainable depends on the availability of a vast amount of scientific knowledge with respect to the species in question (Beissinger and Bucher 1991). At present, this knowledge is almost entirely unavailable. The paucity of information regarding the status, reproductive biology, population dynamics, ecology, and other parameters specific to an overwhelming proportion of parrot species in international trade precludes any definitive assessment of the sustainability of exploitation. Current trade monitoring and controls must therefore rely to a large degree on guesswork and expert opinion. On one hand, this can jeopardize the survival of species in trade. On the other hand, it can constitute a loss of enormous economic potential with respect to wildlife utilization. A serious problem in the short term, this conflict will become worse as pressures on parrot populations increase.

NEW DIRECTIONS FOR THE WORLD'S LARGEST IMPORTER?

Even as the demand for pet birds appears to be growing in the United States, the efforts of a diverse group of non-governmental organizations may lead to a reduction and eventual elimination of most imports of wild-caught birds into the United States for pets. The Cooperative Working Group on Bird Trade, convened by the World Wildlife Fund and TRAFFIC (USA) in August 1988, is composed of representatives from the pet industry, conservation and animal welfare organizations, aviculture, zoos, and avian veterinary associations. Working Group members have been meeting for more than two years to identify and discuss problems associated with the exotic bird trade in the United States, and to develop workable solutions to the problems. The initial result was a series of recommendations calling for the United States government to: (1) facilitate domestic and foreign captive breeding of birds for the pet market; (2) phase out most imports of wild-caught birds for the pet trade over a five-year period; (3) improve enforcement of current trade regulations; and (4) improve the welfare of birds during all phases of the trade process. Draft federal legislation based on these recommendations is being prepared, with the intention of introducing a federal "bird trade bill" to the U.S. Congress as early as 1991. If the Working Group is successful, the importation of wild-caught exotic birds will only be allowed for captive breeding, educational, and scientific purposes. Imports of certain "common or abundant" species may also be allowed if such imports are determined to be beneficial to the "conservation of that species or the ecosystem it inhabits" (Cooperative Working Group on Bird Trade 1990).

The progress of the Working Group is being watched closely both within the United States and internationally. For the first time, "traditional enemies" such as the pet industry and animal welfare groups have worked together to evaluate the bird trade and develop long-term solutions which collectively address their constituencies' concerns. The recommendations of the Working Group also represent the first real effort to give legislative force to CITES Resolution Conf. 1.6, which "urges . . . that all contracting Parties encourage the breeding of animals for this purpose [pets], with the objective of eventually limiting the keeping of pets to those species which can be bred in captivity" (Conference of the Parties 1976). Adoption of stricter import restrictions in the United States could set a precedent for other importing countries. However, it could also result in exports simply shifting to other countries without reducing the total international trade.

TRADE AS AN ECONOMIC AND BIOLOGICAL SUCCESS OR FAILURE

Can and should parrots be seen as renewable resources which, if effectively managed, can be sustainably used indefinitely, much as certain game species are managed in many parts of the world? In theory the answer to this question is "yes." Unfortunately, the realities of the Neotropical psittacine trade may preclude such idealized management programs, at least in the foreseeable future.

In most South and Central American countries, the parrot trade is composed of several to many competing trappers operating in the absence of any regulations (at least enforceable regulations). These trappers are driven solely by a profit motive, each striving to maximize personal income. The result is a clear example of Garret Hardin's "tragedy of the commons" (Hardin 1968). In many instances, especially in the case of rare or declining species, there is an incentive to trap as many specimens as quickly as possible. With a philosophy of "every man for himself," trappers realize that if they do not catch a parrot quickly, someone else probably will. In either case the bird will no longer exist in the wild and therefore will not provide a source of future income.

Obviously the species in the wild, the ecosystem, and human society as a whole are the losers in such a process. And if pursued to its logical conclusion, such a "management program" ultimately results in the loss of income for the trappers and traders themselves. This is precisely where the Neotropical parrot trade, as currently practiced and regulated, is headed. A lack of incentive to conserve is leading to the permanent depletion of psittacine resources.

During the 1980s, campaigns to ban the importation of parrots and other exotic birds, launched by animal welfare and conservation groups, made the pet industry slowly realize that the supply of wild-caught birds for international trade would eventually end. This realization has resulted in an incentive system similar to that operating in exporting countries, namely to maximize immediate profit opportunities without regard to the implications for the species in the wild. This situation is especially dangerous for the slower maturing and reproducing species like macaws, because indiscriminate trapping may lead to the rapid elimination of entire wild populations.

The exploitation of the Hyacinth Macaw is a case in point. In the "early days" of high-volume trade in this species, almost all specimens captured were chicks taken from nests in Brazil. However, as demand and prices increased in the 1980s, there were no longer sufficient chicks available in the main trapping areas to meet the demand. As a result, more and more adult birds were trapped for trade until eventually all the birds traded were specimens from the adult population (Munn et al. 1987, Thomsen unpubl. data). The net effect of this "management system" has been clear: within just 30 years, large areas of prime Hyacinth Macaw habitat have been emptied of birds (Munn et al. 1989). Ironically, during most of this period, Brazil had laws which completely banned the trapping and export of this species. Continued trade in Hyacinth Macaws was only possible because the country of origin was falsely identified on export documents for birds smuggled from Brazil into Bolivia.

Today there is general agreement within the scientific and conservation communities that current levels of exploitation of Neotropical parrots do not ensure the long-term viability of many wild populations. But as has been seen in the case of the Hyacinth Macaw, unilateral efforts to ban the trade in one or more species will remain ineffective as long as even one country is prepared to allow trade to continue unregulated. Multilateral trade control measures, such as those provided by CITES, will also be unlikely to result in effective trade restrictions, as the data required to support such measures have so far been insufficient. Unless a trading regime based on sound biological principles and levels of trade specific to the status of individual species is developed, there will be no success in developing rational exploitation schemes that allow the sustained use of Neotropical parrots as a renewable resource.

LITERATURE CITED

Anonymous. 1988a. Pets in the United States. Pet Business Magazine 14(9): 28–30.

Anonymous. 1988b. Your cagebird customer and the importance of the retailer in consumer buying decisions. Chilton, Wisconsin, Kaytee Products, Inc., Kaytee Educational Service, volume 1.

Anonymous. 1989a. "Operations psittacine" is a success. TRAFFIC (USA) 9(1):5–6.

Anonymous. 1989b. Cuban parrots caught in Miami. TRAFFIC (USA) 9(1): 8–9.

Anonymous. 1990. Argentina establishes bird quotas. TRAFFIC (USA) 10(1):22.

Banks, R. 1970. Birds imported into the United States in 1968. Washington, District of Columbia, U.S. Department of the Interior, Special Scientific Report—Wildlife No. 136.

Barzdo, J., S. Broad, T. Inskipp, & R. Luxmoore (Eds.). 1989. Problems in CITES Implementation: case studies in four selected countries. Lausanne, Switzerland, World Wide Fund for Nature.

Beissinger, S. R., & E. H. Bucher. 1991. Sustainable harvesting of parrots for conservation. This volume.

Clubb, S. L. 1991. The role of private aviculture in the conservation of Neo-tropical psittacines. This volume.

Collar, N. J., & A. T. Juniper. 1991. Dimensions and causes of the parrot conservation crisis. This volume.

Conference of the Parties, Berne, Switzerland. 1976. Conf. Resolution 1.6. Lausanne, Switzerland, Secretariat of the Convention on International Trade in Endangered Species of Wild Flora and Fauna.

Cooperative Working Group on Bird Trade. 1990. Findings and recommendations. Washington, District of Columbia, World Wildlife Fund.

Fuller, K., & A. Gaski. 1987. Update to Latin American wildlife trade laws. Washington, District of Columbia, World Wildlife Fund.

Fuller, K., B. Swift, A. Jorgenson, & A. Brautigam. 1985. Latin American wildlife trade laws, second edition. Washington, District of Columbia, World Wildlife Fund.

Gruss, J. X., & T. Waller. 1988. Diagnostico y recomendaciones sobre la administracion de recursos silvestres en Argentina; la decada reciente. Montevideo, Uruguay, TRAFFIC Sudamerica.

Hardin, G. 1968. The tragedy of the commons. Science 162:1243–1248.

Inskipp, T., S. Broad, & R. Luxmoore. 1988. Significant trade in wildlife: a review of selected species in CITES Appendix II. Volume II: Birds. Lausanne, Switzerland, International Union for Conservation of Nature, and Secretariat of the Convention on International Trade in Endangered Species of Wild Fauna and Flora.

Munn, C. A., J. B. Thomsen, & C. Yamashita. 1987. Survey and status of the Hyacinth Macaw (*Anodorhynchus hyacinthinus*) in Brazil, Bolivia, and Paraguay. Lausanne, Switzerland, Secretariat of the Convention on International Trade in Endangered Species of Wild Fauna and Flora.

Munn, C. A., J. B. Thomsen, & C. Yamashita. 1989. Hyacinth Macaw. Pages 404–419 *in* Audubon Wildlife Report 1989/1990 (W. J. Chandler, Ed.). New York, Academic Press.

Ramos, O. M., & E. Iñigo. 1985. Comercialización de Psitácidos en México. Memoria Primer Simposium Internacional de Fauna Silvestre, vol. 2. México, D.F.

Ridgely, R. S. 1982. The distribution, status, and conservation of Neotropical mainland parrots. New Haven, Connecticut, Yale University, Ph.D. Dissertation.

Thomsen, J. B., & A. Brautigam. 1991. Sustainable use of Neotropical parrots. Pages 359–379 *in* Neotropical wildlife use and conservation (J. G. Robinson & K. H. Redford, Eds.). Chicago, University of Chicago Press.

Thomsen, J. B., & G. Hemley. 1987. Bird trade . . . bird bans. TRAFFIC (USA) 7(2&3):1, 21–24.

Appendix

Neotropical parrots listed in Appendix I of the Convention on International Trade in Endangered Species of Wild Fauna and Flora. This list includes parrots that are threatened with extinction which are or may be affected by international trade.

Common Name	Scientific Name
Red-necked Amazon	*Amazona arausiaca*
Yellow-shouldered Amazon	*Amazona barbadensis*
Red-tailed Amazon	*Amazona brasiliensis*
Red-browed Amazon	*Amazona dufresniana rhodocorytha*
St. Vincent Amazon	*Amazona guildingii*
Imperial Amazon	*Amazona imperialis*
Cuban Amazon	*Amazona leucocephala*
Red-spectacled Amazon	*Amazona pretrei*
Tucuman Amazon	*Amazona tucumana*
St. Lucia Amazon	*Amazona versicolor*
Vinaceous Amazon	*Amazona vinacea*
Puerto Rican Amazon	*Amazona vittata*
Glaucous Macaw	*Anodorhynchus glaucus*
Hyacinth Macaw	*Anodorhynchus hyacinthinus*
Lear's Macaw	*Anodorhynchus leari*
Buffon's Macaw	*Ara ambigua*
Blue-throated Macaw	*Ara glaucogularis*
Scarlet Macaw	*Ara macao*
Illiger's Macaw	*Ara maracana*
Military Macaw	*Ara militaris*
Red-fronted Macaw	*Ara rubrogenys*
Golden Conure	*Aratinga guarouba = Guaruba guarouba*
Spix's Macaw	*Cyanopsitta spixii*
Yellow-eared Conure	*Ognorhynchus icterotis*
Pileated Parrot	*Pionopsitta pileata*
Blue-throated Conure	*Pyrrhura cruentata*
Thick-billed Parrot	*Rhynchopsitta pachyrhyncha*
Maroon-fronted Parrot	*Rhynchopsitta terrisi*

Resumen.—Aproximadamente del 6% al 10% de los domicilios en los Estados Unidos mantienen aves exóticas como mascotas, la mayoría son periquitos y *Nymphicus hollandicus*. Se calcula que de 1982 a 1988 1.8 millones de psitácidos neotropicales fueron exportados legalmente para el comercio de mascotas. Los Estados Unidos fue responsable de casi el 80% del comercio de psitácidos neotropicales, seguido por países en la comunidad económica europea y Japón. Argentina exportó casi la mitad de todos los loros comerciados de 1982 a 1988. Otros países que exportaron legalmente números significativos de loros incluyen Guyana, Surinam, y el Perú. Este comercio multimillonario (en dólares) pone en peligro cada vez más la existencia de poblaciones silvestres de loros y hasta especies enteras. Aunque casi todos los países que exportan e importan son miembros de "CITES," y muchos de los países exportadores tienen reglamentos sobre el comercio, las leyes nacionales e internacionales que deben asegurar que la captura para el comercio no resulte en reducciones de especies por lo general han sido inefectivas. El papel de la destrucción de habitat aparenta ser exagerada y el comercio algo ignorado como causas principales de la reducción de muchos loros, aunque faltan datos concluyentes. Técnicas de manejo intensivo como la reproducción en cautiverio y la explotación sostenible en fincas puede ayudar a satisfacer la demanda para loros mascotas mientras reduce la presión sobre poblaciones silvestres. En los Estados Unidos el "Cooperative Working Group on Bird Trade" está desarroyando legislación inicial que durante el transcurso de cinco años eliminaría la importación de aves capturadas en su habitat silvestre para el comercio de mascotas. Sin embargo, hasta que las medidas para controlar la captura y exportación se basen en la biología de las especies y son adecuadamente aplicadas, el comercio internacional seguramente seguirá reduciendo poblaciones silvestres de loros neotropicales.

10. A Round-table Discussion of Parrot Trade Problems and Solutions

Edited by Frances C. James

Department of Biological Science, Florida State University,
Tallahassee, Florida 32306-1043

The discussion that follows is the edited transcript of a one-hour session held at the American Ornithologists' Union (AOU) meeting on 29 June 1990 at the University of California, Los Angeles. The session was the final part of a full-day symposium on the biology and conservation of Neotropical parrots. Participants who had delivered papers were joined on the stage by the coauthors of their papers and by several additional specialists, 15 panelists altogether. The objective was to discuss with the audience the complexities of the international trade in wild psittacines and to explore solutions.

We heard during the course of the day that the exact extent of the declines in parrot populations had not been well documented, nor was it clear to what extent these declines were attributable to habitat destruction. Nevertheless, it was clear that the thousands of wild birds which are sold each year in the international pet trade are a major factor contributing to population declines. The overall message of the panelists was that this issue deserves much more attention from ornithologists, conservationists, and the general public than it has been receiving thus far.

I served as moderator of the discussion. Later, speakers were given an opportunity to edit the transcripts of their own contributions. I edited the material, with the help of Anne Thistle of Florida State University, only to make it more readable.

Moderator (James): First, I'll introduce our distinguished experts in psittacology: Nigel Collar, Noel Snyder, Scott Derrickson, Rosemarie Gnam, Susan Clubb, Paul Butler, Robert Ridgely, Joseph Forshaw, Marcia Wilson, Steven Beissinger, Donald Bruning, Charles Munn, Jorgen Thomsen, James Wiley, and Enrique Bucher. Members of the audience can direct questions to a specific person on the panel or can ask a general question, and we'll see who wants to answer it.

As an introduction to our discussion, I will summarize the most important things that I learned today. Nigel Collar and Tony Juniper showed us that populations of many species of parrots seem to be declining precipitously. Then Charlie Munn told us that ecotourism shows promise in Peru and elsewhere, and Paul Butler told about his exciting accomplishments with education programs in small communities in the West Indies. Susan Clubb says that the aviculture industry is anxious to work together with biologists and conservationists in parrot conservation. We need to pursue that. Scott Derrickson and Noel Snyder told us about all the difficulties with captive breeding. James Wiley, Noel Snyder, and Rosemarie Gnam summarized the extra complications associated with reintroduction programs. Steve Beissinger's and Enrique Bucher's warnings of how complex the social behavior of parrots is and how little we know about their population dynamics were sobering. Finally, Jorgen Thomsen and Teresa Mulliken presented alarming statistics about the magnitude of the international pet trade and how, in spite of United States' and international laws, the situation seems to be out of control.

One topic that hasn't been discussed is problems with law enforcement in the United States and the magnitude of the illegal trade. I'm going to ask the panel to comment on that before we have comments from the floor. Would someone begin with a statement about the magnitude of the illegal trade?

Thomsen: I can try. It's very difficult to estimate, of course. It's a lot easier to count the birds that we see on the permits. The law enforcement agencies and the Department of Justice in the United States have tried to estimate the magnitude of illegal trade. During the 1980s those estimates have varied from 25,000 parrots being smuggled into the United States on an annual basis to anywhere between 100,000 and 150,000 birds. These estimates are all based on known cases of smuggled birds and on trends known from other criminal activities in the same localities, primarily the Mexican border. The drug trade has been used as a basis for extrapolation to the illegal bird trade. The birds being smuggled are primarily of a few species, to a large extent birds from Central America and Mexico in particular.

I don't have a big picture of the illegal trade. What have always fascinated me are the occasional stories and the specific cases that you hear. One that had alarmed me—I think it was in 1979—was a bona fide, documented case of 20,000 Lilac-crowned or Finch's Parrots (*Amazonia finschi*) that were dropped over the border in gunny sacks. That's essentially the total annual production of baby birds for Nayarit, Sinaloa, and Sonora (Mexico) combined. Those sorts of cases add up. I think 50,000 birds per year is the best estimate of the number of Neotropical parrots smuggled into the United States. Quite high.

Moderator: There's also the document-fraud problem and the trans-shipment problem, which I don't think we've covered either. Would anyone like to comment on that?

Thomsen: Well, of course, document fraud occurs in the bird trade just as in any other wildlife trade. So does trade in birds that are captured in countries that prohibit export, smuggled into countries that do allow export, and then laundered, so to speak, under legal documents there. It's very difficult to estimate the size of that type of trade. It's quite clear that, after Bolivia shut down exports in mid-1984, very few birds came into the United States from Bolivia. But at the same time, Argentina increased its exports, so in fact the total volume of birds exported the previous year by Bolivia and Argentina together was equalled by the following year's export from Argentina alone. We now know from studies in Argentina that a lot of birds that originated from Bolivia were in fact traded through Argentina. But the extent of this type of fraud is very difficult to estimate.

Bucher: Just a comment that reinforces this point. *Brotogeris versicolorus* is a species that occurs only marginally in Argentina. There are only three records in the literature, the last one in the 1950s, but during the last three years Argentina has exported over 3,000 specimens. They probably came from Paraguay.

Moderator: This is apparently a problem in the worldwide trade. It's not just Neotropical parrots. It has led many countries to ban exports.

Thomsen: Yes, that is true, but I also think it's important not to overrate the problem. Illegal trade and laundering of birds are only serious problems if the trade is not sustainable. I think, from listening to the papers today, that the most important lesson is that we either don't know or can't actually prove that large numbers of species in trade are being traded at unsustainable levels. I think what we should discuss today is what to do in that situation. Biological principles are not being applied to this trade. Clearly, the decision to export 30,000 Blue-fronted Amazons (*Amazona aestiva*) a year is not based on surveys and is not based on sound biological principles. I think that's really the key point in this forum.

Bucher: I think that we have to be careful. In some of the cases where you may think that the trade is sustainable, in reality it is so only because there is a moving frontier of agricultural development; the birds are coming from the edge of the original over-mature forest. Once the whole region is developed, then you can expect a sudden crash in population and in exportation. Another point that is important to consider is that in parrots you may have a very big component of nonbreeding birds within the population that trade is exploiting. Consequently, there is no sudden decline in productivity of young at the beginning, because losses in breeding pairs are compensated by nonbreeders that start breeding in a density-dependent fashion. But then you can expect a sudden crash once all the nonbreeding segments of the population have already entered into reproduction, leaving no potential for further compensation.

Questioner: I'd like to make a couple of statements and ask a question, too. My question, which is addressed to the TRAFFIC people, is why did they, unlike the AOU, retain *Amazona ochrocephala* as a single species? I ask this question partly because I live in Guatemala, and Guatemalan birds tend to disappear into Mexico and Honduras. Quite obviously, the west-coast bird would be hard for the Hondurans to smuggle if it were split into the species as it is now done by the AOU. Guatemalan birds tend to go out through southern Mexico, particularly Tapachula. In Guatemala, rural people collect chicks, often very young chicks. These collectors have improved their system in one way in the last 10 years. They no longer cut down the trees. They now use climbing irons to climb the trees, because the number of trees, particularly on the south coast, is very low. The number of *Amazona* parrots—just from visual reports—has probably halved in the last 10 years. In the north, there are still large forests and populations of parrots.

Moderator: Do you have a question for the panel?

Questioner: Yes. We don't seem to have any data from the Latin American countries on domestic consumption. I think that this is a huge hole in the data necessary to make any kind of numerical predictions. I am going to address this problem when I get back to Guatemala. I plan to set up some household surveys in different socioeconomic groups inside of Guatemala City to get some idea of how many parrots are in households there. I think we will find it's a much larger number than many people think. There is a huge internal market. Turning off the external market will probably just drive the internal market price down and may not necessarily reduce the flow that much.

Moderator: Thank you. You make the point that we don't have enough information to set quotas and that we don't know the size of the trade within countries, or the real drain that our trade is causing in the international market.

Questioner: Since we are talking about illegal trade, I will comment on the quota issue. When species are cited in Appendix 1 of CITES, their trade value goes up because they're illegal. I want to know what's being done in the consuming countries to change the fact that any bird that comes into the country is legal once it's there. Many birds come through Mexico, and once they're in the United States, they just flow through the system and nobody does anything about it.

Bruning: I'm not sure I can help you much. Unfortunately it's very true that illegal birds flow through the system and don't get caught. A few do. In a few recent cases there have been some convictions, but it's far too little, too slow, and largely too late. Much of the problem really comes down to the fact that, as long as there are people willing to purchase wild birds, the flow seems to continue. There are also other problems, for example, the mortality question. We need to know the mortality of birds all the way along the trade chain. What we really need now is more ornithologists willing to go out and help us get some of the data that we need to document what is happening. With the support of ornithologists and the public, we could get law enforcement people to do more about enforcing regulations. But it's going to take an all-around effort. I'm not sure that answers your question. It's very unfortunate, but enforcement is nothing like what it ought to be. I'm not sure there is an answer to the problem.

Questioner: I have a question for all the panelists. I'd like to know how many people on the panel support a total ban on the import of wild-caught birds. How many support a partial ban? And no ban?

Snyder: I think you could ask the question, "How many people support a moratorium, which might or might not lead to a ban?" as an alternative. I'll raise my hand on that.

Questioner: What do you mean by a moratorium?

Snyder: A time-limited total ban. In other words, a cessation that after study might or might not lead to selective reopening of trade but would be tied to assessment of the viability of populations for harvest.

Forshaw: I feel somewhat out on a limb here. My experience is in another part of the world [Australia]. I don't wish to set myself up as offering any advice on what is an extremely complicated situation in the Neotropics. However, I'm appalled by the facts and figures that have come out; it's quite obvious that this situation cannot be allowed to continue. If it is, then it will be on all our heads.

A total ban or a moratorium? I don't want to be put in a position to defend a total ban by any nation, including my own, which has had a total ban in operation for 31 years. That is up to each nation to decide. Let me say that I can readily understand nations moving to a total ban when the present situation, as it is now, operates internationally. As far as enforcement is concerned, every enforcement officer that I have met and every enforcement agency has said to me that a total ban is not fully enforcible but that a partial ban is unenforcible. I guess that's one of the problems that we're faced with in Australia. We believe that for our purposes the total ban has worked and has worked well. Sure, we have smuggling, and we have animal welfare problems, and we have people getting around the regulations, but we do not have exportation of the massive numbers of birds that you have from the Neotropics. That says something for a total ban.

It seems to me that we are really talking about the niceties of procedure before we've got the ground rules laid, and I don't think we can operate that way. Therefore, I didn't vote on the question that was put to me for the exact same reasons that Noel Snyder mentioned. I don't know that a total ban would work, but I think we must have a breathing space. We must air out everybody, to get right back to the basics, to the principles that we all operate on as biologists. If we're going to talk about sustained harvesting, we don't harvest before we've got the information. There must be a complete moratorium, and we have to go right back to square one and have everybody sit down and work on deciding where to start.

If it would make that moratorium more palatable, then some of the species that Steve Beissinger and Enrique Bucher mentioned that obviously can withstand trade could be exempted. But if we take that decision, it is taken arbitrarily, not on biological principles. We must accept that. Then we can all stand back and look at the situation. As ornithologists we can only work from the principles of our discipline. I agree with Steve Beissinger and Enrique Bucher that all these other attitudes, pseudopolitical, social, economic, etc., are important. But we are ornithologists, we are biologists. We have to provide the policymakers with the right decisions on the basis of scientific principles, and at the moment we're just not in a position to do that.

Questioner: My name is Laura Simon, and I've been studying the effects of one ban, the New York ban, which many of you know was passed in 1984. It restricts the New York bird trade to captive-bred birds. The law went into effect in 1986, and four years later I'm studying whether the law is working. I'm finding that there are a number of problems inherent in the law itself. More specifically, the continuing trade in wild birds is having negative impacts on the New York law. First, one of the bigger problems is that retailers say they cannot get certain species from breeders because they're just not being bred. Because imported birds are so cheap, there is no incentive for breeders to breed birds like African finches or Blue-fronted Amazons. So New York retailers can't get them. If we allow birds to be imported that can be sustainably utilized, say Orange-winged Amazons (*Amazona amazonica*), are we going to be discouraging breeding efforts because these species will be available so much cheaper? Blue-fronted Amazons are imported as chicks and fledglings, which make just as good pets as captive-bred birds. Because of the price differential, who's going to be breeding these birds? There's really no incentive. I'd like to hear from anybody who has a suggestion.

Clubb: Well, if we look at the economics of the pet bird industry over the last couple of years, and we take into account the possibility of a partial ban on importation in the future, I think we're going to see a change in the economic situation. Certainly people throughout the United States are being educated in the difference between a pet that is a captive-bred bird and one that is a wild-caught bird. I'm not talking specifically about baby Blue-fronted Amazons but about species typically wild-caught as adults. People are beginning to want captive-bred birds for pets. The price difference affects their decisions. If birds are imported in much lower numbers and aviculture counteracts with higher production, the prices of captive-bred birds will drop dramatically every year. This has been happening in the last two years, especially. I think any aviculturist will tell you that the prices are continuing to go down. But with the limited availability of wild-caught birds due to a ban on importation of some type, prices for pet birds will go up. I think that we will see a change in supply and demand, such that the aviculturist who wants mature wild-caught birds for breeding is going to be willing to pay a higher price, whereas a person who wants a pet bird, if they can get that bird for maybe the same price or a little lower, is going to buy a captive-bred one. I think these changes in the economic situation will happen if a partial ban is put in place.

Beissinger: I'd like to add something to this debate. In many instances in conservation we need to consider who benefits from our attempts at regulation. One aspect that we need to consider carefully is the north-south situation within our hemisphere. There are some benefits of a trade in birds. For example, some of the economic effects go back to the local people. Enrique Bucher and I mentioned sustainable development, or ecological economics, an area of conservation that is starting to emerge. In the captive breeding process here in the United States, we are very happy to take Latin American birds and breed them for our own profits, but we are not happy to receive birds that might be bred in a sustainable manner in Latin America, where money might go back into that economy. Realize that if you value a bird in its natural habitat, you also give value to the natural habitat, and that gives some impetus for local conservation of forest habitat. In part I think Nigel Collar's and Tony Juniper's presentation and Joe Forshaw's follow-up comments above suggest that, if the trade doesn't devastate a species, then habitat destruction may eventually do so. We also need to be aware of the long-term picture.

Forshaw: Could I just make a quick comment? Foreign finches are, from our point of view, a long way removed from parrots, but Australian aviculturists are the largest breeders of African finches in the world and also of the Cuban

Finch or Grassquit (*Tiaris canora*). We export them all over the world. Australian aviculturists are allowed to do that because they are nonnative birds. Aviculturists were forced to breed nonnative finches when the ban came down in 1959, and they've been extremely successful. The numbers were very low. Now not only do Australian aviculturists support our own domestic trade, but they support the international trade as well. It's far removed from parrots but I think the principle I'm trying to point out is very applicable.

Bruning: But it's not that far from parrots. European breeders over the last 25 years have become experts at breeding Australian parrots for the same reason. Because Australian parrots were suddenly shut off from the European market by the Australian ban, today you see a very significant number of the Australian species that are traded. Even some species that are regarded as endangered or threatened in Australia are in fact being bred in fairly large numbers in Europe. Even in the United States now.

Questioner: My name is Ruth Russell. One of the solutions to the problems with the New York law, which many of us regard as a model, would be a federal law. I was wondering if anyone would address the proposal made by the recent coalition, which included many avicultural organizations, that would impose a ban on importation in five years but would allow exceptions by permit for breeders, for zoos, and for research. Would anyone care to comment? I guess I'm really hoping that sometime in the near future the AOU will take a position that will support some of these things. I know the AOU's been working on the issue, but we haven't gotten there yet. Other national organizations have taken positions, and the AOU represents the people who seem to me to be the ones who should be taking the lead. Perhaps some of you could speak to that, so that we could get a sense of what this group feels about the future of that plan from such a large consortium.

Moderator: You're talking about the TRAFFIC (USA)-sponsored working group that Jorgen Thomsen and Teresa Mulliken discussed, so he's the one to answer.

Thomsen: Yes, I was in the lucky position to help draft a lot of the language that led to some of the recommendations. This group worked for about two years. During its work, all the recommendations that were developed were confidential and were released just a few months ago. It was an eye-opener for everybody, an educational process. The group included animal welfare groups, the pet industry, avian vets, and scientific and conservation groups. The recommendations addressed a series of questions about the current importation system, quarantines, and so forth, but I guess the overall feeling among this diverse group of constituencies was that the current level of trade is unsustainable. At least, for the cases where we don't have baseline data, the levels are so high that it's quite likely that they are unsustainable.

Therefore the group, together with the industry, recommended that the United States federal legislative system introduce new, improved regulations that aim at phasing out imports of wild-caught birds for the commercial pet trade. The group has consciously made a distinction between imports for the commercial pet trade and imports for breeding purposes. The recommendation is that, after this five-year phaseout, imports be permitted to continue to supplement registered breeding facilities that are producing birds to meet the demand for the same species.

During the five-year phaseout, the group has also recommended that a number of other actions be taken. Clearly, for a number of species, imports into the United States represent a risk to their survival, and there's no reason why the federal system should not ban the trade of those species. At the same time, the group says, if it can be documented later that the same species have populations that can sustain trade, there is no reason why trade shouldn't open up again. There was not a consensus on this final point.

In summary, what the group has recommended is that over a five-year period the import of wild-caught birds for the commercial pet trade should be phased out. The mechanism suggested by the group is an import-permit system instituted by the U.S. Department of Interior so that all bird imports to the United States would actually require an import permit and not just an export permit, which is the case right now for at least some species. Under an import-permit system, you can establish quotas and gradually reduce the trade.

Beissinger: I can speak to the issue of the AOU's moving on this matter. We find ourselves almost in a retroactive rather than a proactive position in the sense that a lot of groundwork has been done already. This working group is a major step toward conflict resolution in these kinds of conservation problems, bringing together a diverse group ranging from the pet trade to conservationists to animal rights people. The AOU, at least the Conservation Committee, has asked me to chair an ad hoc committee that will examine these issues and try to produce some kind of position paper that we as a society might be able to support.

Questioner: My name is John Fitzpatrick. I'm not an expert on parrots, but I have been taking part in a long-term study of a *K*-selected species for 20 years. I've been considering as I listen to these talks whether we have enough information on the Florida Scrub Jay (*Aphelocoma coerulescens*) yet to allow construction of a scenario for its harvest that would keep that population from declining. I don't think we do. That isn't to say that it isn't possible; Steve Beissinger and Enrique Bucher made a very important list of pieces of information that would be required to understand the population biology of a bird as complex and as long-lived as a parrot before one could imagine constructing a system whereby you could harvest it on a sustained basis. It's difficult to identify any species of bird in the world for which we have that information, much less species as difficult to study and as variable as parrots. I submit that we don't have that kind of information for any species of parrot in the New World, and that leads me frankly to commend Joe Forshaw in his restraint in these last few minutes of this meeting. I find it very difficult to avoid a quiet fury that the AOU is so reticent still to recognize what it has to do, which is to proclaim that it is time to stop imports for a period of time. Noel Snyder's idea of five years seems perfectly legitimate. Just plain stop the importation of these birds for a period of time and set out a series of steps whereby we could begin to study species that might be harvestable in the future. To allow the trade to go on year after year while we all sit in a panel like this in a room like this and see the populations decline to me is simply just inexcusable.

Questioner: In response to that comment, will a moratorium or a ban increase smuggling?

Thomsen: I'll take a crack at that question. It was contended that, when the New York law was passed, it would increase smuggling, but I don't think there is any real documented information that it has. Smuggling existed before and will exist after. There is probably good reason to suspect that a ban will increase smuggling in the beginning. At the same time you would have to beef up law enforcement to bring the smuggling down in the long term. If you don't, you're just going to change the problem. A ban would make enforcement easier because it's a lot harder to hide birds if you don't have a huge volume of legal or quasi-legal trade.

Simon: Since the New York law went into effect, there have been three cases of Newcastle-infected birds coming into the state, which is not any different than it was before, according to the U.S. Department of Agriculture. They felt assured that there was no increase in smuggling in New York after the law went into effect. Smugglers target the United States, not New York or any other state specifically. New York buys out of the same pipeline as all the other states.

Forshaw: I'm not sure that we would know whether smuggling increased because we don't know how much there is now. But another point—it will depend to some extent on how the moratorium is put in place. If, as I would hope, it is put in place with the general agreement of all vested interests, then the potential for the rewards to the smugglers may be lessened. In other words, if we all go into the moratorium with the general agreement that it is in the long-term interest of all legitimate parties concerned, then the incentives to smuggle birds might not be so great. That may be idealistic, but we should at least try to achieve it.

Questioner: My question concerns the European community countries. If there is any moratorium in the United States, I believe Europe should have a moratorium at the same time. Otherwise the trade is simply going to change channels, to Europe or maybe even Japan, which I understand is still quite low in this business.

Thomsen: The European community has tried to deal with the question we're debating today. Since they started implementing CITES on a community level in 1984, they have progressively decided on their own either to stop or to impose quotas on import of a number of species. The mechanism they have used is that all wildlife imports into the 12 community states require an import permit. They can decide, at the community level, no longer to issue permits for imports of Blue-fronted Amazons from Argentina. They have in fact done so. In 1987 the European Economic Community (EEC) forced Guyana, which is currently one of the largest exporters of parrots in South America, to stop exporting parrots. They simply threatened an immediate end to imports of *any* wildlife from Guyana.

The United States did not participate. The United States waited until CITES or the secretariat of this treaty said that perhaps the EEC is right and there is a problem in Guyana. Then the United States acted as well. The United States is the largest import market in the world. Restricting imports, for at least some of the more sensitive species, could therefore make a real difference. Japan represents probably only about 10% to 15% of the total trade, if we look at all birds. There are new ideas coming out of Japan these days as well. Certainly restrictions by the United States and Europe alone would represent quite some difference.

Questioner: I'd like to point out that this group is probably the best equipped to do a couple of very important things. The first is to implement some good field studies, so we can get some quality data. I've heard several people today say that all species are declining when in fact we really don't know. To continue to be perceived as a responsible group, you need not only to obtain some good field data but also to refrain from quoting figures based on weak estimates. Doing so can only undermine your individual efforts.

Thomsen: May I ask Bob Ridgely a question? About 10 years ago, Bob did his dissertation on mainland Neotropical parrots. He did a lot of surveying and also looked at trade levels. I think he is quite aware of the species in trade today and the levels. Perhaps he has a couple of comments or perhaps can compare the current situation with that 10 years ago.

Ridgely: Well, that's a major order obviously. I can probably make the most sense of an incredibly complex situation by referring to the country that I know best, Ecuador, where I've been spending a good bit of time in recent years as well as back in the mid-1970s.

There is no question in my mind that certain species have undergone catastrophic declines in Ecuador over the last 15-year period. I would point in particular to *Aratinga erythrogenys*, which occurred in the thousands in southwestern Ecuador. It was a very common, widespread species in the mid- to late 1970s. Now it is at a population level where you really have to look for the odd dozen or two, perhaps 50 in remote canyons with relatively low human population density. In 1977 there were thousands of them passing over Guayaquil every morning and evening. If there is one anywhere near there now, I don't know where it is. Indeed that conure has been very extensively harvested in Ecuador during that period. It is my understanding that they have been smuggled through Peru. I have no information about the current status of Peruvian populations, but I suspect that they have also been affected seriously by the trade. It's devastating to me that this has been happening. It shows what concerted efforts to trap birds and export birds over a decade can do to a population.

To summarize, I think indeed we are in trouble, and I would support a partial ban or partial moratorium. In fact I actually think that a virtually permanent moratorium on import of certain species is called for, until we come up with some sort of data to indicate that sustainable trade is going to be viable in the long run.

Bucher: I would like to add a comment on the need for reliable figures. My feeling is that, although there is a need for surveys and censusing, we also urgently need a more dynamic approach to the problem. We need to know more about the interactions between natural vegetation and parrots, population dynamics and social facilitation, and other aspects that apparently are crucial to the way a typical parrot population behaves. We are still far from knowing enough. So although I think that we need surveys, I will try to leave the message that we should go into a more functional kind of research.

Munn: I'd like to elaborate on that last comment. I think you should actually push it a bit further and do some of the kinds of experiments that Steve Beissinger is suggesting. For example, try to get local people land tenure, and then try to work with them in some experimental projects to see whether they could produce parrots and under what types of circumstances. Do not wait until we have all the biological parameters exactly clear. I don't think we have to worry about whether we're doing everything precisely right in the beginning. These are models that will spread quickly. The international funding organizations, actually the multinational banks, will have to help get the people who are living on the land to own the land. Then you can talk with them about how to manage their resources, which include parrots.

Butler: I think it's important to note, particularly in the presence of so many scientists, the need for research to be applied. As a biologist by training who spent 11 years as a resource manager in a developing nation, I have seen far too many valuable scientific documents sit unused, gathering dust on the shelves of forestry departments around the region. If our work is to translate into action, it must be written in a format that those whose responsibility it is to initiate such action can comprehend. Complex computer models and theoretical data will not be used by resource managers in our islands if their content cannot be immediately understood. Many of our officers lack advanced training, and for them to persuade politicians to take action, they need supporting data that is simple and unambiguous and that clearly spells out the socioeconomic benefits as well as the ecological ones.

Questioner: I'm Nancy Hilgert de Benavides. In Ecuador last year, a foreign avicultural company that has also been to Peru and Guyana asked to open a breeding ranch for parrots and toucans. They asked our permission and our support (i.e., the International Council for Bird Preservation and the local ornithological society). We said "no," and other foundations said "no," but the government is still not sure. I would like to have the panel's opinion so I can go back to my country and push the authorities, I hope, to say "no."

Munn: No! But actually try to get them to work with local people. Once again, don't help some first-worlder to set up an operation to raise birds in captivity in Ecuador that could end up being a screen for laundering wild-caught birds. I'm talking about working with the people who actually live out in the selva. The *campesino* who's living down in the jungle. Work with that person. Get those people land title and then work with them to manage their resources. You can't make progress in conserving parrots and the forests they depend on by dealing with the middleman in the cities.

Forshaw: Can I just follow up from that? I would like to reinforce what Charles Munn has said. If the first-world people want to put money into ranching parrots in Ecuador, then adopt a user-pays principle. Let them put up the funds, but let the Ecuadorians do it in the way Charles Munn has mentioned. That would be the way that I would recommend.

Munn: They also asked in Peru, and the Peruvian authorities are very confused also. I told them the same thing. Why do you want to set up a bunch of first-worlders to make added value off your jungle products and provide no incentive whatsoever for the local people to protect the forest or to find another way to value the forest? It seems like the ultimate absurdity. The bureaucrats scratched their heads and said, "Oh yeah, we'd never thought of that." They should be looking out for the interests of their own country. Presumably that's what they're being paid to do. They seemed to think that it was a great idea to have a captive-breeding operation somewhere in Lima. Actually, for minimal set-up costs, if any, you could, for example, feed females a little bit of food in the wild and take one egg away from each one. It seemed absurd to me that they wouldn't think about that at all. The people who actually live in the forest do understand these issues, much better than the bureaucrats and certainly better than I and many of us sitting here.

Moderator: At this point I want to see whether we can come to a group consensus. On the basis of what we've heard today, I would like the panel to tell us what they would recommend at this point.

Beissinger: I think the biological information suggests that the quota systems presently have no biological basis. As a first step, I think most of the panel agrees that some kind of biological basis for import levels of parrots needs to be established. Until that happens, more drastic measures may be needed to curtail trade, like a moratorium on trade.

Forshaw: I think John Fitzpatrick is perfectly right that it's very difficult to reach the stage where we have sufficient data. I think we need to set our objectives very clearly if we start down this way. We're not talking about surveys. What we're talking about is ascertaining recruitment levels, age-cohorts in the population, and what one could harvest. In other words, we're all used to the waterfowl caveats that govern the hunting fraternity and cover the game bird people and the fishing people. We are looking at another form of utilization of wildlife. We need the same biological principles in place.

It's going to be difficult. It's going to be costly to get the information. The third world countries can't be expected to carry the burden. The user-pays principle must be examined. We must discuss it with the trade industry. Trade obviously has the built-in capacity to pay. Having seen the figures today, I'm more convinced of that than ever. In other words, all the other utilizers of wildlife pay for the privilege to do so. The trade must do so as well. We must set up the mechanisms to govern that whole regime, and we must do so quickly. We all must act in concert or we will have contributed to the extinction of many Neotropical parrots.

11. Toward a Conservation Strategy for Neotropical Psittacines

Noel F. R. Snyder, Frances C. James, and Steven R. Beissinger

Wildlife Preservation Trust International, P. O. Box 426, Portal, Arizona 85632; Department of Biological Science, Florida State University, Tallahassee, Florida 32306-1043; and School of Forestry & Environmental Studies, Yale University, New Haven, Connecticut 06511

Abstract.—The overall status of Neotropical psittacines has been rapidly worsening, despite the recent establishment of new preserves, increased participation in CITES by western hemisphere countries, and some innovative efforts in education, ecotourism, and research. The two main problems are the high rate of habitat destruction and an immense harvest of wild birds for trade. Public education programs about these issues are urgently needed. Other high priorities include accelerated habitat preservation efforts, research, and government regulations to greatly reduce trade.

PARROT CONSERVATION EFFORTS—PAST AND PRESENT

Widespread concern for the conservation of parrots is relatively recent. The first major conference focusing on the problems faced by New World psittacines was convened in St. Lucia only 10 years ago (Pasquier 1981). At that conference, the main threats to parrots were generally acknowledged to be habitat destruction, international and domestic trade, and killing for food and feathers. A number of Caribbean species and several large macaws of the mainland were recognized as particularly imperiled.

Recommendations from the St. Lucia conference centered on stemming the tide of habitat destruction and trade. Participants urged that more areas should be set aside for reserves and that reserves should be adequately staffed by trained wardens. As a step toward better regulation of the bird trade, all countries were asked to join the Convention on International Trade in Endangered Species (CITES). Emphasis was placed on increasing law-enforcement efforts to stop the smuggling of birds across the Mexican border into the United States and to stop the movement of birds from nonexporting countries to exporting countries in Latin America. Other recommendations and proposals included (1) the development of a manual for parrot identification to aid customs officials in enforcing CITES regulations, (2) surveys to determine the status of some species, (3) research to investigate the feasibility of sustained harvest of wild parrot populations, (4) the development of an international registry of captive Caribbean amazon parrots to coordinate captive breeding efforts, and (5) education campaigns to raise public awareness for conservation in Neotropical countries.

Many of these recommendations have been implemented in the past decade. Among the more positive developments, a number of preserves have been created that have benefited parrots in the Caribbean, the Andes, and Brazil (Collar and Juniper 1991). Between 1981 and 1990, seven countries instituted bans on the exportation of their indigenous wild-caught parrots (Thomsen and Mulliken 1991), although with the exception of Bolivia and Mexico, most of these countries had not been important exporters (Roet et al. 1981). Six mainland Neotropical countries have ratified CITES since 1981, and all countries except Mexico are now members (Pasquier 1981, Thomsen and Mulliken 1991). The Cooperative Working Group on Bird Trade was convened in 1988, and has developed recommendations aimed at decreasing mortality of birds during transport and quarantine, and at progressively reducing the importation of wild-caught birds for the pet trade in the United States (Cooperative Working Group on Bird Trade 1990). A few field studies have demonstrated a potential for sustained harvest of parrots (Beissinger and Bucher 1991), and some surveys of parrot populations have been completed in Venezuela (S. Strahl pers. comm.). The ability to care for and breed psittacines in captivity has increased substantially (Clubb 1991). On islands in the Lesser Antilles, innovative conservation programs have been pivotal in conserving several endemic species through changes in public attitudes (Butler 1991). Finally, encouraging starts have been made toward conservation of some substantial blocks of intact Peruvian rain-forest, primarily through macaw ecotourism (Munn 1991).

Yet despite the recognition of the major threats faced by New World parrots, and despite the progress described above, evidence presented in this book indicates that the overall conservation status of these birds has continued to worsen. Almost one-third of the 140 species of parrots found in the Neotropics are now in imminent danger of extinction (Collar and Juniper 1991). Moreover, nearly all of the 98 "nonthreatened" parrot species of the Neotropics are currently thought to be declining in numbers (Collar and Juniper 1991). The family Psittacidae now has a larger proportion of endangered species than does any other major family of birds.

The primary factors threatening most endangered Neotropical parrots continue to be habitat destruction and the bird trade. Collar and Juniper (1991) estimate that 40% of these species are threatened primarily by habitat destruction, 36% are threatened by a combination of habitat destruction and trade, 17% are threatened by the trade alone, and 7% are threatened by a variety of other causes.

Rates of habitat destruction have been accelerating during the past two decades, especially in tropical lowland and highland forests (FAO/UNEP 1981, Myers 1986, Gradwohl and Greenberg 1988, Lugo 1988), where the greatest diversity of Neotropical parrots is found (Forshaw 1989). More than 70% of the Neotropical parrots threatened with extinction inhabit forests of the Atlantic coast of Brazil, the Andean valleys of Colombia and Ecuador, and the islands of the Caribbean—areas that have undergone massive habitat degradation (Collar and Juniper 1991). Additional reserves are urgently needed in these regions.

The bird trade affects almost as many species of parrots as does habitat destruction. Judging from import permits, more than 1.8 million parrots were legally exported from Neotropical countries to world markets between 1982 and 1988 (Thomsen and Mulliken 1991). Furthermore, estimates of pre-export mortality (e.g., Ramos and Iñigo 1985) and illegal smuggling (see Thomsen's comments in James 1991, Thomsen and Hemley 1987) suggest that the actual number of birds removed from the wild during this period must have been several times the number reported on import permits. In addition, none of these figures accounts for the very substantial internal trade in parrots characteristic of many Neotropical countries.

Fewer countries are exporting birds now than earlier, but the number of parrots in legal international trade has grown from less than 100,000 annually in the 1970s (Roet et al. 1981) to more than 250,000 annually in the 1980s (Thomsen and Mulliken 1991). No comprehensive legislation has yet been passed in the United States or in Europe to decrease the large numbers of parrots imported.

Although many of the parrot species being traded are not yet considered at risk of extinction (Thomsen and Mulliken 1991), they too may soon be in danger, because their low reproductive potentials make them highly susceptible to overharvesting (Bucher 1991, Munn 1991). The trade appears to be particularly threatening to species found in lowland mainland habitats (Collar and Juniper 1991).

Other concerns also cry out for attention. Research is urgently needed on the basic biology of most psittacines. Survey work has not been intensive enough even to allow confidence as to whether some species still exist in the wild. Further, the role that captive breeding should have in parrot conservation remains in vigorous dispute. Many aviculturists wishing to participate in parrot conservation have yet to recognize that reintroduction and bolstering of wild populations must be the primary goals of captive-breeding programs, and that long-term captive breeding leads inexorably to domestication, not preservation, of species. Thus far, aviculturists have been slow to cooperate with conservation efforts (Bertagnollo 1981, Clubb 1991, Derrickson and Snyder 1991).

The conservation achievements of the past decade have not outweighed the losses. Many of the same species of parrots are still in trouble, and, unfortunately, more have been added to the list. A decade ago, Warren King's (1977–1979) comprehensive account of endangered birds worldwide for the International Council for Bird Preservation and the International Union for the Conservation of Nature and Natural Resources listed 23 species and subspecies of Neotropical parrots in danger of extinction (9 endangered, 4 rare, 5 vulnerable, and 5 indeterminate). By 1990, Collar and Juniper (1991) considered 42 species to be at critical risk. Although the criteria for listing and the amount of available information were not strictly comparable for these two compilations, the magnitude of deterioration in the status of most Neotropical parrots cannot be mistaken. A few of the Caribbean amazon parrots are slowly increasing in numbers, but most are still declining, and the large mainland macaws and amazons are disappearing rapidly from their ranges. At least two species, the Glaucous Macaw (*Anodorhynchus glaucus*) and Spix's Macaw (*Cyanopsitta spixii*), have been effectively lost from the wild in recent years. Others, such as the Hyacinth Macaw (*Anodorhynchus hyacinthinus*) and Lear's Macaw (*Anodorhynchus leari*), do not appear to be far behind. Neotropical parrots are indeed facing a crisis in survival.

PARROT VULNERABILITY FACTORS

Parrots possess a number of traits that make them vulnerable to direct and indirect human influences and that make their conservation especially problematic:

1. They tend to be highly conspicuous birds because of their bright colors, loud vocalizations, and gregarious habits. These characteristics make them vulnerable to shooting and trapping.
2. Many species are large enough to be worthwhile as game for subsistence hunters.
3. Their food habits often make them competitors with agricultural interests.
4. Their attractiveness as pets is rivaled by few other wild animals.
5. Their usual habit of nesting in natural tree cavities means they are strongly affected by destruction of primary forests.
6. Their harvest for the pet trade frequently involves deliberate destruction of nest sites, which are often in limited supply.
7. Most parrots are residents of lesser-developed regions of the world, where it is difficult to employ conservation measures that would be more practical in regions with greater economic resources. Even with a strong desire to conserve these species, the governments of many countries lack the financial and administrative means to do very much on their behalf.

In spite of these impediments, interest in conserving these birds has increased rapidly in the past decade, and some success has been achieved in preventing the extinction of certain species (Snyder et al. 1987, Butler 1991). Surely many more can be preserved with a continued expansion of conservation efforts. While we remain apprehensive about how successful any conservation endeavors can be in the long term if human populations continue to grow uncontrollably, we see no alternative in the short term but to proceed with whatever conservation techniques are available and effective.

PURPOSES OF THE 1990 SYMPOSIUM

In organizing the Los Angeles symposium, we decided to focus on general topics of concern and promise in parrot conservation, rather than repeat the species-by-species emphasis that characterized the St. Lucia conference. In the past decade, several broad approaches have been developed which offer hope that the progressive declines of many wild parrot populations can be reversed. During the symposium, we sought to feature these approaches and to encourage discussion of their advantages and disadvantages.

The rapidity with which many species are approaching extinction allows very little time for corrective actions and encourages a search for general solutions that may help many species. We do not mean to disparage individual species efforts, as such efforts are certainly worthwhile and are often the most efficient way to preserve whole ecosystems. But we seek to place them in the context of overall efforts to protect biological diversity. There are just too many endangered species beyond parrots, too few resources, and too few able conservationists.

ALTERNATIVE CONSERVATION MEASURES

The chapters in this volume consider a number of approaches for dealing with the parrot conservation crisis. Each has its own importance and relevance to part of the crisis, yet none is applicable to all situations.

Reducing Habitat Destruction

Habitat destruction is clearly the principal threat to many parrot species, and no species can exist in the wild without appropriate habitat. At the same time, we believe that this threat can be overemphasized with some species and that habitat destruction has often been used uncritically to justify unsupportable levels of wild harvest under the argument that "they would die anyway, and we can save them by captive breeding."

As is clear from the establishment of feral populations of dozens of species of parrots in urban areas around the world (Thomsen and Mulliken 1991, Wiley et al. 1991), many parrots are not truly habitat specialists and can thrive in extremely disturbed areas, so long as they are not hunted or captured for the trade. Even where native populations have been stressed by massive losses of habitat, it appears that many species can be conserved in replacement habitats if special attention is given to providing and conserving nest sites and to reducing direct human impacts on the populations.

Nevertheless, we do not mean to imply any lack of concern for either habitat preservation or habitat restoration, as these efforts benefit whole constellations of species in addition to parrots. Clearly, habitat considerations remain a central concern for the preservation of all species in the wild and need to be pursued with the utmost vigor. Collar and Juniper (1991) called attention to many opportunities for reserve creation, especially in regions that could benefit multiple species. Aside from establishment of reserves, many of the other approaches described in this book are also tied closely to habitat preservation and seek to promote habitat preservation by giving value to sustainable uses of natural areas (see Fig. 1 in Beissinger and Snyder 1991).

Reducing the Bird Trade

The bird trade, discussed in depth by Thomsen and Mulliken (1991), is certainly the major cause of decline for a number of species and has several important characteristics. Much of this problem traces to the desires of parrot fanciers and aviculturists in developed countries to possess exotic species. But we must not forget that often there are also strong demands for captive parrots within their countries of origin. The example of the Puerto Rican Parrot (*Amazona vittata*) is instructive in this regard. While the pet trade was surely a major factor in the catastrophic decline of this species in this century, the harvest was stimulated primarily by local rather than foreign demand (Snyder et al. 1987). Even if effective international controls are achieved, internal trade may still exterminate many species.

Because the United States is the largest market for Neotropical parrots, it has been responsible for a substantial fraction of the declines due to trade (James 1990). The United States presently has the ethically schizophrenic policy of prohibiting commercial use of its native bird species while allowing trade in the avifauna of other countries. The reduction in trade in endangered species achieved by CITES has been only partial. Many species listed in CITES continue to be overexploited (Thomsen and Mulliken 1991).

No consensus has emerged as to how the bird trade might best be controlled in the United States. Primary alternatives under consideration include a complete ban on the importation of wild-caught birds, a complete moratorium followed by selective authorization for species harvestable on a sustained basis, and the immediate implementation of a "clean list" that would allow importations of only those species thought to be able to withstand trade. While it seems doubtful that a full consensus can be achieved, the Cooperative Working Group on the Bird Trade (1990) has been struggling valiantly to find a strategy that can be supported by a majority of interested parties. This group was convened in August 1988 by the World Wildlife Fund and included representatives from 13 organizations, among them the National Audubon Society, the International Council for Bird Preservation, the Humane Society, the Animal Welfare Institute, and the American Federation of Aviculture. Its goal has been the development of a comprehensive bill on bird-trade regulation for consideration by Congress of the United States. As of this writing (January 1991), the parties have some remaining differences about the final draft, but they are agreed on major recommendations.

The bill will provide for a 5-year phaseout of the importation of wild-caught birds into the United States for direct sale on the pet market. At the end of this period, some importations for commercial captive breeders and aviculture would still be permitted. The difficult issues that remain unresolved are: (1) regulation of the importation of birds for avicultural captive-breeding programs;

(2) how birds will be marked to distinguish wild from captive-reared birds; (3) how to regulate ranching (sustained harvesting operations); and (4) whether to empower the Secretary of the Interior to selectively halt all imports in cases in which species are not on the Endangered Species list but probably should be. Under the draft proposal, aviculturists who want to raise birds to sell as pets will have to be registered with the U.S. Fish and Wildlife Service, and their facilities will be subject to inspection without notice.

The final proposal has not yet been submitted and may differ in some respects from what we have summarized above. And of course it remains to be seen whether the proposal will find acceptance in Congress. Whatever may develop from the ongoing debate, we wish to emphasize certain aspects of the regulatory problem that need special attention:

1. To succeed, selective import regimes depend on the development of reliable means for discrimination between legal and illegal birds. Such discriminations may involve distinguishing between captive-bred birds and wild-caught birds, or between species that may be imported legally and ones that may not. Experience with such discriminations under existing laws has not been encouraging, mainly because of the gross underfunding of regulatory agencies and the inherent difficulties in making some discriminations. No marking systems for identifying birds are foolproof, and some traders are already highly skilled in "transforming" one species into another by coloring procedures. Furthermore, there are no reliable behavioral means for distinguishing captive-bred birds from those taken from the wild as nestlings and hand-reared.

2. Any solution that involves licensing, complicated regulations, and the creation of a substantial administrative structure poses severe disadvantages from the standpoints of costs and potentials for regulatory abuse. Exactly how regulations are adopted and administered, and how regulatory agencies are overseen are extremely important questions.

3. Any solution that fails to address comprehensively the problem of inadvertent importation of exotic diseases poses great risks. A number of the psittacine diseases that have recently become established in this country have latencies that far exceed standard quarantine periods, and cannot be detected in carrier individuals by any current methods. Several such dis-

eases have had devastating impacts on captive populations and pose threats to native wild populations as well (Derrickson and Snyder 1991, Wiley et al. 1991). This aspect of the bird trade has received far too little attention.

4. The United States should avoid the position of treating native wildlife differently from foreign wildlife.

5. Several practical problems accompany the importation of species that are agricultural pests in their native lands (Bucher 1991). Any exotic species has the potential of establishing itself in the wild in feral populations through escape or release. While species that are pests in their native lands may not become pests in feral populations, certainly they should be viewed as having this potential. Also, species that are not pests in their native lands can become so when introduced elsewhere. The risks are substantial in either case and should be weighed heavily against any perceived benefits of trade.

6. Potential solutions should be carefully evaluated with respect to their impacts on smuggling activities. To the extent that regulations may shift the trade from legal to illegal activities, problems such as the introduction of alien diseases may be exacerbated.

Even a superficial examination of these considerations reveals the great difficulty in creating regulations that may reliably maximize all potential benefits. A total ban or moratorium may seem a logical position from the standpoints of minimizing bureaucracy, ease of enforcement, potential beneficial impacts on wild populations, consistency of ethical positions, and avoidance of importation of exotic pests and diseases. But these benefits could be lost if a total ban results in greatly increased smuggling. Nevertheless, the results of the New York state ban on importations of wild-caught birds are quite encouraging in this regard (Knights 1990, Simon 1990). Since the institution of this ban in 1984, there has been no evidence of increased smuggling and no detectable increase in avian diseases in this state. Moreover, the trade in pet birds has not been hurt—many of the common species in trade are now being bred in captivity.

A selective ban on international imports would require the creation of a substantial bureaucracy, and it could set the stage for enough clever faking of species identities and rearing histories (i.e., wild-caught vs captive-reared) to result in little net progress. Further, it could likewise stimulate smuggling in a compensating way. Selective bans have some attractions in theory, but pose substantial difficulties in practice.

So even though nearly everyone agrees that the present system of regulations is inadequate, the optimal replacement system for lowering pressures on wild populations is still under debate. We believe that any adequate solution will require changing the behavior of consumers. Until it becomes socially unacceptable to own wild-caught parrots, the problem may stay with us no matter what regulations are adopted, and we may see the loss of a substantial number of species from the wild. Recall that the slaughter of herons and egrets for the plume-bird trade in the United States in the early 1900s was halted primarily by a shift in public attitudes (Howell 1932). Similarly, many observers have concluded that reducing demand represents the only real hope for controlling the illicit drug trade.

The primary purposes of the symposium discussions and presentations on the bird trade (Collar and Juniper 1991, James 1991, Thomsen and Mulliken 1991) were to outline the magnitude of the problem and to explore ideas about ways to reduce trade impacts on parrots. An optimal solution to the trade issue can only be achieved with the widest possible discussion of alternatives and their implications. The symposium was not designed to achieve a formal consensus on the trade issue, and no full consensus was evident in either the presentations or the round-table discussion. Nevertheless, most participants expressed support for an immediate moratorium on the importation of wild-caught psittacines into the United States.

The three authors of this chapter are among those who prefer an immediate moratorium on importations of all wild-caught birds into the United States and especially of the 42 species mentioned by Collar and Juniper (1991), some of which are still being traded in numbers (Nilsson 1989, 1990). In theory, we see no reason for opposing sustainable uses of wild populations or trade in captive-bred or ranched birds. However, we are not certain that sustainable harvests can be achieved in practice, and believe no international trade should be authorized without rigorous supporting data as to its sustainability. We recognize the extreme difficulty in distinguishing between captive-reared and wild-caught birds, and believe that if importations are to be allowed for captive-reared or ranched birds in the future, they should be under the supervision of a well-funded international commission with powers to monitor suppliers close-ly to prevent illegal laundering of wild-caught birds through the system. This commission should be funded on a user-pays basis. We also recognize the need for significantly increased law-enforcement efforts, regardless of what specific trade regulations may be adopted. We do not think that aviculturists need to have continued access to wild-caught birds, though we support special importa-tions of birds when they are part of internationally supervised recovery pro-grams, or when they are to be utilized for special scientific or educational pur-poses consistent with the conservation of wild populations. Above all, we favor expanded education efforts to stigmatize the private holding of wild-caught birds in captivity, unless they are part of recognized and controlled recovery progams.

Promoting National Pride

The approach used by Paul Butler (1991) of encouraging residents to develop national pride in their native parrots has proved highly successful in the Lesser Antilles, although Paul cautions against overestimating how widely applicable the approach may be. His approach appears to be well suited for certain char-ismatic species and has the important benefit of generating spinoff protection for entire ecosystems, giving value to these ecosystems that did not exist earlier.

Promoting national pride may not prove successful for species that lack special human appeal or do not share the ranges of appealing species. Never-theless, one can hope to find some charismatic species (not necessarily a parrot) for most ecosystems, so the approach may not be so limited as it might seem at first. For example, a program patterned after Paul's has been extremely successful for the golden lion tamarin (*Leontopithicus rosalia*) in Brazil (Dietz and Nagagata 1986). In his discussion, Paul emphasized that the efficacy of this approach seems to depend on working with relatively small and isolated societies, where everyone knows everyone else and where there is effective local control over conservation decisions.

Ecotourism

The ecotourism approach developed for macaws by Charles Munn (1991) also depends on charismatic species, and further, on charismatic species that can be viewed by the public with reliability. This approach seems especially well suited for locations where macaws assemble in spectacular numbers to ingest clay deposits (macaw licks). Like promoting national pride, promotion of showy concentrations of large parrots can have the beneficial effect of causing communities to value their local ecosystems as sustainable resources. And although it may be difficult to develop a viable tourist industry for less-exciting parrot species, this does not preclude them from being the beneficiaries of tourism developed primarily for more charismatic species sharing their ecosystems.

Some of the sites of spectacular roosting aggregations of amazon parrots would seem to have tourist potential comparable to that of macaw licks, if developed intelligently. But how widely this approach can be used to protect parrots is as yet unclear.

If ecotourism is to be successfully employed to protect forest habitats and birds, then local people must be actively involved in the implementation of programs and receive direct economic benefits. Land tenure for local people may be a prerequisite for success in many regions.

Reintroduction

Reintroduction, as discussed by Wiley, Snyder, and Gnam (1991), is a specialized and highly intensive restoration tool. It can help in specific situations with individual species, and it should always be the goal of captive-breeding efforts conceived as conservation measures. But opportunities for using this technique are limited, and it should not be viewed as a panacea for the plight of endangered parrots.

Reintroduction can be expensive when it is dependent on captive breeding rather than on translocation. Moreover, it should not generally be attempted without good indications that environmental conditions in the region of prospective reestablishment have improved since the species in question disappeared.

Captive Breeding

Captive breeding appears to have a place in parrot conservation, as discussed for private aviculture by Susan Clubb (1991). Unfortunately, its importance has often been oversold (Derrickson and Snyder 1991). The inherent problems associated with financial costs, behavioral and genetic deterioration under captive conditions, programmatic continuity, disease control, and the difficulties in achieving consistent breeding in many species argue for using this technique only with great discretion. Captive breeding has often become a substitute for implementing more effective and long-term solutions, and its promotion as a conservation solution has sometimes been a thinly veiled rationalization for keeping captive birds. Captive breeding efforts that are not fully integrated with reintroduction efforts have little, if any, conservation value, and in fact may instead represent significant drains on wild populations.

Nevertheless, aviculturists have become increasingly interested in conservation efforts for endangered parrots, and they are a resource that could play a significant role in future conservation-reintroduction programs if a number of serious problems could be solved. Principal among these problems are achieving adequate long-term control over disease threats (potentially solvable if aviculturists can become reconciled to housing only single species in their aviaries) and achieving a sound administrative framework for operations (potentially solvable if ownership and control of birds are given up to a centralized authority). These are difficult problems, but not necessarily insurmountable ones.

The notion that captive breeding might replace incentives for wild harvest of many species, without the implementation of truly effective import-export bans, fails to inspire much confidence on economic grounds.

Sustained Harvest

As discussed by Beissinger and Bucher (1991), sustained harvest of wild populations, or ranching, may be feasible for certain prolific and manageable species. In theory, proper management for sustained harvest of nestlings would result in wild populations near carrying capacity. Surely, if there is to be survival of trade in psittacines, it must be constituted on a sustainable basis. Like ecotourism, sustained harvesting could lead to protection of natural habitats and could create economic benefits for local people.

But it remains to be demonstrated that sustained harvesting can be economically competitive for any species if illegal wild harvest and smuggling activities continue to be widespread. The economic temptations to launder non-ranched birds through the system will be substantial. Further, the potentials may be very limited for using sustained harvest with many large and slow-reproducing species or endangered species. Before strong hopes are vested in this approach, demonstration programs are needed that solve its many inherent political and economic problems.

OVERALL PRIORITIES FOR CONSERVING
NEW WORLD PARROTS

Given the overwhelming evidence that New World parrots are in a conservation crisis, what sort of overall strategies should be developed? We believe that an effective conservation effort will have to emphasize four interrelated spheres: education, research, habitat preservation, and governmental regulation. Of the four, education may be the most important, as success in habitat preservation and government regulations will depend on social acceptance in the last analysis. The best tool for achieving social acceptance is education.

A top priority for education must be to make people aware of the values of parrots as wild creatures and the precarious status of wild parrot populations in the Neotropics. Currently, the public is largely ignorant of the fact that many of the parrots that they see in pet stores and in the hands of parrot fanciers are species whose wild populations are critically threatened. Most people are surprised to learn that if they buy a bird that entered the country illegally, they have broken the law. Under present conditions, parrots are still commonly regarded as having cages for natural habitats, and their attractiveness as pets and importance as status symbols constitute two of the most difficult aspects hindering conservation efforts. Even so, we should not be too discouraged about these obstacles. The success achieved by Paul Butler and his colleagues in the Lesser Antilles stands as a clear example of the enormous potential of imaginative educational efforts to overcome such difficulties.

The exposure of elementary school children to information about the problems of the bird trade should be a high priority, not only in importing countries such as the United States, but also in exporting countries, and particularly in local areas surrounding established reserves. Young children are receptive to such information and can become a potent force in educating older family members. Ultimately, the success of governmental regulations in exporting countries is as dependent on social acceptance as is the success of regulations in importing countries, and both are necessary for true reductions in pressures on wild parrot populations.

The pet-bird industry itself will not stand or fall on continued importations of wild-caught birds. With respect to parrots, the industry today is based primarily on two species that are captive-bred, the Budgerigar and the Cockatiel (Thomsen and Mulliken 1991). For the vast majority of pet owners these species fulfill all needs. The major problem lies instead with the demand of hobbyists, aviculturists, and collectors for other species, especially for the rare and exotic species that are not bred routinely in captivity (Clubb 1991). Education efforts should stigmatize the ownership of these latter species and stimulate consumers to accept only birds that have been captive-bred.

With respect to research, we plead for comprehensive field surveys and natural history studies of parrots, especially those species identified by Collar and Juniper (1991) and by CITES, as well as species that are prominent in the trade (Nilsson 1989, 1990). The number of Neotropical parrot species that have received intensive research is very small, and many highly endangered forms have received no attention at all.

For each species, we need to know the relative impacts of habitat destruction and trade, as well as the importance of other limiting factors. Unless research efforts are mounted, conservation efforts will undoubtedly founder for many endangered parrots because the crucial factors threatening endangered species often turn out to be quite subtle and different from what is suspected from the armchair.

Habitat preservation should be viewed as the most important overall objective of conservation efforts for parrots, for it is through habitat preservation that species preservation rises to the level of ecosystem preservation. Habitat preservation can include seminatural environments as well as pristine wilderness. The means of achieving habitat preservation are diverse, ranging from reserve creation by governmental or private agencies to steering economic development in the direction of sustainable practices compatible with the survival of wildlife species. There is no universal formula for successful habitat protection. Conservationists will continue to be challenged to identify and implement solutions appropriate to local conditions, whether they be through ecotourism, or coordinated efforts of private and governmental agencies to directly protect crucial areas, or other approaches.

As Collar and Juniper (1991) have pointed out, priority should be given to protecting areas with the maximum species diversity and with sufficient areal extent to sustain viable populations of all component species. Unfortunately, given our current levels of knowledge, we cannot yet identify such areas for many parrots. The determination of specific areas for habitat preservation remains a critical aspect for future research efforts. Once areas are identified, education programs are essential to generate social acceptance and local support for habitat preservation measures.

Government regulations are important in both countries that have wild parrot populations and countries receiving parrots in international trade. Certainly a high priority must be given to efforts to reform the currently indefensible levels of importation that characterize the United States, but no one should be deceived that the United States is the only offender (Thomsen and Mullikcn 1991).

As a final comment, we caution against despair. It is easy to conclude that the future conservation of Neotropical parrots is hopeless. Yet even on Puerto Rico, a densely populated island with only a small percentage of its native forest left intact, enough habitat has been preserved to offer adequate life support for its endangered amazon parrot. Similarly, on St. Lucia and St. Vincent, enough native forests are under protection to permit survival for their native amazons. Parrots are relatively adaptable birds, so their conservation can be assured with thoughtful efforts. Just as this symposium has drawn together speakers from a diversity of backgrounds and specialties, our future conservation endeavors must incorporate a diverse spectrum of activities, methods, and constituencies. With enough energy and commitment, it still should be possible to conserve nearly all species of Neotropical parrots.

LITERATURE CITED

Beissinger, S. R., & E. H. Bucher. 1991. Sustainable harvesting of parrots for conservation. This volume.

Beissinger, S. R., & N. F. R. Snyder. 1991. Introduction. This volume.

Bertagnollo, P. 1981. Better definition and coordination of captive breeding programs. Pages 57–64 *in* Conservation of New World parrots (R. F. Pasquier, Ed.). Washington, District of Columbia, Smithsonian Institution Press/International Council for Bird Preservation Tech. Publ. No. 1.

Bucher, E. H. 1991. Neotropical parrots as agricultural pests. This volume.

Butler, P. J. 1991. Parrots, pressures, people, and pride. This volume.

Clubb, S. L. 1991. The role of private aviculture in the conservation of Neotropical psittacines. This volume.

Collar, N. J., & A. T. Juniper. 1991. Dimensions and causes of the parrot conservation crisis. This volume.

Cooperative Working Group on Bird Trade. 1990. Findings and recommendations regarding the United States trade in exotic avian species. Washington, District of Columbia, World Wildlife Fund.

Derrickson, S. R., & N. F. R. Snyder. 1991. Potentials and limits of captive breeding in parrot conservation. This volume.

Dietz, L. A., & E. Nagagata. 1986. Community conservation education program for the golden lion tamarin. Pages 8–16 *in* Building support for conservation in rural areas—workshop proceedings vol. 1 (J. Atkinson, Ed.). Ipswich, Massachusetts, QLF-Atlantic Center for the Environment.

Food and Agriculture Organization of the United Nations/United Nations Environment Program. 1981. Tropical forest resource assignment project (in the framework of the global environment monitoring system). Rome, Food and Agriculture Organization of the United Nations.

Forshaw, J. M. 1989. Parrots of the world, 3d revised edition. Willoughby, Australia, Lansdowne Editions.

Gradwohl, J., & R. Greenberg. 1988. Saving the tropical forests. London, Earthscan Publications Ltd.

Howell, A. H. 1932. Florida bird life. New York, Coward-McCann Inc.

James, F. C. 1990. The selling of wild birds: out of control? The Living Bird 9:8–15.

James, F. C. (Ed.). 1991. A round-table discussion of parrot trade problems and solutions. This volume.

King, W. B. 1977–1979. Red data book, vol. 2: aves, part 2. Morges, Switzerland, International Union Conservation Nature and Natural Resources.

Knights, P. D. 1990. Wild bird imports for the pet trade, an EEC overview. London, Environmental Investigation Agency.

Lugo, A. E. 1988. Estimating reductions in diversity of tropical forest species. Pages 58–70 *in* Biodiversity (E. O. Wilson, Ed.). Washington, District of Columbia, National Academy Press.

Munn, C. A. 1991. Macaw biology and ecotourism, or "when a bird in the bush is worth two in the hand." This volume.

Myers, N. 1986. Tropical deforestation and a mega-extinction spasm. Pages 394-409 *in* Conservation biology: the science of scarcity and diversity (M. E. Soulé, Ed.). Sunderland, Massachusetts, Sinauer.

Nilsson, G. 1989. Importation of birds into the United States in 1985. Washington, District of Columbia, Animal Welfare Institute.

Nilsson, G. 1990. Importation of birds into the United States in 1986–1988. Washington, District of Columbia, Animal Welfare Institute.

Pasquier, R. F. (Ed.). 1981. Conservation of New World parrots. Washington, District of Columbia, Smithsonian Institution Press/International Council for Bird Preservation Tech. Publ. No. 1.

Ramos, O. M., & E. Iñigo. 1985. Commercialización de Psitácidos en México. Memoria Primer Simposium Internacional de Fauna Silvestre, vol. 2. México, D. F.

Roet, E. C., D. S. Mack, & N. Duplaix. 1981. Psittacines imported by the United States (October 1979–June 1980). Pages 21–55 *in* Conservation of New World parrots (R. F. Pasquier, Ed.). Washington, District of Columbia, Smithsonian Institution Press/International Council for Bird Preservation Tech. Publ. No. 1.

Simon, L. 1990. New York's crusade for exotic birds. Defenders 65(6):26–38.

Snyder, N. F. R., J. W. Wiley, & C. B. Kepler. 1987. The parrots of Luquillo: natural history and conservation of the Puerto Rican Parrot. Los Angeles, California, Western Foundation of Vertebrate Zoology.

Thomsen, J. B., & G. Hemley. 1987. Bird trade . . . bird bans. TRAFFIC (USA) 7(2&3):1,21–24.

Thomsen, J. B., & T. A. Mulliken. 1991. Trade in Neotropical psittacines and its conservation implications. This volume.

Wiley, J. W., N. F. R. Snyder, & R. S. Gnam. 1991. Reintroduction as a conservation strategy for parrots. This volume.

Resumen.—La situación general de los psitácidos neotropicales se ha estado empeorando aceleradamente, a pesar del reciente establecimiento de nuevas areas protegidas, un incremento en la participación en "CITES" por los paises del hemisferio occidental, y unos esfuerzos novedosos en la educación, el ecoturismo, y la investigación. Los dos problemas principales son la tasa alta de destrucción de habitat y la immensa explotación de aves silvestres para el comercio. Se necesitan programas de educación pública sobre estos temas urgentemente. Otras prioridades de suma importancia incluyen esfuerzos acelerados para la protección de habitat, y el establecimiento de reglamentos gubernamentales para reducir el comercio en forma significativa.

Index

Note: Page references followed by *f* denote figures; page references followed by *t* indicate tables. Birds are indexed by Latin name and by common name.